D1617524

THOMAS GRAY AND LITERARY AUTHORITY

A Study in Ideology and Poetics

THOMAS GRAY AND LITERARY AUTHORITY

A Study in Ideology and Poetics

SUVIR KAUL

Stanford University Press
Stanford, California
1992

Stanford University Press
Stanford, California
©1992 Oxford University Press
Originating publisher: Oxford University Press, Delhi
First published in the U.S.A. by
Stanford University Press, 1992
Printed in the U.S.A.
ISBN 0-8047-2027-4
LC 91-67134

∞ This book is printed on acid-free paper

Contents

Acknowledgements

I should like to thank Rick Bogel, Laura Brown, Walter Cohen, Jonathan Culler, Janadas Devan, Judy Frank, Gerry Heng, Ania Loomba, Sam Otter, Marty Wechselblatt and my editor at Oxford University Press. At different times, as readers and motivators, they helped write this book. Its problems, as well as its occasional felicities, can be traced (directly and without mediation) to their tutelage and friendship. For academic motivation that pre-dates this book, I am grateful to Dr Brijraj Singh, and to his stern admonition that tutorials take precedence over everything but my demise. Vivi Mansukhani helped rescue the index. In the period that this book was written, Alka Mansukhani made possible much happiness. For various domestic pleasures I thank my parents, Kaushalya and Bhavanesh Kaul, and Bhaiyu, Sabi, Urvi and Anal Puri, as also Tia, Kalpana and Thotha Kaul.

Readers will notice the many ways in which my arguments benefit from Roger Lonsdale's edition of *The Poems of Gray, Collins and Goldsmith.* Although my readings of Gray's poems almost invariably differ from his, I am indebted to his editorial and critical achievement.

My first employers, S. G. T. B. Khalsa College, Delhi University, were remarkably generous with leaves of absence, thus allowing me to take up the Leverhulme Visiting Fellowship at the University of Kent at Canterbury, and later to spend a year at the Society for the Humanities, Cornell University. I am grateful to all three institutions for their intellectual and professional support.

A section of Chapter II was published as ' "A Solitary Fly": Thomas Gray and the Construction of Literary Authority,' in the *Yearly Review* of the University of Delhi (1987). A section of Chapter IV was published as 'Why Selima Drowns: Thomas Gray and the Domestication of the Imperial Ideal,' in *PMLA* 105 (1990). It is reprinted by permission of the copyright owner, The Modern Language Association of America.

This book is often about elegiac transitions. For that, and for many other reasons, it feels appropriate to dedicate it to the memory of Avinder S. Brar—reader of books; swimmer in cold waters; keeper, in murderous times, of a public faith.

Introduction

> I can not brag of my spirits, my situation, my employments, or my fertility. the days & the nights pass, & I am never the nearer to anything but that one, to wch we are all tending. yet I love People, that leave some traces of their journey behind them, & have strength enough to advise you to do so, while you can.
>
> —Thomas Gray to William Mason[1]

This book begins with a basic assumption, that the most critically productive way to decipher the traces left by any poetic journey is to read at the intersection of the formal and the ideological. That is, it understands poetic texts to be the products of these two imperatives, and it also holds that the richest critical accounts of, or meanings of, poems are arrived at through an unravelling of the details of their formal and ideological construction. No poet, in this analysis, lives a life separate from the socio-historical processes of time and place; no text, then, exists without its equivalent context.

The reconstruction of 'context,' though, is not to be understood as the deployment of a master discourse of the biographical and historical particulars of time and place that will have a unilateral explanatory force on the subordinate text. Rather, this analysis holds that context and text exist in a mutually constitutive relationship, our knowledge of the former being as dependent on the latter as vice versa. In this it follows Raymond Williams in rejecting the 'simple assumption that there is, on the one hand, a relatively unproblematic body of "literature," with its own inherent and autonomous qualities, and on the other hand, a body of general and summary knowledge which is, correspondingly, "history."'[1] Rather, this enquiry responds to Williams' call for essays that do not 'pretend to be committed to explanatory completeness,' but whose 'emphasis is on literature *in* history: the study of actual works, practices and conditions, in a particular place and period: some "literary," some "historical," but never assumed to belong, by definition, to pre-formed bodies of "literature" and "history."'[2]

This book is concerned with reading Gray's major poems as artifacts whose formal features, representational methods, thematic concerns, and ideological priorities both reproduce, and also produce, the socio-cultural and literary practices of their day. To set the stage for such a reading, Chapter I discusses Alexander Pope's 'An Epistle to Dr. Arbuthnot' (1734) and Edward Young's 'Two Epistles to Mr. Pope' (1730), both polemical poems on contemporary authors, their literary practices, and the market forces that were rapidly transforming a hitherto comparatively homogeneous and allied culture. The discussion shows how poetic debates that seem restricted to defining the proper *literary* qualifications of anyone who would be called 'Poet' are actually shaped by a sharp sense of the social and cultural contingencies and imperatives of literary production. Young and Pope seek to claim for themselves, and legislate general access to, the 'noble title' of Author or Poet—writers they do not care for are represented as tainted professionals, worthy only of the condemnatory label 'Grub Street hacks.' Yet, as the analysis demonstrates, such poems enact not the ease, or even possibility, of defining and enforcing distinctions, but the impossiblity of doing so, with the result that they offer contradictory, occasionally incoherent, testimonials to those authorial and self-presentational anxieties that structure so much early-eighteenth-century English poetry.

Chapter II begins the study of Gray with a set of complementary readings of four early poems: 'Ode on the Spring,' the Eton College *Ode*, the West *Sonnet*, and the 'Ode to Adversity,' all written in 1742. The analytical focus is upon questions of poetic and socio-cultural authority, and on the ways in which Gray's poems engage with the representational techniques by which different poetic and generic conventions enable and empower the poetic voice. His discomfort with some of these methods is read here as an individual instance of the larger vocational crisis brought on by the radically different nature of the new literary marketplace, which threatened to marginalize high-cultural and ideological 'aristocrats' like Gray. The interrelations of formal methods and cultural politics are then detailed further in Chapter III, which reads the *Elegy Written in a Country Churchyard* as an attempt to contest the hegemony of bourgeois social and cultural values, and as a record of the textually and historically inevitable failure of such an attempt.

Chapter IV then traces a portion of the peculiar itinerary followed by Gray's poetic career, an itinerary which connects, most representatively, the contemporary search for poetic authority with the cultural celebration of British mercantile and imperial power. In each case, the hesitations and anxieties that marked Gray's discovery of variously imperial themes and forms are understood here as identifying, and being defined by, the ideological contradictions lived by an eighteenth-century English 'gentleman.' ChapterV concludes this study via an examination of the few poems —satires and translations—Gray produced after he, as it were, stopped writing poetry, and concentrated instead on his private scholarship. These poems continue Gray's flirtation with the poetry of the public voice, but equally, in their suppression (the satires) or their historical anachronism (the antiquarian translations), they repeat the gestures of cultural alienation that mark all of Gray's poetry.

Throughout, this book is especially interested in questions of how best to *read* poems: how to work through the details of the thematic and formal construction of a poem; how to read in this construction histories of literary, cultural, and ideological practices; how to unravel the discursive, representational, and canonical codes that allow (and encourage) poets and readers to make particular sense of poems.[3] Thus, Gray's poems are constantly located within contemporary poetic practices, and their formal and thematic elements are examined as existing not only in an internally dialogic state (that is, within the poem), but also in a (largely agonistic) counterpoint with precursory and contemporary discursive practices. This study also touches upon questions of genre, especially as heuristics that explicate the connections between poetic forms and ideological functions. In all this, the large unasked question, that is of necessity answered only indirectly, and never completely, is this: After the ideological assumptions of the eminently reasonable critical narratives of humanist recuperation are made clear, what critical idioms must be developed in order to write fully, powerfully, and with a genuinely *critical* emphasis, about the texts of the canon, of the 'cultural heritage?' What discourse, that is, will combine best the dual work of explication and demystification, exegesis and critique, that is our task as students and teachers of literature, culture, and history?

LIFE AND LETTERS

Most criticism written on Gray is the work of 'humanist' scholars who seem to have found, and are now celebrating, one of their very own. The tone of such criticism tries hard to match the tone they discover in (their presentation of) Gray, a discovery which involves a (re)creation of the biographical subject through an unproblematic culling of selected quotations from his poetic subjects:

> 'Ah, tell them they are men!' is Gray's sigh as he sees 'the little victims' at play on the fields of Eton, 'regardless of their doom.' 'Teach me to . . . know myself a Man' is Gray's prayer for himself at the end of the 'Ode to Adversity'. Before being anything else Gray desired to be a loving, forgiving, generous, self-scanning human being, and deeper than his humanism is his humanity.
>
> To be a man, however, is, with fatal inevitability, to be melancholy.[4]

Such analyses are not content only to outline the 'sensibility' or 'humanity' of the poet, but work hard to read such constructs as triumphant incarnations of the unchanging and transcendent verities of 'man.' The language of timelessness and existential inevitability is spoken often here, as it is in those frequent moments when the *Elegy Written in a Country Churchyard* is celebrated as the finest achievement of a congruent poetic discourse of human transience, mourning, and the small compensations of fortitude.

There have, of course, been important exceptions to this critical approach, and my analysis not only takes note of them, but is often indebted to them as well. Arthur Johnston, for example, treats Gray as 'Our Daring Bard,' and speaks of his fascination with 'war and the warrior.' Concentrating his analyses on the Welsh and Norse poems Gray translated in his later career, Johnston writes of a growth 'from the poet as hidden and remembered only by a kindred spirit, to the poet as the sole surviving voice of liberty and virtue,' from 'the poet of *memento mori,* longing to warn men of the inevitability of suffering and death,' to 'the poet [a]s a kind of warrior,' a 'prophet' who is the 'father of the powerful spell' that is poetry.[5] Johnston properly emphasises the continuity of thematic elements, and of the evolving figuration of the poet, in Gray's poems, but his article is obviously too brief to do justice to those issues, or to work out the ideological and formal imperatives behind such continuity and evolution.

Similarly, James Steele, in his stimulating account of the interrelations between Gray's politics and his poetry, revises certain biographical assumptions about Gray, and suggests that Gray, 'by virtue of his family background, his wealth, and his wider social and economic connections, was very much a part of the *rentier* stratum of the capitalist ruling class in England. He was in fact a life-long Whig, with firm ideas about what constitutes true liberty, and with a partisan's knowledge of its historic roots. He also had an enthusiastic appreciation of the origin and development of the British Empire and strong opinions as to how it might be most efficiently advanced in his own time.' [6]

While Steele is correct both in his description of Gray's class origins and his politics, he tends to read Gray's poems as more or less seamless expositions of a 'Whig' world-view, especially dedicated to the extension of British imperial power and mercantile magnificence. For instance, he rightly says of the ideological scheme of 'Luna Habitabilis' (an early Latin poem by Gray, to which we will return) that although 'war and gunboat diplomacy will provide the means of conquest [of the moon], Gray's justification for such an action is not merely *force majeure* but the superiority of English scientific knowledge. Gray's Muse Luna is also the goddess of astronomy and geometry, and she naturally assumes in a post-Newtonian age that her citizenship is English (l. 79).'[7] However, Steele does not notice sufficiently those occasions in Gray's poems when the suturing of the formal and the ideological, the poetic and the social, is less than smooth; those occasions when Gray's 'utopian conclusions' include dystopian themes, when the ideological fantasy fissures under the pressure of the social and historical here-and-now. Thus 'Luna Habitabilis' also includes a powerful vision of the particular form the violence of imperial conquest takes: 'the regiment of monsters, and gigantic beasts full of armed men, and the inimitable lightning,' who make British power possible.

All of Gray's poems are marked by such moments of radical ambivalence; some, as we will see in the earlier chapters, draw from such ambivalences structural and thematic features. In each case, I will suggest, it is an understanding of the imperatives of class, rather than party, allegiance that are better indicators of how best to read Gray's poems. After all, symptoms of anxiety, ambivalence, or even resistance can scarcely be traced to a residual 'Tory' cause—for example, all 'Tories' were no more opposed to a strong British overseas presence than all 'Whigs' were enthusiastic supporters of it. As Louis Landa asserts, 'men of Tory persuasion' both praised commerce and engaged in it: 'In Tickell's poem, in *Spectator*, No. 69, in other works praising the glories of maritime commerce, something more than a partisan or factional view emerged. As I have indicated, what we do have in fact is a delectable vision of England's greatness and glory, a vision of splendour and magnificence shared by Englishmen of all persuasions.'[8]

The formal tensions and thematic anxieties both latent and manifest in Gray's poems are then to be accounted for with reference to the ideological contradictions lived by an independent English gentleman in the eighteenth century. Culturally and socially, Gray was alienated from those who did not share the lives, values, and aspirations of aristocrats and their client groups. Personally, as Steele points out, Gray's 'grand tour in a very grand manner, his return to Cambridge with the rank of fellow-commoner, his unwillingness to practise civil law, his gracious declining of a dutiful secretary-ship to the British ambassador to Spain, and his refusal of the reputedly servile poet-laureateship (*Corres.*, II, 543–44) were characteristic of a man of his class. His acceptance of an unsolicited offer of the Regius Professorship of Modern History—a sinecure which Gray described as 'the best thing the Crown has to bestow (on a Layman) here [at Cambridge]' (*Corres.*, III, 1048)—evidently marked the lowest degree to which he would stoop.'[9]

At different points in his life, Gray felt the attractions of a public career and, on each occasion, opted for the life of private ease and academic, cultural, and social refinement. For him, and for others like him, there was no easy co-existence with, and within, the English public sphere as it was being reconstituted in the eighteenth century. The same economic and political energies that had led, in the late seventeenth and early eighteenth centuries, to the increasing concentration of power in the hands of the class to which Gray belonged threatened to (and did) expand that power base till, in the middle and later eighteenth century, it effectively changed socio-cultural and class character. In Gray's case, a family history that combined domestic and overseas trade and investment had made a historically early accession to the *rentier* class possible, but also, more significantly, *via* Eton and Cambridge, it had made possible membership in an aristocracy of connections and aspirations.[10] The cultural and ideological hegemony of this aristocracy, supported by its surrogates in the *haute* bourgeoisie of the day, was questioned and contested as the century grew older, till—represented especially in the rise, and the particular forms and concerns, of periodic literature and the novel—the values, ideas, and practices associated historically with the numerically larger and culturally less cohesive *petit* bourgeoisie came to define the English public sphere. Gray's was a proleptic and defensive (if only partial) awareness of this history—the same socio-economic processes which had 'created' him were, inexorably, marginalising all that he stood for.[11] Gray's poems exist as they do because of, and as, this awareness; that is, they are shaped by its strengths, its blindnesses, and most importantly, by the anxiety-fraught, contradictory ideological visions that result from the conjunction of both.

In the seventeenth and eighteenth centuries, the cultural and self-representational authority of the gentleman-poet was, after all, predicated upon the maintenance of the status of a gentleman, . . . a status which was, as John Barrell reminds us, under both socio-economic and cultural siege. It had seemed perfectly credible early in the eighteenth century for a social essayist to claim the persona of a gentleman-at-large: 'Thus I live in the world rather as a Spectator of mankind than as one of the species; by which means I have made myself a speculative statesman, soldier, merchant and artisan, without ever meddling with any practical part in life. I . . . can discern the errors in the economy, business, and diversion of others, better than those who are engaged in them . . . In short, I have acted in all the parts of my life as a looker on.'[12] As his introduction of himself tells us, the Spectator's freedom from the professions, and his life of leisure, are made possible by the rents from a small hereditary estate, and it is precisely this membership in the class of *rentier* capital that also enables him to represent himself as possessing a point of analytical privilege. As Barrell suggests, such an authority was based on having avoided 'the concentration on one particular activity [that] is inimical to the acquisition of that comprehensive view, the attainment of that elevated viewpoint, from which society can be grasped in terms of relation, and not simply of difference.'[13]

However, as the century continued, such viewpoints of elevation and comprehension were increasingly unable to keep track of the effects of the overwhelming energy of social and economic differentiation that marked the life of eighteenth-century Britain. Myriad new social forms and relations were created, and they (as we will see in one instance, in the study of the relations between Pope and Young and the world of contemporary literary production) threatened any scenario of social coherence that could be written. As we might expect, high-cultural texts especially are marked by a fear of a destabilisation and confusion following upon this unregulated, uncontrolled social differentiation—the older social narratives had no precise explanations for the newly powerful, and clearly contestatory, economic methods, social values, and cultural forms that define later eighteenth-century bourgeois and *petit* bourgeois consolidation. In response to this, as Barrell points out, several important writers (Hume, Goldsmith, Johnson, Adam Smith) strove to acquire a 'knowledge across as many arts, professions, and sciences as possible . . . which aimed to grasp the relations of a multitude of social activities and practices by paying a detailed attention to as many of them as possible; so that a comprehensive knowledge of society may certainly, by the third quarter of the century, be more easily imagined in the man of letters than in the gentleman of fashion.' [14]

Gray can also be located (though in a qualified manner) in this shift from the 'gentleman-author' to the 'man of letters,' a sort of professional of society. He straddled these personae, and consequently, enacted the dualities of such a position. As one of his biographers, William Jones, puts it, Gray's 'tastes fit the tradition of the more literary landed gentry of his time . . . But he had no estate . . . and so he became a gentleman of letters, with chambers at Cambridge as his manor and the whole intellectual world as his estate. He was proficient at poetry and composed occasionally for his own friends, but disdained the profession of writing.' Jones continues: Gray 'would have no profession, even though trained to the law, and so he took to scholarship in order to fill his time in a manner congenial to his tastes and his code of a gentleman . . .

Sensitive to an extreme, he hated to offer his poems to the world. As a result of all these circumstances, he played the gentleman by reading and studying at Cambridge in winter and visiting his friends at their homes and estates in summer.'[15]

Yet Gray was no literary dilettante. He had a trained, academic approach to the nuances of the poetic tradition, and as he grew older, his scholarship (while producing little or nothing) grew prodigious. Being so, he could scarcely write poems without alluding, often critically and in perceptive ways, to the works of poets who had written before him.[16] Time and again, the characteristic discourses of the poetical tradition are deployed and deconstructed, often under the probing pressure of the single question—with what authority can a poet speak languages whose articulation will ultimately (if not even then) result in his marginalisation, or worse, his appropriation by a public culture opposed to the one he values? That is, can the avowedly high-cultural poet really claim for himself an authority that is based on representations of authorship and on linguistic and poetic practices derived from, and legitimised by, different earlier socio-cultural configurations?

One would expect that there might be an empirical answer to such a question, one given by the public reception of a poet's work. Yet for a gentleman-poet like Gray, precisely such a criterion of evaluation represented an unacceptable system of cultural values. The details of the publication of the *Elegy Written in a Country Churchyard* bear this out, as do accounts of Gray's reactions to the public success of the poem. Gray's modern editor, Roger Lonsdale, quotes Dr. John Gregory's report of Gray's comment to him about the *Elegy*: 'which he told me, with a good deal of acrimony, owed its popularity entirely to its subject, and that the public would have received it as well if it had been written in prose.'[17] This remark, made in 1765, is especially poignant, for by this time, Gray's two 'great' *Odes* had been published (1757) and had met with some respect, some attention, but largely confusion and puzzlement. This reception proved traumatic enough for Gray to stop writing poetry almost completely, and to devote himself to scholarly pursuits. As

Jones notes, 'when the public acclaimed the *Elegy*, he bore their approval with indifference, when they criticized his Pindaric odes, he withdrew into his recluse's shell.'[18]

A sense of Gray's own understanding of his cultural sphere may be derived from a letter he wrote to Count Algarotti in 1763, fairly late in his life, well after he had stopped writing poetry:

> I see with great satisfaction your efforts to reunite the congenial arts of Poetry, Musick, & the Dance, wch with the assistance of Painting and Architecture, regulated by Taste, & supported by magnificence & power, might form the noblest scene, and bestow the sublimest pleasure, that the imagination can conceive. but who shall realize these delightful visions? there is, I own, one Prince in Europe, that wants neither the will, the spirit, nor the ability . . .
>
> One cause that has so long hindered, & (I fear) will hinder that happy union, wch you propose, seems to me to be this: that Poetry (w^ch^, as you allow, must lead the way, & direct the operations of the subordinate Arts) implies at least a liberal education, a degree of literature, & various knowledge, whereas the others (with a few exceptions) are in the hands of Slaves & Mercenaries, I mean, of People without education, who, tho neither destitute of Genius, nor insensible to fame, must yet make gain their principal end, & subject themselves to the prevailing taste of those, whose fortune only distinguishes them from the Multitude.[19]

Even after we discount for the polite hyperbole of a near-diplomatic correspondence (Count Algarotti was Chamberlain to Frederick the Great of Prussia), a definite picture of a preferred, historically-specific form of literary and artistic production emerges: the European patron-prince (Frederick), his Maecenas (Algarotti), and creative artists free of the need to 'subject themselves to the prevailing taste' of the rich and uncultured.[20] Frederick was well known as a patron of the arts, as an educated and well-read correspondent of Voltaire's, and as the ideal type of enlightened monarch. Algarotti's interventions might thus encourage an aristocratic culture now waning, or defunct, in Gray's England. Hence, Gray's nostalgic rhetoric is marked by performative excess; it suggests a deep antipathy to those who 'must yet make gain their principal end,' a horror of professional authors and artists, of 'Slaves & Mercenaries.'

In all this, we might consider Gray's special place in eighteenth-century English literary history to be that of the poet whose corpus reveals a historically representative, insistent, troubled engagement with the contradictory vocational attractions of the public and the private, of the anonymous market and of the self-selecting coterie.[21] His work is ambivalent, too, about the great contemporary source of public authority—the celebration of national mercantile and imperial power—out of a concern for its impact on domestic society and culture. His poems are structured by various versions of this dialectical interplay, and are witness to the mid-eighteenth century poet's need for appropriate social, political, and ideological positions from which to establish poetic and cultural authority. But above all, his poems embody his search for a coherent contemporary poetics; for the languages, forms, and representational codes that would enable the gentleman-poet to reassert his sense of the way the world (of letters) should be.

NOTES

1. Thomas Gray to William Mason, August 11, 1758. *Correspondence of Thomas Gray*, eds. Paget Toynbee and Leonard Whibley, 3 vols. (Oxford: Clarendon Press, 1935), ii. 579.
2. 'Editor's Introduction,' in John Barrell, *English Literature in History, 1730–80: An Equal, Wide Survey* (London: Hutchinson, 1983), pp. 10–11.
3. The general project is analogous to Jonathan Culler's description of the efforts made by twentieth-century critics 'to increase the range of formal features that can be made relevant and to find ways of analysing their effects in terms of meaning.' The attempt of contemporary critics to offer increasingly sophisticated readings of poems, particularly of the ideology of form, is thus an extension of Culler's argument that the 'reading of poetry has always involved operations to make the poetic intelligible, and poetics has always attempted, if only implicitly, to specify the nature of such operations.' *Structuralist Poetics* (Ithaca: Cornell University Press, 1975), p. 179.

4. Jean Hagstrum, 'Gray's Sensibility,' *Fearful Joy: Papers from the Thomas Gray Bicentenary Conference at Carleton University*, eds. James Downey and Ben Jones (Montreal: McGill-Queen's University Press, 1974), p. 6.
5. Arthur Johnston, 'Thomas Gray: Our Daring Bard,' in *Fearful Joy*, eds. Downey and Jones, pp. 58, 61–63.
6. James Steele, 'Thomas Gray and the Season for Triumph,' in *Fearful Joy*, eds. Downey and Jones, p. 198.
7. Steele, 'Season for Triumph,' p. 208.
8. Louis Landa, 'Pope's Belinda, The General Emporie of the World, and the Wondrous Worm,' *South Atlantic Quarterly* 70 (1971), p. 221. Lee Elioseff also argues against the notion of a 'Whig' aesthetics: 'The more common practice has been to identify 'Whig' aesthetics with particular issues in both politics and criticism. The Tories were identified with a defense of the *status quo* and security, and the Whigs with "progress and an expanding future," which the Tories held to be an argument for excessive irregularity . . . . [However, the] pattern of crossing party lines in key issues is prominent enough to make the use of differences of opinion on general political questions an uncertain guide to the definition of Tory or Whig aesthetics.' *The Cultural Milieu of Addison's Literary Criticism* (Austin: University of Texas Press, 1963), pp. 128–29. But see Samuel Kliger, 'Whig Aesthetics: A Phrase in Eighteenth Century Taste,' *ELH* 16 (1949), pp. 135–50.
9. Steele, 'Season for Triumph,' pp. 200–01.
10. Steele, in 'Season for Triumph,' makes a similar point: 'Gray's sense of distance from the common people (*Corres.*, II, 852), his amusement at the pretensions of a "broken Tradesman" (*Corres.*, II, 758–59), and his political fear of the collective strength of petty-bourgeois craftsmen [*Corres.*, II, 875] were also in line with a bourgeois definition of liberty which ever since the crushing of the Levellers had formally excluded men not in possession of substantial wealth' (p. 204). It should be clear that the 'bourgeois definition' Steele writes of here is derived from, and shared with, the ideology of those he earlier calls 'the capitalist ruling class in England' (p. 198).
11. Laurence Goldstein has a comparable analysis of Pope and the ideological implications of the debate over 'Caesarism' in the earlier eighteenth century: Pope 'praised Caesar Augustus in the advertisement to his *Epistle to Augustus* for carrying out the royal responsibility: "the Increase of an *Absolute Empire*." But his adaptation of Horace's

poem contains a contemporary note: "to make the poem entirely English, I was willing to add one or two of those [qualities] which contribute to the Happiness of a *Free People*, and are more consistent with the Welfare of *our Neighbours*." The exact prescription of parts for a working harmony eluded People, in part because the new age of commercial expansion brought into ascendancy a class of people which offended his taste. Many intellectuals, like Pope, were uncomfortable with the implications of their sincere desire for a commercial empire.' *Ruins and Empire* (Pittsburgh: University of Pittsburgh Press, 1977), p. 45.

12. Joseph Addison, *The Spectator* 1, Thursday, March 1, 1710–11, in *Works*, ed. Richard Hurd, 6 vols. (London: George Bell & Sons, 1880), ii. 230–31.
13. Barrell, *English Literature in History, 1730–80*, p. 183.
14. Barrell, *English Literature in History, 1730–80*, p. 207. I should make clear that unlike the four public men of letters Barrell lists, Gray was very much the private student of nature and culture. Johnson, for instance, made his polymathic abilities the basis for his social and cultural position; Gray, on the other hand, discovered in natural history, entomology, history, and literary history compensations for his perceived lack of similar authority.
15. William Powell Jones, *Thomas Gray, Scholar: The True Tragedy of an Eighteenth-Century Gentleman* (Cambridge: Harvard University Press, 1937), p. 146. Jones calls his book 'the critical biography of an eighteenth-century poet who preferred to be known as a "gentleman"' (p. 29).
16. S.H. Clark offers a similar insight: 'I feel that the interpretive bias of Gray's poetry cannot be too strongly stressed: reading him gives a sense not of the re-enactment of feeling, but of modes of assessing feeling, an emotional hermeneutic. The verse often seems stilted, assembled rather than written, because it refuses to focus back on to a posited point of origin. The "sacred source" of sentiment proves unknowable: instead we get a sequence of discrete analytical moments.' '"Pendent Homo Incertus": Gray's Response to Locke. Part One: "Dull in a New Way",' *Eighteenth-Century Studies* 24 (1991), p. 279. Clark argues for a reading of Gray's poems that would see them as 'reactive, a series of rigorous meditations on the Lockean self,' particularly insofar as they enact the crises of self that follow from Locke's notion of the 'individual entropy' to which memory (the basis of Augustan rationalism) is subject (pp. 274, 280). While I agree

entirely that in Gray's poems 'the poetic voice must diagnose its own uncertainty, probe its own lack of authority' (p. 279), I locate the sources of such uncertainty not only in Gray's reading of Locke but largely in his response to the changing matrix of contemporary literary and poetic production. However, as Clark suggests, Gray's socio-cultural and professional dilemmas could certainly have found intellectual analogues in Locke's ideas.

17. Lonsdale writes: 'In spite of, or perhaps because of, its popularity, G. rarely mentioned the *Elegy* after its publication . . . Yet if G. at times disliked being a popular author, the "affecting and pensive" Mr Gray, he was not entirely indifferent to the *Elegy's* success. A marginal note . . . in the transcript of the poem . . . lists, with evident satisfaction, the various edns it passed through.' A small, scholarly marginal note—that is all that the enthusiastic public reception of the poem merited from Gray. *The Poems of Thomas Gray, William Collins, Oliver Goldsmith*, ed. Roger Lonsdale (London: Longman, 1969), p. 113. Future references are to this edition.
18. Jones, *Thomas Gray, Scholar*, p. 146.
19. Gray to Count Algarotti, September 9, 1763. *Correspondence*, ii. 810–11.
20. Later in the same letter, Gray's remarks on the progress of architecture in England confirm this vision of royal patronage: 'Charles had not only a love for the beautiful arts, but some taste in them. The confusion, that soon follow'd, swept away his magnificent collection, the artists were dispersed or ruin'd & the arts disregarded till very lately. The young Monarch on the throne is said to esteem & understand them: I wish he may have the leisure to cultivate, & the skill to encourage them with due regard to merit, otherwise it is better to neglect them.' *Correspondence*, ii. 812.
21. In a recent article, Linda Zionkowski argues that 'Gray's verse, particularly his odes, does not display alienation from "culture" or "society" in general, but rather argues specific anxieties over the poet's function during this period of commodified texts and expanding readerships.' 'Bridging the Gulf Between: The Poet and the Audience in the Work of Gray,' *ELH* 58 (1991), pp. 332–33. As my analysis will show, I am in complete sympathy with Zionkowski's overall argument, though my readings of Gray's poems differ from hers, particularly in the ways in which we map the dislocations (and the recuperations) of the authorial voice in the poems.

I

The World of Letters

The Legitimation and Regulation of Cultural Authority

Shut, shut the door, good John! fatigu'd I said,
Tye up the knocker, say I'm sick, I'm dead,
The Dog-star rages! nay 'tis past a doubt,
All *Bedlam*, or *Parnassus*, is let out:
Fire in each eye, and Papers in each hand,
They rave, recite, and madden round the land.
—Pope, 'An Epistle to Dr. *Arbuthnot*' (1734)

Shall we not censure all the motley train, . . .
The college sloven, or embroider'd spark;
The purple prelate, or the parish clerk;
The quiet quidnunc, or demanding prig;
The plaintiff tory, or defendant whig;
Rich, poor, male, female, young, old, gay or sad
Whether extremely witty, or quite mad;
Profoundly dull, or shallowly polite;
Men that read well, or men that only write;
Whether peers, porters, tailors, tune the reeds,
And measuring words to measuring shapes succeeds
For bankrupts write, when ruin'd shops are shut,
As maggots crawl from out a perish'd nut.
His hammer this, and that his trowel quits,
And, wanting sense for tradesmen, serve for wits.
By thriving men exists each other trade;
Of every broken craft a writer's made:
—Young, 'Two Epistles to Mr. Pope' (1730)

Poems that announce themselves as letters—Epistles—foreground their circuit of communication. By specifying both addressee and sender, they nominally limit, and provide a structured context for, their reception. In doing so, they are more particular and formally overt than other poetic modes like the lyric, whose privacy is based on the fiction that it is addressed to no one, or even the epic, whose public, declamatory stance is predicated upon its claim to speak to all people, that is, to speak to another kind of anonymity. These distinctions are, of course, not absolute: the lyric that is 'overheard' is more often than not published, and the epic often comes with a Preface Dedicatory that defines its ideal reader or reading community. The poem-as-epistle shares in this fictive and presentational paradox or dualism, which it inscribes into its very title. How- ever, there is no question that the two or more proper names of the addressee(s) and the author are meant to have a public resonance strong enough to make the cultural context of the particular poetic discourse clear. The names inscribed are meant to situate the poem socially, to validate its thematic concerns, and to anchor its polemical and ideological positions.

These names, then, act as a special, and even more categoric, instance of what Michel Foucault describes as the 'effect' of the (name of the) author: 'It points to the existence of certain groups of discourse and refers to the status of this discourse within a society and culture. The author's name is not a function of a man's civil status, nor is it fictional; it is situated in the breach, among the discontinuities, which gives rise to new groups of discourse and their singular mode of existence . . . [it] characterize[s] the existence, circulation, and operation of certain discourses within a society.'[1]

Both Edward Young's 'Two Epistles to Mr. Pope' and Alexander Pope's 'An Epistle from Mr. *Pope* to Dr. *Arbuthnot*' use names to nominate an exclusive elite of poets and authors, and to simultaneously characterise and sanction the particular discourses associated with this elite. In Young's poem, Swift, Addison, and Pope—'Our age demands correctness; Addison/ And you this commendable hurt have done' (ii. 133-34)[2]—are the eighteenth-century writers whose methods and personae set the standard for authentic authorial practices. Pope names into existence an entire cultural community—'*Granville* the polite,/ And knowing *Walsh*,' 'Well-natur'd *Garth*,' '*Congreve*,' '*Swift*,' 'The Courtly *Talbot, Somers, Sheffield*,' 'mitred *Rochester*,' 'St. John's,' and '*Dryden*' (ll. 135–41)[3]—whose support authenticates his claim to poetic authority, and, by extension, their own.

This positive community is reinforced by the presence, in these poems, of a negative group, people who do not get things right. Young uses no proper names, only literary pseudonyms, satirising Codrus, Lico, and Clodio as those who 'languish for an author's name' (ii. 97), but whose motives and abilities deny them this desire. Pope piles up a long list of proper names and pseudonyms: *Arthur, Pitholeon, Curl, Codrus*,[4] *Colly, Henley, Moor, Bavius, Philips, Sapho, Tibald, Bufo, Balbus, Sporus, Welsted, Budgel* are all writers, booksellers, patrons who represent the wrong kind of cultural establishment.

Both Young's and Pope's epistles are poems (to use Young's sub-title) 'concerning the authors of the age.' This theme, and, especially in Pope's case, the desire to win every topical literary battle, can explain the anxious profusion of names in these texts. The form of the catalogue of names—part real, part fictional; part proper, part pseudonymous—is shaped by the strategy of attack followed by Young and Pope in their battles. They refuse to allow that the tribe of contemporary writers is so numerous that it represents a qualitative and distinct historical shift in the nature and status of the profession;[5] their way to contain the problem is to locate it in a recognisable literary-cultural tradition of upstarts and pretenders, Codrus and Bavius giving way to Cibber and Philips. That way the entire weight of canonical culture can be brought to bear upon this new threat, and past 'victories' offer reassurance of present success.

Rhetorical and polemical triumphs do not come quite so easily though, as an examination of these poems will show. The threat registered is too strong, its origin too close to home to allow for containment without contamination.[6] But first the threat. For Young, a scatological cum literary flood is at hand:

> at parties, parties bawl,
> And pamphlets stun the streets, and load the stall;
> So rushing tides bring things obscene to light,
> Foul wrecks emerge, and dead dogs swim in sight;
> The civil torrent foams, the tumult reigns,
> And Codrus' prose works up, and Lico's strains.
> Lo! what from cellars rise, what rush from high,
> Where speculation roosted near the sky;
> Letters, essays, sock, buskin, satire, song,
> And all the garret thunders on the throng! (i. 3–12)

Pope's vision of Codrus's insensitivity too is of theatrical apocalypse:

> take it for a rule,
> No creature smarts so little as a Fool.
> Let Peals of Laughter, *Codrus*! round thee break,
> Thou unconcern'd cans't hear the mighty Crack.
> Pit, Box and Gall'ry in convulsions hurl'd,
> Thou stands't unshook amidst a bursting World.
> (ll. 83–88)

Even when we take into account the rhetorical overkill of eighteenth-century satire, and remind ourselves that Young could have profitably followed his own maxim—'Unless you boast the genius of a Swift,/ Beware of humour, the dull rogue's last shift' (ii. 179–80)—we are left with the impression of a world under siege: 'Shut, shut the door, good *John*!'

Both Young and Pope are clear about what is at stake in this battle.[7] Now 'Millions of wits, and brokers in old song' (i. 58) all 'languish for an author's name' (ii. 97). Young's own sentiments are clear: 'An author! 'tis a venerable name!/ How few deserve it, and what numbers claim!' (ii. 15–16). For those who dare stake their claims, Young has better names: 'vipers,' 'insects,' 'flies' (i. 22, 29,

30). As lines 39-54 of the first *Epistle* show, Young is worried not only about the quality of the lines being produced ('how few deserve') but even more about the fact that there is no check on who can set up shop as a writer ('what numbers claim!'). Accordingly the greatest part of the first *Epistle* is given over to examining not the quality of contemporary production—how and why the prose is 'heavy' and the verse 'immoral' (ii. 65-66)—but the social relations of production, beginning with the question 'What glorious motives urge our authors on?' (i. 69).

The answers are various: one poet

> loses his estate, and down he sits,
> To show (in vain!) he still retains his wits:
> Another marries, and his dear proves keen;
> He writes as a hypnotic for his spleen:
> Some write, confin'd by physic; some, by debt;
> Some, for 'tis Sunday; some, because 'tis wet. (i. 71–76)

This account of idiosyncratic psychological and material reasons leads to two extended 'characters' of would-be authors, Lico and Clodio (i. 81–122). Both, it seems, write for money:

> Has Lico learning, humour, thought profound?
> Neither: why write then? He wants twenty pound:
> His belly, not his brains, this impulse give. (i. 81–83)

Clodio, 'His fortune squander'd, . . . / for bread his indolence must quit,/ Or turn a soldier, or commence a wit' (i. 111–114).

Pope's poem is also concerned about the ease with which anyone can become a 'Man of Ryme' (ll. 15-18). All those who apply to him are not only bad writers—'I read/ With honest anguish, and an aking head' (ll. 37-38)—but also those who would make money from their writing, either from Pope or from his intercession with others. One wants 'Friendship, and a Prologue, and ten Pound' (l. 48); *Pitholeon* seeks an introduction to a patron (ll. 49–54); a 'stranger' sues for commendation to the stage or to Lintot; and

One from all *Grubstreet* will my fame defend,
And, more abusive, calls himself my friend.
This prints my Letters, that expects a Bribe,
And others roar aloud, 'Subscribe, subscribe.' (ll. 111–14)

The last line in particular focuses the general irony of Pope's diatribe against professional writers. As Ian Watt points out, Pope was 'able to assert his independence from patronage through the new resources which the booksellers had made available . . . Pope set out to beat venal booksellers and hacks at their own game. By an extraordinary example of the interpenetration of opposites . . . Pope turned his aristocratic friends, not into patrons, but into publishers—he set Lady Burlington, the Earls of Orrery, Islay and Granville, and the Viscount Simon Harcourt to soliciting subscriptions, dispatching and storing books, keeping accounts and collecting money, and he also made the Earl of Oxford, the Earl of Burlington and Lord Bathurst proprietors of the copyright of *The Dunciad*.'[8]

Both Young and Pope were obviously aware that their condemnation of 'restless men, who pant for letter'd praise' (l. 21) and who wish to gain preferment or make a living by writing, could easily be turned on themselves. Their poems thematise this anxiety, offering elaborate justifications for why they write, then or ever. Young's poem is forced out of him:

O Pope! I burst; nor can, nor will refrain;
I'll write; let others, in their turn, complain:
Truce, truce, ye Vandals! my tormented ear
Less dreads a pillory than a pamphleteer;
I've heard myself to death; and, plagu'd each hour,
Shan't I return the vengeance in my power? (i. 13–18)

At the end of the second *Epistle*, in which he sets up a curriculum of corrective advice for would-be poets, Young hears the voices of those whom he has addressed:

"Who's this with nonsense, nonsense would restrain?

> Who's this (they cry) so vainly schools the vain?
> Who damns our trash, with so much trash replete?
> (ii. 217–19)

In the face of such predictable criticism, Young offers a well-worn defence, invoking 'Time' as the impartial judge:

> Time is the judge; time has nor friend nor foe;
> False fame must wither, and the true will grow.
> Arm'd with this truth, all critics I defy;
> For if I fall, by my own pen I die. (ii. 231–34)

His vision of a stoical death is his attempt to transcend the basic contradiction of his position, for the disease he claims infects 'the writing tribe' (ii. 229) contaminates him too.

Pope's attempt to explain his genesis as a writer is more artful, claiming both a power beyond himself—a natural gift—and a need for an 'idle trade' (l. 129),[9] to 'help me thro' this long Disease, my Life' (l. 131):

> Why did I write? what sin to me unknown
> Dipt me in ink, my Parents' or my own?
> As yet a child, nor yet a Fool to Fame,
> I lisp'd in Numbers, for the Numbers came. (l. 125–28)

To explain his decision to publish, Pope enumerates all those who praised and encouraged him (the list is quoted on page 18), who 'With open arms receiv'd one Poet more' (ll. 135-42). There is, of course, no mention that he too might have written to make a living. It is precisely the professionalisation of the vocation of author that Pope must distance himself from, and his way of doing so is to claim the approbation of an aristocratic cultural and social circle as the guarantor of his authority.

Thus, not all authorship is bad. Certain kinds of writing and publication are acceptable, but, for the most part, contemporary production needs to be censured. Young, who calls critics 'snarlers' (ii. 235) when they address him, nevertheless believes in 'just judges' (i. 148) and 'censors' (i. 159):

Teach them, ye judges! with an honest scorn,
And weed the cockle from the generous corn.[10]

(i. 151–52)

Standards are to be maintained, and Young specifies the types of writing that he does not approve of. He does not like hagiographers who write solely for patronage (i. 175–85),[11] nor those who lack principles, and in their writing 'love, and hate, extempore, for gold' (i. 202). He reserves a special ire for party writers, calling them 'vipers,' who 'poison' and pour their 'politics through pipes of lead,/ Which far and near ejaculate, and spout' (i. 212–13).[12] There is little that is surprising here—this is the standard vituperation indulged in by both sides of the literary and political controversies of the day.

For Pope, over two decades after the critical prescriptions of *An Essay on Criticism*, bad writing is to be judged primarily by its social and moral effects:

Curst be the Verse, how well so'er it flow,
That tends to make one worthy Man my foe,
Give Virtue scandal, Innocence a fear,
Or from the soft-eyed Virgin steal a tear! (ll. 283–86)

Pope continues to use these categories throughout this passage (ll. 283–304), ending with an attempt to salvage his poetry from the reader who 'reads but with a Lust to mis-apply,/ Make Satire a Lampoon, and Fiction, Lye' (ll. 301–02). Of particular interest here is line 302, which registers the anxiety of the practising poet about the fine margin that separates the properly 'literary' genre ('Satire' or 'Fiction') from the improper and self-serving form ('Lampoon' or 'Lye'). The writing and publication of *The Dunciad* (1728) would have taught Pope that this tenuous separation could be exploited, both by writer and by (mis)reader.[13]

Thus, in his own defence, and in a characteristic form of self-definition (in that he uses negations and oppositions rather than positive assertions), Pope writes:

> Not Fortune's Worshipper, nor Fashion's Fool,
> Nor Lucre's Madman, nor Ambition's Tool,
> Not proud, not servile, be one Poet's praise
> That, if he pleas'd, he pleas'd by manly ways,
> . . . .
> That not for Fame, but Virtue's better end,
> He stood the furious Foe, the timid Friend. (ll. 334–43)

As I will go on to argue, such an attempt at defining authorship and cultural authority through moral negations is structurally characteristic, ideologically necessary, and historically contingent—and as such, it offers us one important way of understanding what was at stake in so many of the literary and cultural controversies of the early and mid-eighteenth century.

In Pope's poem, the recourse to moral binarisms in his attempt at self-definition as an author, or, more accurately, Self-distinction from Other authors, follows from the fact that he was primarily interested in making and maintaining socio-cultural, rather than more specifically literary, distinctions. Pope did describe this poem as a 'just vindication from slanderers of all sorts, and slanderers of what rank or quality soever,'[14] but it is still surprising that he is at his most scathing in the character of 'Sporus,' Lord Hervey (ll. 305–33), who was better known as a courtier and Whig politician than as a writer. The portrait of 'Bufo' (ll. 230–50), a composite of Bubb Dodington and the Earl of Halifax, is also a condemnation, as I have said before, not of shoddy literary production, but of the social relations of production gone awry. Most revealing of all, perhaps, is Pope's study of Addison as 'Atticus' (ll. 193–214), where he is careful to qualify his cultural resentment with outright praise for Addison's literary abilities:

> Peace be to all! but were there One whose fires
> True Genius kindles, and fair Fame inspires,
> Blest with each Talent and each Art to please,
> And born to write, converse, and live with ease:
> Shou'd such a man, too fond to rule alone,

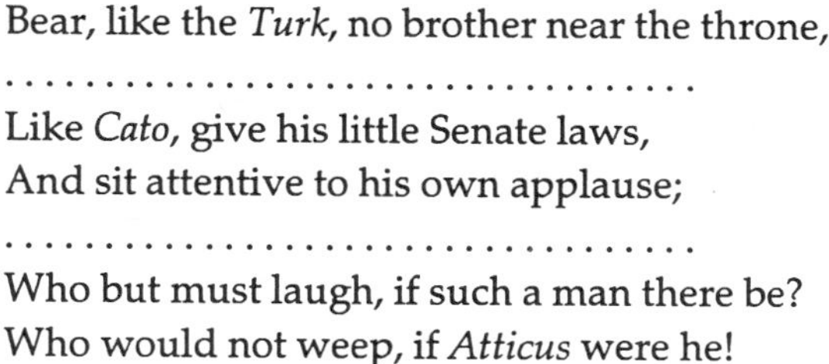

> Bear, like the *Turk*, no brother near the throne,
> . . . .
> Like *Cato*, give his little Senate laws,
> And sit attentive to his own applause;
> . . . .
> Who but must laugh, if such a man there be?
> Who would not weep, if *Atticus* were he!

The problem with Atticus lies not in what he writes, but in the fact that he runs his literary and cultural kingdom parsimoniously, that he keeps it closed to those whose talents threaten his stature.

Line 200, about Addison's jealous 'hate[red] for Arts [in other writers] that caus'd himself to rise,' emphasises the essentially social nature of the Pope-Addison quarrel. Addison had been particularly successful at achieving exactly what Pope had been engaged in—a career-long attempt to parlay his abilities as a writer into a role as *the* contemporary arbiter of cultural and social values. For Pope, in fact, Addison was more a figure to identify with than to scapegoat (and perhaps to scapegoat precisely because of the threat presented by such an identification): 'But after all I have said of this great man, there is no rupture between us: We are each of us so civil and obliging, that neither thinks he is obliged: and I for my part treat with him, as we do with the Grand Monarch; who has too many great qualities not to be respected, tho' we know he watches any occasion to oppress us.'[15]

When Pope does mention those writers he wishes to distinguish himself from, he rarely does more than name them:

> And has not *Colley* still his Lord, and Whore?
> His Butchers *Henley*, his Free-Masons *Moor*?
> Does not one table *Bavius* still admit?
> Still to one Bishop *Philips* seem a wit? (ll. 97–100)

The Dunciad had, of course, done much of Pope's work for him, and these names function primarily as echoes of their presence in the Empire of Dulness. However, even when Pope does specify literary grounds for taking exception to writers, he describes first those who would be *critics*: 'From slashing *Bentley* down to pidling *Tibalds* . . . / Each Word-catcher who lives on syllables' (ll. 164–66).

The only passage in which Pope actually describes literary failures is lines 179–88, where he condemns plagiarism ('pilf'red Pastorals'), writing for money, and the mutilation of generic distinctions:

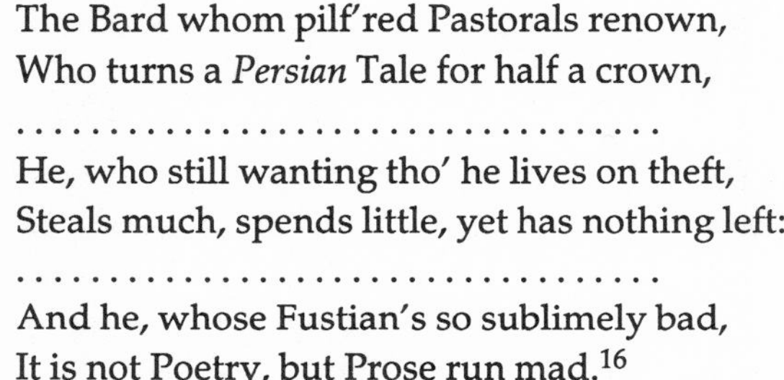

The Bard whom pilf'red Pastorals renown,
Who turns a *Persian* Tale for half a crown,
. . . .
He, who still wanting tho' he lives on theft,
Steals much, spends little, yet has nothing left:
. . . .
And he, whose Fustian's so sublimely bad,
It is not Poetry, but Prose run mad.[16]

Pope's choice of literary scandals is symptomatic in that, except for the last one, they are all concerned with social and legal definitions of authorship.[17] 'Sporus,' 'Bufo,' 'Atticus,' the 'pilferer,' the 'hack' all name problems generated by the collapse not of literary standards but of the traditional social relations of cultural production. Here, Pope denounces the invasion of the bastions of high culture by the laws of the market, and the consequent conversion of the values and models of aristocratic, coterie culture into the supposedly degraded cultural activity of the 'professionals' and the London bourgeoisie.

In terms of English literary history, Pope's response is of particular significance because many of his works, and especially *The Dunciad*, were instrumental in the creation of the 'legend of Grub Street,' which, as Watt reminds us, was primarily 'an early and revealingly hostile social definition of a new professional class.'[18] Pope was not always so confident that he could consistently scapegoat those who represented to him the commodification of the literary-cultural tradition. In attack against them, he wielded his satire, and also invoked a community of social and cultural aristocrats to define and support his authorial status. However, in the absence of absolute (or even demonstrably 'literary') criteria with which to demonstrate the superiority of the older, elite conception of the author and of authorial activity, Pope was occasionally, as the 'Epistle to Dr. *Arbuthnot*' reveals, to go on the defensive. In order to examine the radical nature of his defense, however, a digression into Pope's poetic vocabulary and discursive method is necessary.

In *An Essay on Criticism* (1711), Pope attempts to derive, from the discourse and canonical authority of Classical humanism, a model of values and ideals that will define and regulate the activity of literature. He needs this authority to organise a canon and a tradition of literary inheritance, and to suggest that the history of literature (as delineated by him) is also the history of culture, morality, and politics.[19] More immediately, however, Pope also needs to foreclose the possibility that contemporary arguments about the arbitrariness of literary judgements (as indicated, for instance, in the history of critical controversies or in historical changes in aesthetic speculation) might question and render abortive his cultural project. Thus, in *An Essay on Criticism*, as later in *The Dunciad* and in the 'Epistle to Dr. *Arbuthnot*,' Pope anchors his critical prescriptions in an ethico-moral discourse, and claims as absolute literary criteria and evaluations that are necessarily judgemental and relative.

Pope begins his poem about the qualities required of a good poet or critic (ll. 1–2) by grounding poetical 'true *Genius*' and critical 'True *Taste*' in what is meant as an incontrovertible assertion: 'Both must alike from Heav'n derive their Light,/ These *born* to Judge, as well as those to Write' (ll. 11–14).[20] If Pope formulates specific literary maxims based on critical precepts (as, for example, in lines 305–327 or 337–83),[21] he also claims that these are subsidiary to moral and social concerns. A writer must combine 'Taste, Judgement, Learning' with 'Truth and Candor' in a manner collegial enough that readers go beyond the respect due to his '*Sense*' and seek his '*Friendship* too' (ll. 562–65). These moral and social concerns are specific to a certain kind of polite society, whose cultural paradigms can be easily violated, for instance, both by those who write too much, and by those who read too much: 'The *Vulgar* thus through *Imitation* err;/ As oft the *Learn'd* by being *Singular*.'[22] (ll. 424–25). If the former were to be quarantined into Grub-Street, the latter were, equally surely, to be remaindered in *Duck-Lane* (l. 445).

Pope's conflation of social, moral, and literary-critical categories is obviously not singular—an entire tradition of discourse is characterised by such practice. Critical problems arise, however, when commentators take this rhetorical strategy at its face value, accepting and internalising its constructions as 'natural' and prediscursive. Paul Fussell, for instance, allows that 'the humanist assumes that ethics and expression are closely allied,' that 'when a man has himself in order, when he has become proficient at what Adam Smith calls 'self-command,' the man's writing will naturally reflect his internal clarity and coherence. Good writing becomes thus, as it does to the Pope of the *Epistle to Dr. Arbuthnot* or *The Dunciad*, an index of moral virtue.'[23] What I am arguing, of course, is that the terms need to be reversed, that Pope cannot establish the category of 'good' writing unless he can ground it in the non-negotiable, undefined, ethical category, 'good' man.[24] As we have already seen, Pope's effort is to identify the ethical category—Good Man—with a particular, canonical tradition of literary figures, and further, to connect this tradition to a specified contemporary network of social and cultural personalities. Thus, for Pope, the discursive forms of 'humanism' become strategies for local self- and group- legitimation.[25]

An Essay on Criticism was published in 1711 and was the work of a young poet who was laying claim to membership of the elite that constituted what is often erroneously described as the 'republic' of letters. Pope's credentials were strong (he could already claim allegiance to William Walsh, for instance), and his methods in the poem reflected his confidence. He was especially shrewd in understanding that he who legislated, however loosely, the standards of 'Criticism,' could lay claim to have kept the 'professionals' (and the pedants) at bay. As the debate on 'Taste,' and on aesthetic principles generally, that raged through most of the eighteenth century testifies, Pope demarcated precisely the site of cultural contestation that would mark the progress of bourgeois ideologies in England.[26] As is well known, he went on to stage-manage the local drama of this debate, or rather, of the name-calling that sharpened its intensities. Years later, the 1728 *Dunciad* would enact the vituperative public triumph of his literary methods, but also his bitter private intimations of the inevitable loss of social hegemony of the class with which he so strongly identified.[27]

By 1734, and the writing of 'The Epistle to Dr. *Arbuthnot*,' it was clear that neither the creation of ideologically invested critical programs nor the wholesale naming and condemnation of practicing writers was capable of preventing a substantially larger number of aspirants from laying claim to the status of poet, author, man of letters. 'The Epistle to Dr. *Arbuthnot*,' then, registers Pope's awareness of the irredeemable changes in the social relations of literary and cultural production even as it actively resists these changes. As we have seen, Pope sought to legislate a particular, exclusive, *socio-cultural* definition of authorship, and thus to condemn all those who fell outside its pale, both pedants and professionals. Later in the poem, confronted with the realisation that it is impossible to prevent the name of author from being appropriated by a variety of undesirables, Pope defends himself, and his sense of the vocation, by abdicating it, by refusing to be called Author if that means he will be one of an impossible many:

> Why am I ask'd, what next shall see the light?
> Heav'ns! was I born for nothing but to write?
> Has Life no Joys for me? or, (to be grave)
> Have I no Friend to serve, no Soul to save? (ll. 271–74)

The rhetorical reversal represented by line 272 (but prepared for by lines 125 ff.) is quite remarkable. Earlier (lines 13-14), those who had been 'born' to write were the blessed; here, those who are 'born' (for nothing but) to write are the damned, separated from the 'Joys' of life.

It is, of course, appropriate that line 274 should confirm that, for Pope (as for any 'humanist' critical program), 'literary' terminology must give way, under pressure, to fuzzy moral generalisation or truism. Cultural specificity is sacrificed as Pope deploys a vocabulary of ahistorical tropes (a 'Friend to serve,' a 'Soul to save'), and the urgent debate about propriety and authority is declined in favour of a bland pastoralism. Such pieties, however, extract their own price—towards the end of the poem, the man who would have been Poet must claim as a *linguistic* ideal his 'Un-learn'd' father, who 'knew no Schoolman's subtle Art, / No Language, but the Language of the Heart' (ll. 398–99).

The phrase 'Language of the Heart' is resonant with the historical opposition between such claims of natural (moral) Authenticity and those of any kind of manipulative (poetic) Artifice. Here, Pope associates his father with the precise topos of simple and truthful linguistic performance that signifies the morally superior opposite of the subtle and artful literary practices that allowed the poet to move above his father's class. If Pope's father came by his moral and linguistic authenticity because he was 'un-learn'd,' Pope is himself suspect because he so successfully practices the 'subtle Art' of Poetry. This paradox results from more than a simple confusion in poetic vocabulary, and suggests more than a dutiful son allowing his filial sentiments to get the better of his literary-critical logic. It is also symptomatic of Pope's ambivalence towards the socio-cultural processes that permitted upward mobility, for similar processes now threatened his sense of social cohesion.

Significantly, this topos of sincerity goes together with lines which describe his father's 'long' life as one 'to sickness past unknown, / His Death was instant, and without a groan' (ll. 402–03). There is an eerie echo here. Earlier, in explaining why he wrote, Pope had said: 'The Muse but serv'd . . . / To help me thro' this long Disease, my Life' (ll. 131–32). There are strange notions of contamination and causality at work here—the person who spoke the language of moral authenticity (and not, that is, the language of poetic artifice) lived a wonderfully healthy life and died instantly, 'without a groan.' The description of the poet, on the other hand, links his writing with his 'long Disease, my Life,' and with a tainted and even morally ambiguous origin: 'What sin to me unknown / Dipt me in ink, my Parents' or my own?' (ll. 125–26). The central humanist construction (Good Man = Good Writer / Good Writer = Good Man) erected by the poem is scarcely tenable any more, victim once again to the critical incompatibility between the literary and the moral.

'The Epistle to Dr. *Arbuthnot*,' then, describes a long and inevitable personal, ideological, and historical itinerary, one that moves from the aggressive defence of the Poet's name and status of the opening lines, to the passive, melancholy retreat of the last fourteen lines, where Pope seeks only two 'Blessing[s]'—to be a dutiful Son and a comforting Friend—'the rest belongs to Heav'n' (l. 419).[28] By the close of the poem, in Pope's seeming abdication of vocation, it is tempting to read the door that is shut (in the first line) in an attempt to keep out the most obvious manifestations of the effects of historical change on poetry—professional poets—as, in fact, shutting out the very conditions of possibility of poetry. As the 1743 *Dunciad* amply shows, for Pope, the life of the poet could only, finally, be the life of engagement—defensive and besieged perhaps, but definitively engaged.

This tour through the embattled displacements of the authorial self in Pope, and through the modes of discourse that underwrite these slides in the rhetoric of self-presentation, can be recreated by elaborating similar moments in Young. Perhaps one example will serve. 'The black militia of the pen' (i. 310) that so disturb Young are characterised in a variety of vituperative terms. Their manners are 'abandon'd;' they 'draw their venal breath' through 'meagre jaws;' they are marked, Cain-like, as 'murderers of fame' who are different from men; worse, they are men who 'oftener changed their principles than shirt.' These, clearly, are not quite 'literary' critiques, except in the sense that we have already seen operating in Pope, where the literary is, by definition, a particular style of social and cultural behaviour, allegiance, and belonging. Once such a norm has been breached, the professionalisation of letters appears to Young in its most horrific form, as the Protean figure of slippery, threatening cheangeability that escapes social accountability:

> How justly Proteus' transmigrations fit
> The monstrous changes of a modern wit!
> . . . .
> He's now a serpent, and his double tongue
> Salutes, nay licks, the feet of those he stung;
> What knot can bind him, his evasion such? (i. 239–52)

The answer to the last question is quite clear. In the absence of the power of select patronage, or rather, in the presence of the power of the market, the modern wit, the 'swine obscene,' can sup where and as he will (i. 245–46). Young's evasion of this answer takes the form of a well-known rhetorical ploy—what cannot be controlled by social or cultural fiat must be contained in recognisable tropes of moral failure and condemnation. Among other monstrous forms, 'modern authors' ('Made up of venom, volumes, stains, and stings!') resemble snakes, corrupters of a cultural Eden: 'Thrown from the tree of knowledge, like you, curst/ To scribble in the dust, was snake the first' (ii. 253–60).

Both Young and Pope were well aware of the socio-economic or material bases for the narrative of exclusion and condemnation they were writing. Johnson, sensitised to this by his own experiences as a professional writer (and by those of writers like Richard Savage, who were friends), wrote of Pope's imagination being 'too full' of the fortune he had made, and of the regrettable obverse of his delight 'in talking of his money': 'The great topic of his ridicule is poverty: the crimes with which he reproaches his antagonists are their debts, their habitation in the Mint, and their want of a dinner. He seems to be of the opinion, not very uncommon in the world, that to want money is to want everything.'[29]

Young, as does Pope, writes into his text an anticipatory defence against just such criticism, converting, as we might expect, the socio-economic into the moral, rewriting the material condition of poverty as the spiritual sin of pride: 'I reverence misfortune, not deride;/ I pity poverty, but laugh at pride' (i. 127–28). His attack on pride is brief, though, and he ends the first epistle with a revealing tableau, which features impecunious contemporary poets enmeshed in the paradoxical, even perverse, economic and power relations that characterised the eighteenth-century market commodification of literature. These would-be poets ('O merry melancholy fate!') soon *beg* 'in rhyme, and warble through a grate,' and are reduced to abject recipients of charity:

> The friend through pity gives, the foe through spite;
> And though full conscious of his injur'd purse,
> Lintot relents, nor Curll can wish them worse.
> So fare the men, who writers dare commence,
> Without their patent, probity, and sense. (i. 281–88)

Young's recasting of the publishers Lintot and Curll as reluctant *patrons* here seems almost poignant, a sad attempt to reconceive the laws of the market as the spirit of *noblesse oblige*.

Pope's cognizance of an objection like Johnson's takes the following form: 'I question not that such authors are poor, and heartily wish the objection *were removed by any honest livelihood*. But Poverty here is the accident, not the subject . . . Not but poverty itself becomes a just burden of satyre, when it is the consequence of vice, prodigality, *or neglect of one's lawful calling*; for then it increases the public burden, fills the streets and highways with Robbers, and the garrets with Clippers, Coiners, and Weekly Journalists' (my italics).[30] As my earlier discussion of line 129 of 'The Epistle to Dr. *Arbuthnot*' shows (see note 9), for Pope, terms like 'honest livelihood' and 'lawful calling,' were, in the context of his discussions of authorship, moral imperatives designed to attack what he perceived as the primary problem, the overpopulation of the 'idle trade' of letters. A more accurate index of Pope's attitude might be three lines in 'The Epistle to Dr. *Arbuthnot*,' which sum up his criteria for distinguishing himself from other writers, or, more locally, for explaining why he chose not to respond to their 'venal quill[s]:'

I never answered, I was not in debt:
If want provoked, or madness made them print,
I wag'd no war with *Bedlam* or the *Mint*. (ll. 153–55)

For Pope then, Satire—the literary form whose originary moment is the desire to Name the Other—is the chosen vehicle of his attempts to define, intimidate, and distance 'the Race that write.' Young's first Epistle follows suit, but the second takes a somewhat different attitude, attempting an accommodation through acculturation. That is, it tries to educate instead of condemn, and this by setting out 'Some needful precepts how to write, and live!' (ii. 12). Interestingly, this move from the satiric to the didactic is paralleled, or perhaps made possible by, a topographical shift—the second Epistle is written 'From Oxford.'[31] This material realignment of perspective seems to allow Young the rhetorical distance that he earlier needed satire to create. He claims that the *genius loci* of Oxford now empowers him, and enables him to think (but not for long, as we shall see) that he can socialise—teach how to write, and *how to live*—erring literary 'owls:'

All write at London; shall the rage abate
Here, where it most should shine, the muses' seat?
. . . .
Let these instruct, with truth's illustrious ray,
Awake the world, and scare our owls away. (ii. 1–10)

The first piece of advice that Young offers is designed, appropriately enough, to restrict the quantity of poetic production, and thus to alleviate one of the primary symptoms of the contemporary market-dictation of literary culture. He invokes dead authors, telling those who would 'gain the bays' (ii. 22; we hear the language of canonicity resonate in that phrase) to consult 'the laurell'd shade' (ii. 24), but for a quite unexpected reason. Fontaine and Chaucer, Sidney and Waller, he says, would all wish to destroy 'The sprightliest efforts of their wanton thought' (ii. 22), that is, all their poems 'That boast of nought more excellent than wit' (ii. 28).[32] Very quickly then, the terms of analysis and evaluation are deployed, and in a not-so-fine sleight of hand, morality is aligned with the injunction not to publish much. What follows is an extended attack on Wit (which, of course, remains undefined, and seems to describe little more than the ability to write), to which are opposed 'plain sound sense' (ii. 83), 'Prudence' (ii. 85), and 'strong judgement' (ii. 89).

It is unnecessary to rehearse the various twists and turns that Young's argument takes in its effort to seamlessly articulate the rhetoric of moral rectitude with the prescription to be so critically fastidious that little gets published: 'We praise for what you burn, and what you spare:/ The part you burn, smells sweet before the shrine'[33] (ii. 140–41). Shaping the sonorous, meaningless ebb and flow of moral cliche and critical truism—'Clear be the style,' 'Easy the conduct,' 'Striking the moral, and the soul divine,' 'Thus virtue's seeds, at once, and laurel's, grow,' (ii. 201–08)—is the powerful undertow—the primary equation of 'good' writing with 'good' man: 'Would you restore just honors to the pen?/ From able writers rise to worthy men' (ii. 215-16).

As we have seen in Pope, and as Young's first Epistle makes clear, 'good' men ('worthy men') exist in a particular, precisely specified social avatar, as an alliance of the culturally twice-born that represents itself (to itself, and to all those who will listen) as the repository and guardian of *all* value. The narratives of self-congratulatory self- (or group-)representation that we have read accompany the scapegoating rituals of satire precisely because, in this moment of cultural 'crisis,' it is not enough merely to name the Other.[34] The structural changes were so deep, the revolution in the social and economic relations of literary production so drastic, that the reaction to it demanded the simultaneous elaboration of an alternative, backward-looking canonical and social configuration. Both Young's and Pope's texts are centrally involved in such a critique and such a creation, an involvement all the more convoluted (and ideologically invested) because it demanded the repudiation or revision of their own histories as traders in the word. It is no wonder then that Young can hear, at the end of the critical accommodation he has preached at 'the writing tribe,' the clear and derisive question: 'Who's this with nonsense, nonsense would restrain' (ii. 217).

The presence, in the poem, of this mocking signal of the relativity of literary distinctions (one poet's 'sense' is another poet's 'nonsense') should remind us of just how necessary it was for both Young and Pope to articulate their ideas of legitimate poetical authority in the discourse of (classical) humanism. We have seen how this rhetorical conflation of the ethical and the literary works to stabilise their critical programs, and we have charted how, in the face of the transformation of the public domain of letters, both Pope and Young emphasise doggedly their 'moral' resistance to any change in the social definition or activity of the author.

Perhaps the best instance of this tension between the ethico-moral and the social 'definitions' of authorship is to be found in a different text though, Young's *Conjectures on Original Composition* (1759). Young, still in search of the sources of the writer's authority, has recourse to Orphic dicta: 'I borrow two golden rules from *Ethics*, which are no less golden in *Composition*, than in life. I. *Know thyself*; 2dly, *Reverence thyself*.'[35] The writer who follows these rules will 'soon find the world's reverence to follow his own. His works will stand distinguished; his the sole Property of them; which Property alone can confer the noble title of an *Author*; that is, of one who (to speak accurately) *thinks*, and *composes*; while other invaders of the Press, how voluminous, and learned soever, (with due respect be it spoken) only *read*, and *write*.'[36]

Young's argument here is difficult to unravel. The forms that self-knowledge and self-reverence might take are not made clear, nor are we told about meditative or reflective methods which could lead to such understanding. An ethical knowledge of the self, however, is considered necessary for both authorial originality and for 'sole Property' over the text—the name of Author, that is, is predicated upon authentic Selfhood. Further, such an author is defined 'accurately' as one who '*thinks*, and *composes*,' as opposed to other writers, however voluminous or learned, who 'only *read* and *write*.' Its argument aside, this passage reminds us forcefully that, like Pope, Young grounds his analysis of the sources of a writer's authority in the prescriptions of ethics, striving to keep at bay the competing claims of learning or professionalism ('other invaders of the Press').

There is another suggestion in the passage that might be fruitfully followed up: Young's claim that the 'sole Property' over the text, 'which Property alone can confer the noble title of an *Author*,' is derived from authentic self-knowledge, rather than from the obvious source of literary property: copyright or any equivalent professional practice. If we remember the Foucauldian suggestion that the socially and culturally powerful 'idea' of author follows that of legal definitions of authorial property, then we are in a position to see what Young was arguing against. The Statute of Anne of 1709 made literary property rights a feature of copyright, which obviously suggested a specific, socio-legal definition of authorship.[37] Literary authority, that is, became subject to practices that were derived from the world of professional writers and publishers. Young's discourse of moral imperatives and ethical universals, then, seems deployed once again in defence against the professionalisation of the vocation of letters. Once property-rights become the dominant source of literary authority, Young must seek to rescue this language of 'property,' and thus posits the ethically aware self as the only source of *authentic* literary property and authority.

Young's attempt to delink literary propriety from professional property by arguing the priority of self-knowledge is, however, not an entirely arbitrary invocation of manifestly asymmetrical categories, for such a metaphysics of identity and property is the ideological telos of many eighteenth-century discussions of Authority. Underlying such claims is ultimately Locke's 'property-centered' definition of the political and existential subject: 'To understand Political Power right, and derive it from its Original, we must consider what State all Men are naturally in, and that is, a *State of perfect Freedom* to order their actions, and dispose of their Possessions, and Persons as they see fit, within the bounds of the Law of Nature, without asking leave, or depending on the Will of any other Man.'[38] Locke equates the original and natural state of man with the absolute right to alienate possessions and person: the definition of subjectivity and identity, that is, operates with a prior conception of property-rights and possessions. To argue then, as Young does, that an authentic self is the only guarantor of cultural and literary authority is to signal the prior premise, that such selfhood is predicated upon the possession of property. Thus even as Young's critical prescriptions seem to shift the debate away from socio-cultural and onto ethico-moral grounds, they in fact maintain a class-based, socially proprietory, and proper, conception of authorship.

The need for such a metaphysics, for such prescriptions, was born of a reaction to the contemporary commodification of literary practice and the corresponding change in the social relations of cultural production. In a recent essay, 'Lessons from the 'Literatory': How to Historicise Authorship,' David Saunders and Ian Hunter offer a summary account of this socio-cultural phenomenon that deserves to be quoted at length:

In the new divisions of literary labour and status made possible by the technology of print, in the new types of moral and economic activity arising from the book trade, and in the new forms of legal regulation that began to organise this milieu, it was no simple matter to delineate the person of the expressive author in contrast to that of the artisanal book producer, to differentiate the economic interests of writers from those of publishers, or to determine the relation between a writer's legal personality (as copyright holder or as responsible for obscene libel) and his or her ethical or artistic personality (as creator or moral authority). Moreover, when these distinctions began to be instituted, it was not as a sign of the emergence of the authorial subject or its illusion; it was as a set of makeshift solutions to problems arising from new circumstances and from the unforseen interactions of legal, economic, technological, and ethical institutions. The literatory, in short, is an emblem not of the necessity of the expressive author but of his or her monstrous contingency.[39]

In keeping with the general argument offered by Saunders and Hunter, my reading of Pope and Young suggests that it is the specifics of the historical moment that mark such attempts at authorial self-definition as different from earlier (and later) versions of self-representation in English literature, even when those fables of authorial identity were also directed against, and based on distinctions from, contemporary literary practitioners or systems. To take one example (as recounted by Richard Helgerson), Spenser, Jonson, and Milton were all poets responding to the lack of a distinguishing name for 'a writer of [a] particularly ambitious sort,' and the general lack of a 'system of authorial roles in which that ambition might make sense.'

> "Poet" had, they felt, been taken over by lesser men performing a lesser function, and there seemed no way of getting it back . . . They dismissed the usurpers as poetasters, versifiers, or riming parasites and elevated the great writers as *vates*; they translated 'poet' into 'maker,' equated it with "priest," "prophet,". . . But all their efforts to establish a single term that would unequivocally denote the function they strove to exercise ended in failure. The necessary distinction could thus be made only with the circumlocution of self-presentational gesture.[40]

There are structural similarities between the poetic responses to the pre-commodified seventeenth-century literary system that Helgerson describes, and those to the very different conditions of literary production in the early and mid-eighteenth century that we have been analysing. Self-definition based upon a distinction from usurping others, for example, can be understood as based upon 'the dialectical relation' of the poets under discussion to the poetical practices of their day. However, the nature of the distinctions drawn changes drastically, qualitatively. In the first instance, all the poets mentioned, as well as those they dismissed (Chapman, Daniel, Drayton, Wither, Davenant, and Cowley, among others), could see themselves as part of 'the collective project of creating a national literature,'[41] and their quarrel lay in defining a system of authorial roles that would accommodate, in its hierarchies, differing ideals and ambitions. The homogeneity of value and aspiration that shaped this issue is precisely what was threatened in the eighteenth century, when it was not the courtly 'poetaster' who was the irritant but the professional man of letters, the 'Grub-Street Hack,' whose numbers bespoke a radical transformation of not just the literary system, but of the ideological scaffolding of ideals, values and traditions that offered it structure and support. Thus, the defensive locutions of authorial self- and group- presentation in our period included representations of the other that were correspondingly harsher, more condemnatory, and, importantly, class-based and socially and culturally reactionary. When Pope and Young saw the enemy, they knew (or they claimed to know) that he was not one of them. It was such a recognition that focused their attack, and shaped the slippery terrain of cultural and ideological contestation that we will next negotiate in an attempt to locate Thomas Gray.

To prepare the way, we have William Mason's comment on Gray in a discussion of the poet's letters:

> The Reader will have gathered, from the preceding series of letters, that the greatest part of Mr. Gray's life was spent in that kind of learned leisure, which has only self-improvement and self-gratification for its object: He will probably be surprized that, with so very strait an income, he should never have read with a view to making his researches lucrative to himself, or useful to the public. The truth was, Mr. Gray had ever expunged the word *lucrative* from his own vocabulary. He may be said to be one of those very few personages in the annals of literature, especially in the poetical class, who are devoid of self-interest, and at the same time attentive to economy; and also, among mankind in general, one of those very few economists who possesses that talent, untinctured with the slightest stain of avarice. Were it my purpose in this place to expatiate on his moral excellencies, I should here add, that when his circumstances were at the lowest, he gave away such sums in private charity as would have done credit to an ampler purse: *But it is rather my less-pleasing province to acknowledge one of his foibles; and that was a certain degree of pride, which led him of all other things, to despise the idea of being thought an author professed* (my italics).[42]

Mason's letter to Horace Walpole, written when they were

discussing a posthumous edition of Gray's works, repeats this sense of Gray's punctiliousness:

I always thought Mr Gray blamable for letting the booksellers have his MSS gratis. I never saw anything myself beneath the dignity of a gentleman in making a profit of the productions of one's own brain. I frequently had disputes with him on this matter, which generally ended in a laugh—he called me covetous and I called him proud . . . [Gray] had cetainly much better have taken the profits, and bestowed them on such benevolent purposes, for which his purse was never, till of late, sufficient to answer the demands of his heart and which might have been assisted by this means had he not thrown it away on the most undeserving of all objects, *printers and booksellers*, and those rich ones into the bargain.[43]

Mason's idea that gentlemanliness is not compromised by commercial contact with the literary marketplace, and indeed that there is a kind of moral imperative for high-cultural authors to make money off odious '*printers and booksellers*' found a receptive ear in Walpole. 'I not only agree with your sentiments, but am flattered that they countenance my own practice,' Walpole replied, and then wrote that he had sold certain editions he printed at his Strawberry Hill Press only in order to meet the expenses of running the press and in order to raise money for charitable causes. Confident that he has escaped the taint of commercialism, Walpole then goes on:

I am neither ashamed of being an author, or a book seller. My mother's father was a timber-merchant, I have many reasons for thinking myself a worse man, and none for thinking myself better: consequently I shall never blush at doing anything he did. I print much better than I write, and love my trade, and hope I am not one of those *most undeserving of all objects* printers and booksellers, whom I confess you lash with justice. In sort, Sir, I have no notion of Gray's delicacy; I would not sell my talents as orators and senators do, but I would keep a shop, and sell any of my own works that would gain me a livelihood, whether books or shoes, rather than be tempted to sell myself.[44]

The spirit of *noblesse oblige* that allows Walpole to celebrate his merchant ancestry and to claim for himself the status of a gentleman author and printer came easier to the son of a Prime Minister than it did to Gray. As this correspondence shows, Walpole, Mason and Gray each in different ways had to come to terms with the world of commercial literary production. There was no possibility of ignoring the literary marketplace: Walpole claims to be a participant in this culture and yet safe from its excesses; Mason suggests a combative accomodation with its economics, where authorial and editorial payments become a way of lessening the publisher's indecent profits; and as Mason reports, Gray shied away from any kind of contact. His expunging of the word '*lucrative*' (italicised in Mason) from his authorial vocabulary, his creditable participation in acts of *private* charity, his horror 'of being thought an author *professed*'—the Gray that emerges here is nicely representative of the class and value-system that defined itself against the commercial, public, and professional claims of the eighteenth-century English bourgeoisie.

NOTES

1. Michel Foucault, 'What is an Author?' in *Language, Counter-Memory, Practice*, ed. Donald F. Bouchard (Ithaca: Cornell University Press, 1977), pp. 123–24. This essay also reminds us that we must 'study not only the expressive value and formal transformations of discourse, but its mode of existence: the modifications and variations, within any culture, of modes of circulation, valorization, attribution, and appropriation. Partially at the expense of themes and concepts that an author places in his work, the "author-function" could also reveal the manner in which discourse is articulated on the basis of social relationships' (p. 137).
2. Edward Young, *Poetical Works*, 2 vols. (London: Bell and Daldy, 1866), ii. 311. Future references are to this edition.
3. Alexander Pope, *Poems*, ed. John Butt (New Haven: Yale University Press, 1953), p. 105. Future references are to this edition.
4. The name Codrus is a good example of how the Foucauldian 'author-function' works. Pope suggests that it is 'the name of a poet ridiculed by Virgil and Juvenal: "but it is generally believed, that . . . Codrus is altogether a fictitious name . . . [applied] to those poetasters who annoyed other people by reading their productions to them".' Pope, *Poems*, p. 101, note 85. Satire creates a 'Codrus,' who is then repeatedly

invoked to conveniently characterise the circulation and operation of an entire tradition of 'ridiculous' literary practices. Further, this invocation of the improper literary name establishes the later satirist (Pope) in the line-up of canonical proper names (Virgil, Juvenal) who have felt the need to castigate similar, perhaps identical, opponents.

5. The social history of this shift is available in a variety of narratives and need not be rewritten here. First, there is Pope himself, describing why he wrote *The Dunciad* (1728): 'He lived in those days, when (after providence had permitted the Invention of Printing as a scourge for the sins of the learned) Paper also became so cheap, and printers so numerous, that a deluge of authors cover'd the land . . . At the same time, the Liberty of the Press was so unlimited, that it grew dangerous to refuse them either: For they would forthwith publish slanders unpunish'd, the authors being anonymous; nay the immediate publishers thereof lay sculking under the wings of an Act of Parliament, assuredly meant for better purposes.' 'Martinus Scriblerius of the Poem,' *The Dunciad*, ed. James Sutherland (3rd ed.; New Haven: Yale University Press, 1963), p. 49. Martha Woodmansee argues that the very idea of 'author' was the 'product of the rise in the eighteenth century of a new group of individuals: writers who sought to earn their livelihood from the sale of their writings to the new and rapidly expanding reading public . . . in an effort to establish the economic viability of living by the pen, these writers set about redefining the nature of writing. Their reflections on this subject are what, by and large, gave the concept of authorship its modern form.' 'The Genius and the Copyright: Economic and Legal Conditions of the Emergence of the "Author",' *Eighteenth-Century Studies* 17 (1984), p. 426. See also Alexandre Beljame, *Men of Letters and the English Public in the Eighteenth Century*, trans. E.O. Lorimer (London: Kegan Paul, Trench, Trubner & Co., 1948); A.S. Collins, *Authorship in the Days of Johnson* (London: Robert Holden & Co., 1927); Michael Foss, *The Age of Patronage* (Ithaca: Cornell University Press, 1971); Ian Watt, *The Rise of the Novel* (Berkeley: University of California Press, 1957), pp. 35–59; Pat Rogers, *The Augustan Vision* (New York: Barnes and Noble, 1974), pp. 76–86; James Sutherland, *A Preface to Eighteenth Century Poetry* (Oxford: Clarendon Press, 1948), pp. 44–63. Raymond Williams has a useful statistical survey of the changing socio-economic, educational and professional backgrounds of 350 writers born between 1470 and 1920 in *The Long Revolution* (New York: Columbia University Press, 1961), pp. 230–45. For a full and exhaustively documented survey of

the physical, economic, political, intellectual and professional topography of 'Grub Street' see Pat Rogers, *Grub Street* (London: Methuen & Co., 1972). Leo Lowenthal's and Marjorie Fiske's 'The Debate over Art and Popular Culture: English Eighteenth Century as a Case Study,' in Leo Lowenthal, *Literature, Popular Culture and Society* (Englewood Cliffs: Prentice-Hall, 1961), pp. 52–108, is a long and largely successful reading of the social and ideological bases of the aesthetic and literary controversies of the day. A similar cultural-materialist account of this socio-literary predicament informs Alvin Kernan's *Printing Technology, Letters and Samuel Johnson* (Princeton: Princeton University Press, 1987).

6. In *The Politics and Poetics of Transgression* (Ithaca: Cornell University Press, 1986), Peter Stallybrass and Allon White offer a similar insight. In their study of how 'a division of culture was inscribed into the definitional structure of poetic authorship,' the authors suggest that the 'position of transcendence' claimed by the 'master-poets' is based on an 'act of discursive rejection' which is 'marked out by nothing so much as the poet's attempt to found an illusory unity above and beyond the carnival. *In each case however, this apparently simple gesture of social superiority and disdain could not be effectively accomplished without revealing the very labour of suppression and sublimation involved.* Such a project is constitutive, not contingent' (pp. 123–24; my italics).

7. Young certainly thinks martial metaphors appropriate here:

   Sore prest with danger, and in awful dread
   Of twenty pamphlets levell'd at my head,
   Thus I have forg'd a buckler in my brain,
   Of recent form, to serve me this campaign:
   And safely hope to quit the dreadful field
   Delug'd with ink, and sleep behind my shield. (ii. 237–42)

8. 'Publishers and Sinners: The Augustan View,' in *Studies in Bibliography* 12 (1959), p. 19. For some financial details of these (and other) subscription lists see W.A. Speck, 'Politicians, peers and publication by subscription 1700–50,' in *Books and their Readers in Eighteenth-Century England*, ed. Isabel Rivers (New York: St. Martin's Press, 1982), pp. 47–68.

9. Line 129: 'I left no calling for this idle trade,' contains an interesting reversal of terms. Impelled by the need to keep the professions separate and sacrosanct (see lines 15–18, and Young, i. 34–54), and to keep people in the trades they were meant for (born into?), Pope calls writing an 'idle trade,' and any other trade a 'Calling.' The moral

valence of the latter word is no doubt meant to be especially persuasive, as is the suggestion that only people with leisure or a lifelong illness should engage in the 'idle trade.'

10. This is a metaphor whose alignment may indeed have slipped away from Young: 'generous corn' suggests that there is much of value to be saved, but Young's overall point is that most contemporary writing is in fact weed or 'cockle.'
11. If this is not hypocritical, it certainly is unintentionally ironic in the context of Young's literary career, in which he used dedications and inscriptions in a constant search for patronage. In a curious and rather pathetic letter to the king's favourite, Mrs. Howard, Young listed the qualities required for preferment: 'Abilities / Good Manners / Service / Age / Want / Sufferings and Zeal} for his majesty.' He lists his qualifications under each category, writing that he has turned fifty, wants a 'manner of preferment,' and 'As for *zeal,* I have written nothing without showing my duty to their majesties, and some pieces are dedicated to them.' Quoted by Rev. J. Mitford, 'Life of Young,' in Young, *Works,* i. xxxvi–xxxvii.
12. Bertrand A. Goldgar, in *Walpole and the Wits* (Lincoln: University of Nebraska Press, 1976), reminds us of the pension Walpole granted Young, and of Young's *The Instalment,* a poem so fulsome in praise of the Prime Minister that a contemporary reviewer concluded 'either that our Author had a malicious design of *traducing* this *eminent Patriot,* under a pretence of *extolling* him; or else, that he . . . has the worst knack at *Flattery* of any Man living' (p. 39). Goldgar also quotes Swift's lines from the *Craftsman* (13 February 1726/27):

    Whence *Gay* was banish'd in Disgrace,
    Where *Pope* will never show his Face;
    Where Y[oung] must torture his Invention,
    To Flatter *Knaves,* or lose his *Pension.*

13. See, for a history of published interpretations of, and 'complete keys' to, *The Dunciad,* including Pope's own *Dunciad Variorum* in 1729, James Sutherland's introduction to Pope, *Dunciad,* (especially pp. xxiii–xxix).
14. In a letter to John Caryll, December 31, 1734. Quoted by Sutherland in Pope, *Dunciad,* p. xxii.
15. Letter to James Craggs, July 15, 1715. Quoted by Sutherland in Pope, *Dunciad,* p. 110.
16. Here, Pope's desire to claim a definitional purity for Poetry seems

defensive, apotropaic. It relies implicitly on a high-cultural criterion of 'Taste,' which can tell 'Poetry' from 'Prose run mad.' Watt, in 'Publishers and Sinners,' suggests that at this time, 'the more directly commercial context of literature, unintentionally perhaps, but inexorably, favoured the most ephemeral literary forms over poetry, traditionally and actually the most perennial' (p. 17). Pope's implicit hierarchy of forms (those who write bad Poetry are actually writing Prose/those who are writing Prose are actually writing bad Poetry), is then yet another exclusionary gesture designed to distance himself from 'market-variety' writing.

17. See, for a cogently argued account of similar issues in relation to Swift, Neil Saccamano, 'Authority and Publication: The Works of "Swift",' in *The Eighteenth Century* 25 (1984), pp. 241–62, especially pp. 246–50. Once the Statute of Anne of 1709 granted writers property rights over their writing, critics and readers could not 'legitimately interpret a work written by one person but bearing the name of another; nor could we simply ignore plagiarism. Once an author's name has been joined to a work, a reader or critic is obliged always to recognize literary property rights and consequently theft' (p. 248). Saccamano's argument is made in the context of Foucault's observation that it was in the seventeenth and eighteenth centuries that a 'totally new conception was developed when ... "literary" discourse was acceptable only if it carried an author's name . . . The meaning and the value attributed to the text depended on this information.' Foucault, 'What is an Author?' p. 126.

18. Watt, 'Publishers and Sinners,' p. 17. Another way of charting the evolution of coterie cultural and critical values into less consensual, because broader-based, standards of evaluation is to follow the elaborate theorising of the concept of 'Taste' in the early eighteenth century. Sheldon Rothblatt provides a summary of this process: 'By the middle of the eighteenth century, as the patronage system in the arts began to decline in importance, it could no longer be assumed that the patron and the artist, writer or composer, held shared assumptions. The means for determining what Taste was and how it was to be acquired underwent a corresponding change ... The result was a concept of Taste far more relative then it had been in the idealist writings of Shaftesbury . . . a subjective definition began to appear in the definition of Taste and to threaten it with its plural form . . . In retrospect we can see that the Eclectic Style was a clear and direct response to an opening consumer market.' *Tradition and Change in*

English Liberal Education (London: Faber and Faber, 1976), p. 50. See also M. H. Abrams, 'Art-as-Such: The Sociology of Modern Aesthetics,' in *Bulletin of the American Academy of Arts and Sciences* 38 (1985), pp. 8–33; Joan Pittock, *The Ascendancy of Taste* (London: Routledge and Kegan Paul, 1973), especially pp. 2–29, and Robert C. Holub, 'The Rise of Aesthetics in the Eighteenth Century,' in *Comparative Literature Studies* 15 (1978), pp. 271–83.

19. This takes the form of an orthodox Progress of Poesy (ll. 683–722). Alexander Pope, *Pastoral Poetry and An Essay on Criticism*, ed. E. Audra and Aubrey Williams (New Haven: Yale University Press, 1961), pp. 317–323. Future references are to this edition.

20. We should notice the alignment of divine providence (1.13) to sanction a version of cultural aristocracy: 'These *born* to Judge, as well as those to Write' (1.14).

This desire to legislate a foundational notion of the cultural elite within attempts to formulate 'new' and ostensibly historically sensitive accounts of aesthetic values (in that the language of universals is now based on pseudo-empiricist observation) is itself a response to the dissolution of elite culture in the early and mid-eighteenth century. Aestheticians were aware of the dubiousness of such a project, as a comparison of these passages from David Hume will show: 'Thus, though the principles of taste be universal, and nearly, if not entirely the same in all men; yet few are qualified to give judgement on any work of art, or establish their own sentiment as the standard of beauty.' Hume lists those qualities as are necessary: 'Strong sense, united to delicate sentiment, improved by practice, perfected by comparison, and cleared of all prejudice.' Yet his very next paragraph asks 'but where are such critics to be found? By what marks are they to be known? *How distinguish them from pretenders?* These questions are embarrassing; and seem to throw us back into the same uncertainty, from which, during the course of this dissertation, we have endeavoured to extricate ourselves' (my italics). 'Of the Standard of Taste,' *Four Dissertations* (1757; reprinted, New York: Garland Publishing Inc., 1970), pp. 228–29.

Peter Hohendahl, in 'Literary Criticism and the Public Sphere,' summarises the antecedents of attempts like Hume's: the concept of taste was, in the seventeenth century, 'closely linked to the culture of the social elite. Good taste, mediated by both heredity and environment, distinguished the lifestyle of the aristocracy from the lifestyle of other levels of society; superior taste was the basis of their claim to cultural leadership. This concept was a powerful instrument in the hands of the ruling class.' *The Institution of Criticism* (Ithaca: Cornell University Press, 1982), pp. 49–50.

21. These lines, especially 340–343, are a good example of the way Pope transformed what were originally closely observed, technical 'Thoughts' on '*the defect in Numbers* of several of our Poets' (my italics), into a moral and ideological condemnation of their practices:

    [The Muse's] *Voice* is all these tuneful Fools admire,
    Who haunt *Parnassus* but to please their Ear,
    Not mend their Minds; as some to *Church* repair,
    Not for the *Doctrine*, but the *Musick* there.

    For Pope's earlier technical discussion see his letter to Cromwell, November 25, 1710, in *The Correspondence of Alexander Pope*, ed. George Sherburn, 5 vols. (Oxford: Clarendon Press, 1956), i. 106–08.

22. Joan Pittock offers a quick summary of this general phenomenon: 'For the Augustan, good taste as the purlieu of a select minority in a mass civilisation was thought to be endangered by the practice of writers who had not been trained by education or upbringing to appreciate the best models. In this context the single-minded pursuit of scholarship to the possible detriment of good manners might be as damaging as lack of education. So in the "The Dunciad" Pope ridiculed both Bentley and Defoe—the one for his pedantry, the other for his ignorance.' *Ascendancy of Taste*, p. 11.

23. Paul Fussell, *The Rhetorical World of Augustan Humanism: Ethics and Imagery from Swift to Burke* (Oxford: Clarendon Press, 1965), p. 7.

24. Such an imperative can also be seen at work in the relation of two other categories—Nature and Art (The Rules)—central to Pope's effort:

    Those RULES of old *discover'd*, not devis'd,
    Are *Nature* still, but *Nature Methodiz'd*;
    Nature, like *Liberty*, is but restrain'd;
    By the same Laws which first *herself* ordain'd. (ll. 88–91)

    Nature is to Art as Good Man is to Good Writing: mutually apprehensible, mutually translatable. Of interest too is the ease with which Pope can establish the continuity and interchangeability of Art, Nature, and Politics ('*Liberty*') in this passage. This is the ideological nexus at its discursively most fluent, "discovering" (not "devising") alignments, effacing contradictions. On this last couplet, and for a reading of the ideology of Pope's aesthetics in general, see Laura Brown, *Alexander Pope* (London: Basil Blackwell, 1985), pp. 49–68.

25. Patrick Parrinder emphasises a similar understanding: 'the gentility and decorum of neoclassical criticism was always something of a facade. The Man of Taste reflected the ethos of the patrons rather than of the authors themselves. To take their doctrines only at face value would be to forget that their ultimate source lay not so much in the Roman Empire, as in the writer's precarious position in eighteenth-century society.' *Authors and Authority* (London: Routledge and Kegan Paul, 1977), p. 13.
26. Robert M. Krapp analyses the contemporary rewriting of the opposition between 'Wit' and 'Sense' as another facet of such ideological contestation. 'Class Analysis of a Literary Controversy,' *Science and Society* 10 (1946), pp. 80–92.
27. Book iii, especially Settle's prophecy of the empire of Dulness, derives its power from the fact that, for Pope, it is less a 'vision' (1.358) than a contemporary social and cultural reality. Pope's 'Arguments to the Books' attests to this specificity: Settle 'prophecies how first the nation shall be overrun with farces, opera's, shows; and the throne of Dulness advanced over both the Theatres: Then how her sons shall preside in the arts and sciences, till in conclusion all shall return to their original Chaos.' *Dunciad*, p. 56.
28. I am not suggesting that the abdication of the name of Poet in favour of Son, or Friend, is any more absolute, or any less rhetorical and strategic, than the earlier claim to legislative, definitional authority over the activity of literature. The end of the poem enacts a variation on one of the many humility topoi that Pope employed for self-presentation; nevertheless, its deployment here generates a specific and historical resonance. We all know Pope went on to write many more committed, partisan poems, and we can keep in mind Johnson's comment: 'Pope had been flattered till he thought himself one of the moving powers in the system of life. When he talked of laying down his pen, those who sat around him entreated and implored, and self-love did not suffer him to suspect that they went away and laughed.' 'Alexander Pope,' in *Lives of the English Poets*, ed. John Wain (London: J.M. Dent & Sons, 1975), p. 353.

Pope's strategic assumption and abdication of authority might be seen as an overt instance of the internally contradictory, doubling rhetoric necessary to the effective construction of literary identity and authority. As Fredric Bogel has suggested, literary authority has 'an *inherently* dramatic or histrionic character,' and must be enacted in order to be stable and successful. That is, absolute or foundational rhetoric does not establish literary authority quite as well as the careful staging of 'internal division and imperfection.' *The Dream of my Brother: An Essay on Johnson's Authority*, English Literary Studies Monograph 47 (British Columbia: University of Victoria, 1990), pp. 62–63.

29. Johnson, 'Alexander Pope,' p. 377. Sutherland quotes, as having a good deal of justification, a contemporary complaint in a 'Letter signed W.A.,' (*Mist's Journal*, June 8, 1728): Pope 'reproaches his Enemies as poor and dull; and to prove them *poor*, he asserts they are *dull*; and to prove them *dull* he asserts they are *poor*'. Pope, *Dunciad*, p. xlviii.
30. 'A Letter to the Publisher Occasioned by the present Edition of the Dunciad,' Pope, *Dunciad*, p. 15. For an essay representative of those who read Pope's moral discourse on its own terms, see Hugo M. Reichard, 'Pope's Social Satire: Belles-Lettres and Business,' *PMLA* 67 (1952), pp. 420–34.
31. In the chapters that follow, my analysis of the *Elegy* will take into account the fact that Gray wrote, and spent his life, at Cambridge. The same problematic distance from the 'rage' of public authorship obtains in his case, with powerful thematic and formal consequences for his poetry.
32. There is a scarcely disguised polemic at work in Young's choice of poets here. The corpus of each of these poets contains significant thematic and formal materials that would resist recuperation into any simple theory of the moral-didactic basis of poetry. That they are shown suffering in the hereafter, wishing they had written less 'wanton' verse, is just one instance of the wish-fulfilling imaginative fables that Young, paradoxically, felt compelled to write.
33. Both Pope and Young tender similar practical advice about restraining the urge to publish. Pope suggests a piece be kept 'nine years' (1.40), and Young tells the writer to 'zealously prefer four lines to six' and to

    Write, and rewrite, blot out and write again,
    And for its swiftness ne'er applaud your pen. (i. 118–20)

    The space for irony is limited here. As Pope's references make clear, those poets who turn 'a *Persian* tale for half a crown' (1. 180; see Sutherland's explanatory note in Pope, *Dunciad*, p. 109), or who live 'high in *Drury-Lane*/*Lull'd* by soft Zephyrs thro' the broken pane,' and who publish quickly 'Oblig'd by hunger and Request of friends' (ll.

41–44), must be condemned. Such exhortations to artistic correctness carried a very sharp and immediately recognizable polemical charge.

34. Structurally, of course, the satiric naming of the Other is always simultaneously and reflexively (if only implicitly) an identification of the Self. What Pope's and Young's texts of thematised cultural crisis make explicit then, is the more general underlying structure of the genre of Satire, which is involved as much in the presentation of the proper self as it is in the representation of the improper other.
35. *Conjectures on Original Composition* (1759; fac. rpt., Leeds: The Scolar Press, 1966), p. 52.
36. Young, *Conjectures*, p. 54. Young's tone here is far from that of his *Epistle*—this is the language of accommodation, of pseudo-respectful critique. It is now 1759, and though rearguard skirmishes continue, the battle has long been lost. In fact, Young's project in the *Conjectures*, with its new emphasis on 'Genius'—which 'has ever been supported to partake of something Divine' (p. 27)—and 'Originality'—'True Poesy, like true Religion, abhors idolatry' (p. 67)—can be read as an attempt to 'conjecture' into mysterious, interior spaces the sources of poetic authority that were earlier seen as predicated upon a particular social usage. This more 'romantic,' magical notion of the authorial self attempts to preserve a spiritual distance from the products and processes of contemporary literary production; earlier, in the *Epistle*, such a distance had been *legislated* into tenuous existence.
37. Only suggested (rather than legislated), because the Act, being the product of parliamentary efforts made by publishers, was directed primarily at protecting their interests, and was concerned with authorial rights only secondarily. However, as John Feather suggests, the '1710 Act did, even if only in the preamble,' recognise the existence of authors: 'there could be no doubt of the logic of the argument that if a copy was a property then the author was the maker of the property and had to be paid for it.' *A History of British Publishing* (London: Croom Helm, 1988), p. 76. Perhaps I should point out that the Copyright Act of 1710 discussed by Feather is the same legislation referred to by other historians as the Statute of Anne of 1709.
38. John Locke, *Two Treatises of Government* ed. Peter Laslett, rev. edn. (New York: New American Library, 1965), p. 309.
39. David Saunders and Ian Hunter, 'Lessons from the "Literatory": How to Historicise Scholarship,' *Critical Inquiry* 17 (1991), p. 485. This essay offers a thoughtful and nuanced account of the constitution of 'auth-

orship' that argues that 'the delineation and attribution of authorial personality is governed not by the logic of subject formation but by the historical emergence of particular cultural techniques and social institutions' (p. 483).

40. Richard Helgerson, *Self-Crowned Laureates* (Berkeley: University of California Press, 1983), pp. 2–4.
41. Helgerson, *Self-Crowned Laureates*, p. 15.
42. William Mason, *The Poems of Mr. Gray. To Which are Prefixed Memoires of his Life and Writings by W. Mason, M.A.* (York: A. Ward, 1775), p. 335. Mason goes on to connect Gray's never publishing his edition of Strabo, which was 'written in that exact manner, as if intended for the press' (p. 336), or finishing his History of English Poetry, or writing up any of his scholarly work, to this resentment.
43. Mason to Walpole, September 21, 1771. *Horace Walpole's Correspondence with William Mason*, eds. W.S. Lewis, Grover Cronin, Jr and Charles H. Bennett, 2 vols., (New Haven: Yale University Press, 1955), i. 21–22.
44. Walpole to Mason, September 25, 1771. Walpole, *Correspondence*, i. 23–24.

II

A Solitary Fly
Gray and Poetic Persona

> There is a sense in which it is true to say that the poems Gray wrote between June 1742 and June 1750, between the 'Ode on the Spring' and the 'Elegy,' are finished segments of a single poem.
>
> —Arthur Johnston, 'Our Daring Bard'[1]

There are two figures that reappear in Gray's poems: that of the 'wondrous sage' and that of the 'solitary fly.' These figures, antithetical in scope and purpose, are ultimately masks for the poet, names under which the poetic self is dramatised in several of Gray's poems. The 'sage' is the poet as seer, claiming inheritance from the traditions of the vatic and the demi-urgic, possessed of a vision that lays clear the mysteries of the past and the future, proclaiming the ways of fate and fortune in a strong, prophetic voice. The 'fly' is the poet as retiring and shy moralist, kin, in his distance from the 'ardour of the crowd,' to the Horatian *beatus vir*, yet never happy, for he is constantly reminded of his insight that all must eventually 'their airy dance/ . . . leave, in dust to rest.' In Gray's poems, these figures represent alternative, and opposed, conceptions of the poet's vocation; the choice being between the public, declamatory authority of the oracle, and the private, muted tone of the marginal commentator. Different moments in the poems project or chose between one or other of these personae, these voices, without ever being able to repress the tensions involved in making such a choice, such that the very act of choosing, of maintaining boundaries, generates the anxieties that these (seemingly) clear-cut, well-defined choices are meant to efface. But to say that is to leap too far ahead. First, we must examine the genesis and particular manifestations of these figures of vocation.

THE WONDROUS SAGE

In one of Gray's earliest extant translations, that of Canto XIV, verses 32–9, of Tasso's *Gerusalemme Liberata,* we find a magical presence:

> when lo! appears
> The wondrous sage: vigorous he seemed in years,
> Awful his mien; low as his feet there flows
> A vestment unadorned, though white as new-fall'n
> snows;
> Against the stream the waves secure he trod,
> His head a chaplet bore, his hand a rod. (ll. 11–16)

The effect that Gray is achieving here, as he transforms Tasso's holy man, a Christian hermit, into a John the Baptist-like prophet, is enhanced by the context described in the previous lines.[2] Ubald and Charles the Dane, on their mission to rescue Rinaldo, are confronted by an impassable, rain-swollen river. This obstacle is no ordinary one, as is made clear by the description of the raging torrent—the physical barrier, a 'flood Tempestuous,' is powerful enough to provide a physical analogue of the moment of spiritual blockage crucial to an experience of the (Longinian) sublime. As the knights stand 'irresolute' in the face of this sublimity, Gray introduces his sage, 'wondrous' and 'awful,' such that the sage becomes part of these (super)natural phenomena. The 'seer' walks towards Ubald and Charles 'on no hardened plain' (l. 23), but over the boiling waters—the knights are transfixed in response to all this: 'fixed in wonder stood the warlike pair' (l. 25). As it turns out, this sage can not only part the waves, but he is also the one to tell the knights all they need to know; he is the one to relieve 'their care' and to unfold 'Great things and full of wonder in [their] ears' (l. 35). He is, by his own definition, 'no common guide' (l. 29), but one in whom these men of public station and action must put their trust as he leads them into 'Earth's inmost cells and caves of deep descent' (l. 50), where he has his grotto. En route, the knights are led by the 'secret source' (l. 51) of the world's greatest rivers, and along passages 'where ripening minerals flow' (l. 57)—all of which serve, of course, to emphasise the powers of the sage.

The importance of this figure of the sage for Gray, as also its later repetition in forms that allow us to characterise it as a representation of poetic voice, will be the subjects of future discussion. At this point, it is useful to speculate about what else might have made the sage an attractive emblem of poetic authority. There is, no doubt, the seduction of extraordinary power, derived from sources unspecified and unknown, at once secret and sublime. This is no disembodied power though, purely that of the oracular voice, but in fact has an instrumental capacity, a causal relationship with the progress of events. This instrumentality, this abililty to guide men of action who have lost their way, is of particular importance, for it is powerful in two complementary ways: it makes things happen, and it also, crucially, enables the hermit, the recluse, to be the figure of public authority. Thus, it is precisely (and we shall see why this is so), the figure that would work most convincingly and powerfully for Gray, enacting for him the possibility that the man in seclusion could, in the moments of gravest crises, be transformed into the enabling factor, rising from obscurity to declaim to, and direct onwards, an astonished, receptive world. Before we can attempt to unravel this dialectic of the private and the public, and account for the force of the figural translation of one into the other, it is necessary to examine that other representation of poetic voice in Gray's verse: the 'solitary fly.'

THE SOLITARY FLY: *ODE ON THE SPRING*

On May 5, 1742, Richard West included an 'Ode' in a letter he wrote to Gray. In his response, Gray described West's poem as 'light and genteel,' (which is a precise characterisation) and accepted its invitation to 'join with mine thy tuneful lay, / And invocate the tardy May' (ll. 5–6), by writing his own 'Ode on the Spring.' Gray's poem begins as a studied response to West's ode, matching its propriety and correctness with a derivative, or rather, densely allusive text. The first ten lines are clearly an extension of Gray's compliment to West upon his ode: 'She [the month May] cannot choose but come at such a call:'[3]

> Lo! where the rosy-bosomed Hours,
> Fair Venus' train, appear,
> Disclose the long-expecting flowers,
> And wake the purple year!
> The Attic warbler pours her throat,
> Responsive to the cuckoo's note,
> The untaught harmony of spring:
> While whispering pleasure as they fly,
> Cool zephyrs through the clear blue sky
> Their gathered fragrance fling.

As Lonsdale suggests, these lines are 'a deliberate attempt to evoke earlier descriptions of spring, particularly in classical literature,'[4] the sheer density of their inter-textual reference exfoliating into a displaced account of the vernal fecundity that Gray wishes to evoke. The phrase 'purple year' (l. 4) for instance, suggests the generative power of spring not through any descriptive aptness, but rather because it invokes a long tradition of similar naming that goes back to Virgil's *Eclogues*.[5] These opening lines, then, evoke the energising brightness of spring in and through the poetic conventions that have long celebrated that energy. The logic of such displacement is perfectly in keeping with the mannered, affected quality of the tone and method of West's ode, whose referent is clearly rhetorical technique and literary convention more than the specific season or nature. Gray and West, then, engage here in a dialogue which is of a kind with so many of the letters and juvenalia that circulated among the members of the 'Quadruple Alliance': self-consciously clever in the displays of their developing sensibilities, disingenuous in their ironic, yet ostentatious, assumption of the trappings of scholarship and learning, celebratory of their having established a community of like-minded literary souls.[6]

This community is important because in a great deal of Gray's work, the logic of the representation of the poet, as of the dramatisation of poetic power or impoverishment (these being functions of each other), is derived from the literary logic of poetic conventions and topoi, the accumulated force of past practice shaping Gray's own efforts. A good example of the power of convention is available in lines 11–20 of the 'Ode on the Spring.' The first seven lines of this passage (ll. 11–17), seem to extend Gray's account of the coming of spring by describing the shade created by the 'oak's thick branches' or by the 'rude and moss-grown beech.' This shade is where, the poet says

> With me the Muse shall sit, and think
> (At ease reclined in rustic state). (ll. 16–17)

What is interesting, given the theme and development of the poem so far, is that the Muse is going to think of public vanity and pride:

> How vain the ardour of the crowd,
> How low, how little are the proud,
> How indigent the great! (ll. 18–20)

Nothing in the poem has prepared us for such moralising; thus far, the ode has been concerned with celebrating the coming, and not at all the transience, of spring. At this point, then, these moral musings are not a product of the descriptive or thematic logic of the poem, but seem triggered by the conventional figuration of the shade of trees as the space most conducive to poetic contemplation.[7] The primary progenitor text here, as in so many other cases, is Virgil's *Eclogues*, where Tityrus, 'under the spreading, sheltering beech,' 'lazing in the shade,' composes 'woodland musings on a delicate reed.'[8] As the contrast with Meliboeus's situation makes quite clear, there is a causal connection between this shade, provided, as it is, by Augustus's patronage, and Tityrus's song—Tityrus can be a shepherd-poet only because of the protection provided by the 'spreading, sheltering beech.' By the eighteenth century, this political suggestion had been largely lost, and in Gay, Mallet, and Thomson the poet seeks shelter for a more mundane reason, to escape the noon-day sun. Gray's poem lacks any such heat,[9] but what he does require is a conventional way to introduce into his ode the figure of the musing poet, and he chooses as his vehicle the topos we have just described.

To say this is clearly to beg the question: why is it so necessary for Gray to represent in this poem, ostensibly an ode on the Spring, the figure of the poet? The answer, one that this argument will be concerned with throughout, is that there is little verse that Gray wrote that is not explicitly concerned with the figure of the poet, either represented as such or as a clearly identifiable surrogate (the sage of the translation from Tasso), and that very often, the specific details of the poem (setting, occasion, incorporated myths, apostrophic invocations) are, as it were, glosses on the central questions: what is the role of the poet and of his poetry, what are the roles the poet must play in order to ensure a role for himself and his poetry, what are the sources of authority that a poet might claim for himself, and what is the authority that contemporary society will allow the poet?

To return to the poem: the next twenty lines of the 'Ode on the Spring' (ll. 21–40) take, for their view-point, 'Contemplation's sober eye' (l. 31), a position very different from the outright celebration that marked the first ten lines of the poem. In this view, it is transience, not fecundity, that is the true characteristic of Spring, such that the 'insect youth' now gaily on the wing are condemned to 'end where they began':

> Alike the busy and the gay
> But flutter through life's little day,

In fortune's varying colours dressed:
Brushed by the hand of rough Mischance,
Or chilled by age, their airy dance
They leave, in dust to rest. (ll. 35–40)

Lonsdale's annotation to lines 35–36 tells us that the 'comparison of frivolous pleasure seekers to ephemeral summer insects is common in eighteenth-century poetry,' and he lists examples from Pope and Thomson.[10] However, it is not only 'frivolous pleasure seekers' that the poet-moralist wishes to distinguish himself from here. Not just 'the gay' but also 'the busy' are compromised alike by time and mutability, all the activities of the entire 'race of man' (l. 32) being reduced to an equivalent pointlessness by the actions of fortune, mischance, and death. This, of course, is a position that can scarcely allow the poet, one of the race of men, to claim an exemption for his efforts. Nor is such an exemption claimed here. The last stanza spins around to view the 'poor moralist,' the 'solitary fly,' from the point of view of the 'sportive kind,' so that the judgmental distance claimed by the former now lengthens into isolation and a separation from community. The moralist's position is undercut, his loneliness set against the 'frolic' (however ephemeral) enjoyed by the rest, his morality no defence against the passing of time and of youth. The moralist's sun sets untimely, his 'spring is gone' too soon—ironically, the very 'rosy-bosomed Hours' (l. 1) that the ode was written to welcome are now seen as a time the moralist cannot celebrate or even enjoy.

The pathos in these last lines of the poem is dissipated not only by the self-conscious cleverness of the moral twist contained in them (Johnson called the conclusion 'pretty'[11]), but also by the tone and diction of the entire poem, which resembles nothing so much as a set-piece, an exercise in debating the nature of what is usually called 'universal moral experience,' using only the language, conventions, and tropology clearly identified with the traditional discourse of that debate. The language of inter-textual allusion here follows and displays the logic of poetic formulation and re-formulation, with an emphasis on the latter. The effect of this studied and artificial (in both the weak and strong sense of the word) language is to call attention to itself in a way that can only interfere with the immediacy of the moral debate it enacts.

Another way to understand the dynamics of this poem is to notice how the 'Ode on the Spring' is presented rhetorically as an enactment of that moral process of learning and understanding which usually results in a deepening of stoical distance and detachment. The sense of moral process, of ethical purposiveness, is of course sharply ironised in the final gesture of the poem, its mocking representation of the marginality of the poet-moralist. Yet, this marginality is not the final comment on the poet or on the aspiration of poetry—contained within the poem, this ironic representation of the poet is only provisional, and actually the last step in the process of the 'self-actualisation' of the Poet.[12]

I use 'self-actualisation of the Poet' as shorthand for the entire intricate process of subject positioning in the writing and reading of poetry discussed by Anthony Easthope in *Poetry as Discourse.* I quote briefly: ' . . . on Derrida's showing, discourse is "a sort of machine," and subjectivity in poetry—"the Poet"—can never be more than an *effect* of discourse, a god or ghost produced (by the reading) from the machine.' Further, subjectivity 'must be approached not as the point of origin but as the effect of a poetic discourse.'[13] The discursive effect of reading or speaking—phenomenalising—the poem creates our sense of The Poet. This is of course the obverse of the view that sees the poem as The Creation of the poet, who is seen as its *a priori,* unproblematic 'point of origin.' The full effect (set up by the reading or the speaking of the poem) no doubt is a product of the oscillation between both these processes of creation, where the reader's encounter with the machine produces the 'god or ghost,' who in turn is seen as producing the machine. My sense of Gray's poems is that such a double effect is one that is exploited constantly in them, especially as a final compensatory mechanism when the poem's express theme is the marginalised poet or his impoverished authority. Within each poem, there are various rhetorical moves made to distance the thematised figure of impoverishment from the idea of the Poet as creator of the poem, just as, in his later poems, there are moves made to effect an identification between this idea and the figure of vatic power who is dramatised in them.

In the 'Ode on the Spring,' the process by which the authority of the poet is preserved is at least partly predicated upon the power of the writer of the poem to create the figure of partial understanding (the poet-moralist) and to locate it within the precise context that will show off both the strengths and the weaknesses of such understanding.[14] In this rhetorical grid, metaphor is the trope of moral insight (the moralist knows all men are flies), and irony the trope of blindness (the flies know that he too is one of them). The Poet's true power comes then, not from a claim of having viewed all, and understood all (that is the tenuous position of the moralist); not from the learning process that is the metamorphosis of the musing 'me' in line 16 into the 'solitary fly' of line 44 (that too is the moralist); but from his being able to write this metamorphosis, to create its figures and its tropes, and to represent them in the firmly structured order of narration that is the form of the process poem.

If this is so, then for Gray in the 'Ode on the Spring,' the poet as authority is actually the poet as author, and one of the primary implicit structures of the poem must stem from the need to separate the representation of the poet (in the poem) as limited moraliser from the activity of Poetry itself, that is, from the act of writing and representation that is the practice and the prerogative of the Poet. The distinction I am making here is identical with those made by Easthope in his analysis of '*deictics* or *shifters*, linguistic forms that exhibit the "spatio-temporal perspective of the speaker".' Following Roman Jakobson, Easthope distinguishes between 'the *enounced* (*énoncé*, the narrated event); the *enunciation* (*énonciation*, the speech event); subject of the enounced (the participant of the narrated event); subject of the enunciation (the participant of the speech event, the speaking subject, the producer of meaning)'. Easthope goes on to suggest, in Lacanian terms, that 'the subject of the enounced is . . . a smaller circle contained inside ("concentric" to) the subject of the enunciation, a larger circle, which lies outside it (is "ex-centric" to it) . . . *Subject of the enounced and subject of enunciation are two different positions for a speaking subject which is split between them in discourse.*'[15]

In the 'Ode on the Spring' the subject of the enounced is clearly the moralist-poet designated by the 'me' of line 16, the 'I' of line 41, and the 'solitary fly' of line 44, who functions as the narrator, the explicit speaker. Most critics have allowed for an easy identification of this subject of the enounced and the subject of the enunciation (the implicit speaker, the Poet, 'Gray'). I am suggesting, however, that this poem resists such easy identification, an identification that requires the effacement of all the rhetorical traces of enunciation, of the speech act. Instead, it incorporates markers of the speech act, allegories of enunciation (like apostrophe and personification), rhetorical devices (like quotation and allusion), that call attention to their own status, and thus to the status of the poem as fictive utterance. This reflexiveness about language and representation is, as might be expected, not categoric or absolute, but functions rather as the antithetic pole to that provided by the seemingly transparent discourse of the subject of the enounced. My reading of this poem emphasises that it embodies these disjunctions and exists within these antitheses, and that Gray's technique in his early poems eschews synthesis in favour of a foregrounding of the *techne* that is the writing of poetry.

The separation of the narrator (the explicit speaker) and the speaking subject, or of the poet in the poem and the larger activity of poetry itself, does not come easily for Gray, as we can see both in this poem and in others he wrote later, where the figure of the gloomy solitary, both distinguished by, and marginalised by, his sensitivity, exerts a powerful seduction, one that Gray is not always able to resist successfully (possible reasons, both social and psychological, will be examined later). In the 'Ode on the Spring,' the traces of this seduction are the personal pronouns—the 'me' of line 16 and the 'I' of line 41— which stand, with disconcerting ease, for both the solitary moralist (the implied speaker, the subject of the enounced) and the Poet (the author, the subject of enunciation). These pronouns work to efface the distinction between these two subject positions—the thematised moralist-poet and the Poet who is the effect of this poetic discourse—an effacement that totally endangers any claim that might be posited, explicitly or implicitly, to full poetic authority.

If the personal pronouns are the traces of identification between the two subject positions, key personifications are the mechanisms of resistance, of distantiation between them. The Muse is not invoked in its most common eighteenth-century form, as that numen of poetry that will give confident voice to the poet-figure who lacks such confidence. Instead, the Muse is here an autonomous presence, distinct from the poet, pictured sitting by his side and, significantly, not portrayed as inspiring the poet to think, but thinking on its own (ll. 16–20). This personification serves to rob the poet-figure, the 'me' (l. 16), of voice, for the lines that follow can be seen as the thoughts of the Muse rather than of this poet, who is, at best, seen as ventriloquising them. This subversion of the stature and status of this figure is reinforced in line 31:

> To Contemplation's sober eye
> Such is the race of man:
> And they that creep and they that fly,
> Shall end where they began.
> Alike the busy and the gay
> But flutter through life's little day,
> In fortune's varying colours dressed:
> Brushed by the hands of rough Mischance,
> Or chilled by age, their airy dance
> They leave, in dust to rest. (ll. 31–40)

These moral observations are attributed to Contemplation, another personification that is distinct, at least figuratively, from this poet. Then, in a move in keeping with the pattern and logic of the attempt to rhetorically limit and distance the poet-figure in the poem, when he is once again allowed his identity and his voice, it is only in a situation of peripeteia, of observational reversal, one in which this figure is at the receiving end of things:

> Methinks I hear in accents low
> The sportive kind reply:
> Poor moralist! and what art thou?
> A solitary fly!
> Thy joys no glittering female meets,
> No hive hast thou of hoarded sweets,
> No painted plumage to display:
> On hasty wings thy youth is flown;
> Thy sun is set, thy spring is gone——
> We frolic, while 'tis May. (ll. 41–50)

Ironically, yet perfectly appositely, the poet-figure is now granted a name, but it is the name of 'poor moralist' or of 'solitary fly,' both names that obscure his earlier figuration and significance, names that repress the possibililty that this marginalised figure will be identified any more with the Poet who writes (creates and is created by) the 'Ode on the Spring.'

Thus, in the larger rhetorical economy of the poem, a structure of identification and distantiation characterises the play between the two subject-positions—the Poet (the subject of enunciation) and the poet-moralist (the subject of the enounced). The most dynamic, unsettling, moments in the poem are those that mark this pattern of attraction and resistance, those that enable the poem to achieve its primary affect—Gray as gloomy solitary—and those that enable it to achieve its final effect—Gray as Poet, transcending the solitary. The movement of the enunciation, of the speech act, establishes the difficult trajectory of transcendence upon which the authority of the poet is ultimately based. At the end of the poem, the abstraction 'Poet'/'Gray' substitutes for the more fully realised particular 'the poor moralist,' but not before the ambivalent attractions of the figure of the solitary are played out.

In my reading of the 'Ode on the Spring' I have shown how the poem records a shift away from the celebration of the coming and fecundity of spring to moralising about its transience and about the analogous mutability of man (ll. 1–20). The poem turns away from the mode and discourse of pastoral to the themes and language of moral-humanistic, didactic meditation. I have also suggested that this shift is intricately tied up with, and even generated by, an anxiety about the poet's voice and vocation, especially if this vocation is to be based on the dubious ground of a professional ethical purposiveness.[16] The authority of the persona of the moralist, and of his discourse of moral discovery turns out to be as slippery as that of the celebrant of pastoral convention, the former being limited by social isolation just as the latter is silenced by the natural transience of spring. This vocational anxiety is underscored by the fact that it appears not simply as the dialectic of attraction and resistance that marks the thematisation of the poet-moralist, but also in the obvious foregrounding of the over-determined vocabulary and figures most clearly associated with the discursive practices of 'ethical' English poetry.[17] The stilted awkwardness of this allusive, echoing language is a product of Gray's attempts to work with the basic materials and tools of poetry, tempered and moulded as they had been in the separate smithies of English literary history.[18]

In my analysis of Gray's poem, it should be clear that I am working with the idea that the elements of form—genre, topoi, vocabulary—are performatively potent, and encode histories of cultural and ideological usage even as they enact literary functions. To that extent, my understanding is similar to Coward and Ellis' definition of any recognisable 'mode of writing' as being 'pre-eminently social,' and hence 'a use of language which pre-dates the writer and forms the writer like language itself: it is a sociolect.'[19] Thus, in my argument, for a poet to use language typical of a poetic form (or disuse, or use in particular ways) is to confront its conventions and to reshape its logical structures, both as established by past practice and by a specific history of critical and public reception. All 'poetry,' but especially the work of a formally literate poet, engages, in more or less self-conscious ways, in an acceptance or a critique (or both at once), of the methods, expectations and achievements of chosen genres, as well as of their claimed or perceived position within the hierarchy of poetic and cultural forms. To write a particular poetic form, or to construct an ensemble of forms, is also to comment on a history of ideological affiliations, and to the continuing relevance of this history to the cultural politics of the present time. Genre (and any other formal unit) is, like language, always determined by, and determining of, the strategies of contestation that characterise ideological oppositions.

In that, my reading of the poem's concerns and energies suggests emphases different from those summarised by Lonsdale when he describes the ode as staging 'the antithesis of the busy world and the contemplative life [which] was to be dramatized again, more seriously and powerfully, in the *Elegy*, as was the poet's uneasiness about the choice he was attempting to make between them.'[20] Of course, in an obvious sense, such an antithesis is being set up, and even briefly explored in the ode, albeit in a conventional and rhetorically largely unimaginative manner. Such an antithesis, as Lonsdale shows, informs all of Gray's corpus. What my argument claims, however, is that in the 'Ode on the Spring' (and, in similar ways in 'Ode on a Distant Prospect of Eton College' and the 'Sonnet on the Death of Mr Richard West'), Gray is centrally interested in (re)articulating and manipulating the essentially overdetermined figures and vocabulary of conventional moral ode and elegy, multiplying allusion and quotation, invoking image and phrase, echoing topos and trope, till it is clear that he is concerned with the elaboration and communication not so much of personal or universal moral experience as of its poetic representations, its canonical methods and discourse. That is, he is interested more in investigating a poetics than an ethics, where the latter is the occasion for the former.

To say this about, for example, the Eton *Ode* is to controvert most critical opinion that has read it primarily as an instance of Gray's ethical, humanistic and psychological development and/or as an expression of what Gray himself described as his 'white Melancholy, or rather Leucocholy.'[21] Jean Hagstrum, ventriloquising Gray, says 'To be a man is to be condemned to pain, the pain of the passions,' and (about the Eton *Ode*), 'The true man was Gray Agonistes, and the true poetry was carved in a language where emotions press powerfully against cool lapidary statement.'[22] Such a formulation is clearly informed by a critical understanding that Paul de Man calls 'the traditional scheme . . . according to which language is a tool manipulated by extra-linguistic impulses rooted in a subject,' a scheme that 'can be dislodged by the equally reasonable alternative that the affective appeal of text could just as well be the result of a linguistic structure as its cause.'[23] To attempt to characterise the individuality of Gray's poetic style by focusing on the individuality of the poet's psyche or inner life is to misunderstand the construction of the (speaking) figures in Gray's poems. As Eric Rothstein suggests, 'Eighteenth-century poets, quite unlike modern poets, rarely seek to complicate this speaking figure by giving him (or themselves, through him) a sharply individual voice, an "authentic" expression of a singular psyche.'[24] In fact, as my argument suggests, Gray 'complicated' his representations of the poet precisely by making them sharply conventional. One way to think of this is to see the problematic that engaged Gray and engendered his poetry as a search not only for voice but for vocation; the crisis is social, not simply individual.

Lonsdale, in his Chatterton Lecture to the British Academy for 1973, 'The Poetry of Thomas Gray: Versions of the Self,' suggests that Gray's poems are 'an enquiry into the ways in which a private poetic self could be expressed or dramatized.' What Lonsdale calls 'Versions of the Self' I examine as 'representations of the poet,' thus concentrating, in Lonsdale's terms, on how Gray 'dramatized' not only the dilemmas of the 'private poetic self' but also aspects of the public vocational crisis of some mid-eighteenth century poets. Also, I see the peculiar nature of such 'dramatization,' its recourse to particular forms, vocabularies and idioms, as far more problematic and interesting than what Lonsdale describes, and explains away, as Gray's 'inhibited preoccupation with the self': 'The perpetual but inhibited preoccupation with the self in Gray's poetry may be explicable simply in terms of the theoretical pressure on a poet of his generation to avoid morbid self-centeredness and to express the truths of common human experience.'[25]

This image of the man who suffers and the mind that creates is evident in Lonsdale's introduction to the 'Ode on the Spring' too, where he catalogues the death of West, Gray's quarrel with Horace Walpole, the fall of Robert Walpole from the Prime Ministership, the death of Gray's father and the financial insecurity attendant upon that as 'considerations [that] lie behind the poetry that [Gray] wrote in this uniquely prolific period in the summer of 1742, and in particular the *Ode* on Eton.'[26] There is no question, of course, that this is true. The reasons why Gray would choose to write poems about transience and mutability ('Ode on the Spring'); the mindless innocence of childhood and the inevitable horrors of adulthood and age (the Eton *Ode*); death and the loss of dear ones (the West *Sonnet*); the virtues of stoicism and adversity ('Ode to Adversity') in this, his summer of '42, are quite clear. What biographical data do not explain, however, is why his poems took the forms that they did, why he choose the idiom and vocabulary that he did, and what he was trying to do when he wrote as he did.

Critical discussions of these issues have always crystallised around the vexed question of the poetic diction of Gray's poems (as indeed they have in the case of many other eighteenth-century poets). Disagreements have been sharp; compare, for instance, Hagstrum's ideas about Gray's language quoted above with those of Donald Davie, who has this footnote in a manifesto-book entitled, appropriately enough, *Purity of Diction in English Verse*: 'This poem ['On Lord Holland's Seat near Margate, Kent'] seems to me, together with the fragmentary "Education and Government," the only writings of Gray in which the diction is chaste in Johnson's sense or any other. The effect of Gray's example (e.g. in his Odes) was decadent and disruptive; and I can find little of value in his other poems.'[27] Even when critics have not been so dismissive, they have felt the need to be defensive, to make, as F. W. Bateson does, 'an apology for the eighteenth century' in their explication of the otherness of 'poetic diction.' For Bateson, 'poetic diction' is what made the 'early Pope, Thomson, Young, Gray, Collins, and Smart what they are,' and he seeks to right an imbalance when he suggests that these poets must be read not 'in spite of their diction' but with an appreciation of its function. However, his way of learning the latter is to claim that eighteenth-century poetic diction should be treated as a foreign language and its incomprehensible words looked up in a dictionary.[28]

Analysts of the diction of Gray's poems have usually chosen to quote, as prologue or as triumphant conclusion, Gray's pronouncements on 'stile':

> The language of the age is never the language of poetry . . . Our poetry . . . has a language peculiar to itself; to which almost every one, that has written, has added something by enriching it with foreign idioms and derivatives: Nay sometimes words of their own composition or invention. Shakespeare and Milton have been great creators this way; and no one more licentious than Pope or Dryden, who perpetually borrow expressions from the former.[29]

Following upon the first sentence quoted above, discussions have often dealt with the possibility (or impossibility) of being able to distinguish accurately between what might be the language of the age (is it its conversation? its prose? how do we factor in dialectal variations, both regional and class-based?) and that which is the language of its poetry. This is clearly a thankless and perhaps even a pointless task—at its best it can produce an awkward taxonomy of language use; at its worst, it results in embattled value-judgements that seek to separate the 'pure' from the 'impure,' the 'awkward' from the 'natural,' or finally (in a revealing tautology), the 'poetic' from the 'inflated and artificial' or the 'vulgar and prosaic.'[30]

Gray's comments should lead us to think about the connections between the 'language peculiar to' poetry and the continued practice of poets, both in their enriching of this language by their inventiveness, and in their establishing a visible tradition of 'licentious' borrowing and quotation. This tradition, based on imitation and allusion, is clearly what permitted Gray, or might permit us, to speak of a language of poetry that is different from the language of the age. In his somewhat unfortunate 'Life of Gray,' Dr. Johnson seems not to have understood this. His claim that 'Gray thought his language more poetical as it was more remote from common use' is of a piece with his generalisation when he censures Gray's 'cant' in 'The Progress of Poesy': 'An epithet or metaphor drawn from nature ennobles art: an epithet or metaphor drawn from art degrades nature.'[31] Johnson was aware, as Davie points out, that 'this tug away from 'common use' can come only from art, from the usages of previous literature,'[32] but he clearly saw such an inheritance as suspect, and in need of the restraint exercised by some standard of 'common use.' Both strictures function on the premise that the language of common use has as its referent, and its ground, 'Nature,' and that by this token alone this language possesses an enabling and ennobling authority that the language of art-usage and art-tradition does not. Johnson's categoric statements about language, art and nature are meant to anchor his moral and evaluative critical priorities—if, however, we avoid privileging the undefined (because undefinable) referent called 'Nature' over the referent of poetic practice called 'Art,' then we are in a position to examine Gray's poems as an effort at a poetics more than at an ethics.

ODE ON A DISTANT PROSPECT OF ETON COLLEGE

The Eton *Ode*, I will argue, re-enacts some of the key generic, formal and verbal disjunctions that characterise the 'Ode on the Spring,' and for many of the same reasons. The latter took as its point of departure the conventions of pastoral and the pieties of moral discourse, while the Eton *Ode* tropes on the formal elements of the prospect poem, and then goes on to engage critically with the language of moral exemplarity typical of a humanist and ethical poetics. Shaping these concerns is Gray's sharp sense, at once literary and historical, of the vocational crisis of the contemporary poet, which gets played out in these poems in the representation of a poet-moralist as the figure of poetic impoverishment and cultural isolation. As in the 'Ode on the Spring,' the form of the Eton *Ode* stages the tension between poetic voices, between subject-positions, in a way that allows both the symptomatic enactment of vocational anxiety and the containment of such anxiety via the ironic turn that closes off the poem.

The first ten lines of the *Ode*, the address to the 'distant spires' and 'antique towers' (l. 1) of both Eton and Windsor, replay the conventional opening characteristic of a sub-species of loco-descriptive poem: the prospect poem. In his invocation of Eton and Windsor, and in the mention of 'Henry's holy shade' (l. 4), Gray assembles a brief iconography of English aristocratic history, and, with the inclusion of 'the hoary Thames' (l. 9), seems poised to do what prospect poets did—allegorise the particular landscape or vista into an account of politics, history, or society. The strongest tradition of such allegorisation was of course represented by poems such as Denham's *Coopers Hill*, Waller's *On St. James's Park* and Pope's *Windsor Forest*, which worked, as Brendan O Hehir suggests, by 'insistently interpreting emblematically . . . particular places, scenes or events,' by constantly 'reading hieroglyphs presented . . . by nature and history.'[33] Even the lesser, more subjective and introspective prospect poem, best represented by Dyer's *Grongar Hill*, began its moralising on the affairs of men only upon describing some emblem in the landscape such as 'Huge heaps of hoary moulder'd walls' (l. 83), that could have occasioned such thoughts.[34] As Ralph Cohen puts it, 'the perceptual reconsiderations implicit in such works as *Coopers Hill* and *Upon Appleton House* tied the idea of vision to that of history. Distance, prospect, spectator views—these joined the vocabulary of vision to that of history and society.'[35]

In the eighteenth century, perhaps the version of this ideological poetic 'vision' most practiced was the Georgic, especially as written by poets like Thomson and Dyer.[36] In these celebrations of the social harmony and economic power of a 'Happy Britannia,' the expansiveness and confidence of the poets is authorised directly by their optimistic intuitions of national unity and by the mercantile and imperial expansion of England. In their poems, both the celebration and its causes are presented as views available to those who are able to ascend to a noble prospect of society. The metaphor here is spatial—as (the distance of) the prospect lends seamless charm, order, and regularity to the landscape, the landscape becomes the emblem of both domestic and colonial social order.

In another significant version of such a vision, the lessons of time enable the allegorisation of the landscape, as the poet reads social and cultural emblems of the past for signs of the present and the future. In these cases, the poet's posture is occasionally 'defensive' rather than celebratory (or, might one say it, offensive!). The term defensive is Ian Watt's, who, in describing such poems, says that 'the Augustan writers often looked back as a way of measuring the deterioration of the present; they were obsessed with decline . . . This is closely connected with the value which the Augustans placed on history: the contemplation of the civilisation of the past could guide man in the present.'[37]

Both these metaphors of prospect and of retrospect, of vision and of revision, share a common concern—an insistent engagement with ideas of historical change and social and political development. Gray's prospect poem, however, resists both the forward-looking, confident vision, and the backward-looking vision of decline and warning. Instead, it collapses what begins as a spatial and historical view—that of Eton and Windsor—into a temporal and ahistorical vision, and this vision is not of the global or national past, but is a far more restricted memory of childhood and of the individual life.

From line 11 onwards, the Eton *Ode* steers its separate course. Instead of an allegory of history or education, or even a more personal meditation that would derive its sermons from the particular stone-castles that enclose the vista, we are presented with a subjective, even idiosyncratic, heavily mannered and stylised discourse on the thoughtless paradise that is childhood and the inevitable, unrelenting woe that is the rest of life. The associations of memory provide the entry into subjectivity here, or rather, into the theme of the mournful, musing poet, just as the convention of the recumbent *poeta*, in contemplative shelter from the hot sun, had authorised a similar turn in the 'Ode on the Spring.' The turn is sharp enough to suggest a generic discontinuity, and in fact did provide a deviant model for future writers of topographical verse. As Robert Aubin observes, 'most of the elements of [the Eton *Ode*] are well-worn—the opening address, very slight historical retrospection in the reference to the founder of Eton, the genre sketch of the children at play, the presence of abstractions and moralizing. The all-important innovation is the introduction in a developed form of the "early memories" theme which for the first time in local poetry is not merely glanced at but dwelt upon lovingly.'[38]

As the opening invocation dissolves into sighs of pastoral nostalgia, we learn that the poet spent a 'careless childhood' in these 'fields beloved,' a 'stranger yet to pain!' (ll. 11–14). The 'gales' that blow from this 'pleasing shade' (l. 11) soothe the poet, and breathe for him 'a second spring' (l. 20). Nostalgia here has restorative powers, perhaps because the 'pleasing shade' of pastoral poetic practice echoes the earlier phrase 'Henry's holy shade' (l. 4). King Henry VI founded Eton College, and Gray invokes his ghostly presence as a reminder of noble attitudes towards, and support for, education and culture. The repetition of 'shade' (as sign of patronage and of pastoral) suggests Gray's awareness that the pastoral tradition is as much a set of vocational, as of poetic, expectations, and that it takes a system of patronage and a concensual culture to make either feasible. In the 'Ode on the Spring,' lines 11–14 allude to Virgil's iconic portrayal of the Augustan shade that made Tityrus's song possible; in the Eton *Ode*, lines 4 and 11 bring together a similar literary-historical suggestion. Eton, pastoral nostalgia, patronage—in 1742, these must have been overdetermined connections for Gray. In the eighteenth century (as perhaps now), the 'shade' offered by Eton would include the high connections that promised both future social and economic advancement and cultural support. At the time that this *Ode* was written, it was this shade, in the figure of the estranged Walpole, that seemed withdrawn from Gray.

This second stanza (ll. 11–20), is also the bridge that connects the opening invocations of the poem with the moralising that follows. In these lines, the pastoral discourse of the self in privileged communion with nature is, as we have seen, qualified by nostalgia, by a sense of loss. However, for all the poignance of the retrospection, it is too briefly engaged in to develop the 'early memories' theme. In fact, the rest of this poem, from the third stanza (l. 21) onwards, speaks a language different from these ten lines, a shift perhaps most simply exemplified by the disappearance of the key deictics of the self, the personal pronouns 'I' (l. 15) and 'my' (l. 18) that individualise and focus the nostalgia-affect of the first stanza. In the second stanza, the foregrounding of the figure and emotions of the poet bears witness once again to Gray's insistent need to thematise sympathetically the figure of the solitary poet, his sensibility ravaged by the pain of life and society. As the 'Ode on the Spring' shows, Gray identifies with this figure, but only within an oscillation of which the antithetical pole is the need to resist and distance such identification. In the Eton *Ode*, the prime moment of distantiation, again effected by showing the poet-figure to be in some key way limited and flawed, is arrived at only in the last stanza, and our discussion of it must be postponed similarly.

Dr. Johnson, in a wonderful moment of literal-mindedness, took Gray to task for the appeal to 'Father Thames' in line 21: 'His supplication to Father Thames, to tell him who drives the hoop or tosses the ball, is useless and puerile. Father Thames has no better way of knowing than himself.'[39] This is true, except that to read this appeal as anything but a rhetorical move designed to shift the burden of voice, and hence of declamatory authority, away from the already 'weary soul' (l. 18) of the poet-figure (the subject of the enounced) is to misread its function. In the analysis of similar moments in the 'Ode on the Spring' (ll. 16–21 and l. 31), we have seen how the effort to apparently ease and strengthen the speech of the poet-figure by having him ventriloquise the inspired utterance of traditional personifications of poetic power works actually to delimit and weaken this figure, who is represented as already considerably enervated. I argued there that this is one of the rhetorical methods by which the subject of enunciation (the Poet) is distanced from the subject of the enounced (the thematised poet-figure). In the Eton *Ode* too, almost as soon as the pathos generated by the sympathetic representation of the poet-figure in the second stanza tends to become the primary affect of the poem, and thus to encourage (as do the personal pronouns 'I' and 'my' of lines 15 and 18) the complete identification of the subject of the enounced with the subject of enunciation, this figure of 'Father Thames' is introduced, a personification whose rhetorical status quickly sanitises such contagion. As the invoked numen of place, authority, tradition, and voice, this personification both puts the thematised poet, so to speak, in his place, as well as authorises the shift of the poem to its primary theme, the meditation upon childhood, age, and the agonies of life.

Meditation is probably not a good word for the rest of the Eton *Ode* (especially lines 51–90), for it cannot even begin to account for the almost fearsome excesses of word and phrase, image and personification that characterise these stanzas. The awkwardness and stilted diction of lines 21–50 are of a kind with Gray's manifest attempt to foreground the literariness of the language of the poetic tradition. Jan Mukarovsky, in his theorising of 'standard language and poetic language,' argues that the

> function of poetic language consists in the maximum of foregrounding [aktualisace] of the utterance. Foregrounding is the opposite of automatization, that is, the de-automatization of an act; the more an act is automatized, the less it is consciously executed . . . Foregrounding is, of course, common in the standard language, for instance, in journalistic style, even more in essays. But it is here always subordinate to communication: its purpose is to attract the reader's (listener's) attention more closely to the *subject matter* expressed by the foregrounded means of expression . . . In poetic language foregrounding achieves maximum intensity to the extent of pushing communication into the background as the objective of expression, and of being used for its own sake; it is not used in the services of communication, but in order to place in the foreground the act of expression, the act of speech itself.[40]

In my understanding, Gray foregrounds expression primarily by working with the language and rhetorical conventions most clearly associated with a tradition of poetic discourse. Thus, for him, 'de-automatization' consists precisely of the insistent use of that which has been schematized, automatized as poetic discourse, but to a point where the schema is so overloaded, so overdetermined that it reveals its own outlines and its constructions; its strategies of derivation, exclusion and inclusion; its affiliations and allegiances, both literary and ideological; in short, its own genealogy and history.

Accordingly, no attempt is made to particularise or render in any specific detail the children who play in the lap of Father Thames. Periphrases and a formulaic vocabulary ('a sprightly race,' 'idle progeny,' 'bold adventurers,' 'the rolling circle') derived from the conventional languages of poetry suggest that it is not the activities of children, as much as poetic representations of childhood, that is the subject here. These lines enact the irony of such representations, the fact that their characteristic diction functions analogously to the distance imposed by the (temporal) prospect, occluding rather than clarifying, blurring hindsight rather than sharpening insight. Gray problematises the authority claimed by the prospect poet, then, not simply by refusing to write the historical or political or social allegory expected of a prospect poem, but also, more characteristically and acutely, by insistently writing a language that clearly embodies (and reveals) the rhetorical and ideological investments of this tradition of poetry. In spatial terms, the 'prospect' was used to provide a seamless view of natural harmony; ideologically, it was made to stand for the point of superior reference from where the unseemliness of social and existential discord could be smoothed over; rhetorically, as Gray shows us, it encouraged a lexicon and a glossary that attempted to efface (gloss over) all the contradictions that engendered such discourse.

Such an effacement included not just political and social contradictions though, but also those of any other intellectual and ideological endeavour. In producing this rhetorical effacement, as Geoffrey Tillotson has shown us, eighteenth-century periphrastic vocabularies functioned very often as necessary neologisms, 'nomenclature' informed by the assumptions and categories of the theories of ethics, physico-theology, science, that spawned them.[41] Necessary, because they set up the taxonomy and system conceptually central to the discourse that articulated them, and often provided its rhetorical foundations. Poetic diction, or the construction of poems using vocabularies identified with specific discourses, thus needs to be read as a sign of the building of entire (ideological) systems. As Tillotson puts it, 'the reasons why eighteenth-century poets use the diction are among the main reasons why they write poetry at all.'[42]

Hence, in the Eton *Ode*, another reason that the representation of the playing, heedless children is not particularised is because Gray is aware that these children do not really exist in the language of ethical-humanist didacticism except as figural exemplars that act as foundations of a discourse of sententious observation and moral maxim.[43] They are, as emblems of the rhetorical tropes and methods of ethics, 'little victims' (l. 52), who are necessarily prefigured as such (to twist the meaning of the line somewhat), 'regardless of their doom' (l. 52). It is interest in this kind of figuration (*pre*figuration, *re*figuration) that energises the poem from line 51 on, as Gray proceeds to write the secular sermon whose text is the sermon from Menander: 'I am a man; a sufficient excuse for being unhappy.' The power of such didactic discourse is clearly dependant on the skill with which it can elaborate and embellish its chosen theme, as well as the consistency with which it can illustrate its claims to marmoreal, monumental truth. The line from Menander becomes then, for Gray, the pretext for an exploration of the possibilities of such discourse, for a search for the sources of its energy, its claims to truth, and thus, finally, its will to unimpeachable authority.

Gray does this, as is usual with him, by taking the path of greatest (literary) resistance, overloading the rhetorical circuits of such discourse, testing its capacities, its strengths and its weaknesses. Lines 51–90, which function as an account of the many horrors that 'black Misfortune' (l. 56) arranges in ambush for men as they travel the path of life, are scarcely interested in providing a persuasive or moving, or even coherent account of human lives that are inevitably traumatised by transience, mutability, and death. This is the poetry, instead, of frank, and rapid overstatement, where the effect sought for is produced not by sustained particularisation or detail, but by a cumulative excess of conventional figures. Here, Love pines while jealousy 'inly gnaws the secret heart' (l. 67); Infamy grins while hard Unkindness 'mocks the tear it forced to flow' (l. 77); Madness laughs wild as Poverty 'numbs the soul with icy hand' (l. 89). Such cataloging has tested severely even Gray's friends: Thomas Quayle, always sympathetic to Gray, is reluctantly led to conclude that 'it cannot be denied that very many of the beings that swarm in his odes do not differ in their essential character from the mechanical figures worked to death by the ode-makers of his days; even his genius was not enough to clothe them all in flesh and blood. In the "Eton College" ode there is a stanza given over to a conventional catalogue of the "fury passions," "the vultures of the mind"; and similar thin abstractions people all the other odes.'[44]

Quayle is quoted at length here to suggest the ground which critics of Gray's diction have traversed. Perhaps most pithy of all is Coleridge's observation that Gray converts 'mere abstractions' into personifications by typographical fiat,[45] a (rhetorical?) gesture that was clearly too transparent to be acceptable to the program of mystified, 'organic' poetic usage that the later poet was developing. The only criterion for critical evaluation seems to have been the question of whether Gray was able to flesh out his 'mechanical figures' or not. Critics have not asked whether that might in fact not have been the effect Gray was trying to achieve at all. Nobody, that is, except Jean Hagstrum, whose analysis of the Sister Arts (painting and poetry), leads him to conclude that Gray's 'other imagistic effect, like Collins' (or the Wartons'), is created by personified abstraction: a pictorially conceived moral quality is presented as in an allegorical painting, attended by a train of minor but related personae.' Hagstrum calls this configuration an 'allegorical ideogram,' which illustrates 'this tendency to present moral and psychological meaning in visual allegory.'[46] What Hagstrum tells us, then, is that the grounds for explaining, and rendering valid, such poetic usage lie outside poetry, and in that other tradition of representation that is painting. For Hagstrum (to rewrite his insight in the vocabulary of semiotics), the 'personified abstraction' in Gray's poems is a signifier whose signified is to be located in the conventions of allegorical painting. Usage and effect, that is, are underwritten by prior usages and effects.

This reflexivity in relation to the other arts is clearly a feature of Gray's self-reflexiveness and his near-obsessive concern with the validity and authority of different kinds of poetic figuration and diction. The staccato yet insistent unidimensionality of the personified images in these lines in the Eton *Ode* refuse the question: can these not be made to come alive, can they not be rewritten to serve as emblems of the organic unity of rhetorical figure and thematic meaning? They are in fact signifiers designed to frustate the desire for seamless signification, paper cut-outs that can be misperceived as three-dimensional sculptures only if the conditioned eye both supplies foreground and background, and suppresses empirical observation in favour of the blinkers of particular received conventions. That is, to believe that Gray attempted, and failed, to create a gallery of personifications informed by a moral and didactic purpose is to fill in the blanks, to create meaning by not reading the text at hand except as a specific illustration of a broader context (the ethical discourse of poetry/the poetical discourse of ethics), whose every rhetorical form and referential gesture is well known and clearly understood.[47] It is to accept, at face value and without a sense of the disruptions of form and fiction, the ability of this discourse to first generate meanings (through characteristic topoi and tropes, 'ideograms'), and then to fix these meanings (through repetition, convention, hermeneutic tradition) in forms that exist prior to, and which override nearly at will, further refiguration. It is to grant a discourse an authority beyond itself, to grant its signifiers a transcendent signified that obviates the necessity of reading to unravel more particular signification.

Thus, lines 51–90 of the Eton *Ode* are to be read not so much literally, as an impassioned account of the life and death of the average Etonian, but literarily, with a sense of how poets have chosen to represent, as Menander did, 'unhappy man.' Lines 61–90, for instance, about the 'fury Passions'—the passions as Furies: already we have the key to representation—are indebted to Virgil, Statius, Chaucer, Spenser, Shakespeare, Dryden, Pope, and Thomson for their construction.[48] Here, as elsewhere in Gray, allusiveness is so strongly foregrounded that it becomes a technique for the reconstruction, through a kind of echoing, of an entire canonical tradition of poetic discourse. Such a recovery of inheritance and lineage is usually part of an attempt to claim its authority and its power, and this is clearly why Gray is so deliberate in his enactment of the process by which it works. However, as I have argued earlier, Gray's poem re-enacts in order to investigate, ventriloquism being a way of understanding how poetic voices operate. In the Eton *Ode*, then, the nostalgia of the thematised poet-figure (the subject of the enounced) is far more than a nostalgia for childhood or for a pre-lapsarian innocence. It is also a yearning for an entire tradition of poetic discourse that successfully claimed for its representations (of 'man,' of the 'passions of man') a 'truthfulness' based on their status as exemplars, as figures that were the necessary foundations of ethical and moral didacticism. That is, his is a nostalgia for a tradition in which the ground for the authority of the poetic lexicon—exemplarity—is unquestionably secured by its being the foundational trope of the larger discourse of ethics.

Accordingly, the conclusion reached by the poet-figure:

To each his sufferings: all are men,
Condemned alike to groan;
The tender for another's pain,
The unfeeling for his own (ll. 91–94),

is basically a retelling of the epigraph from Menander. There is an important shift in tonal quality in these lines though, the frenzied figuration of the previous forty lines being replaced by quiet platitudes that are meant to alert us to the fact that they represent the end-results of this entire meditation on life. The nature of the musing tone echoes that of the whimsical nostalgia of the second stanza, and serves to reinstate the figure of the poet. The slightly developed personal retrospection of lines 11 to 14 is here replaced by another kind of retrospection, as the poet-figure assumes the posture of the moralist who, having surveyed the histories of individual lives, can now formulate maxims for the public good. Particularly interesting here is the seamless ease with which the topos of retrospection allows the transformation of the tentative text of the personal memories of the poet-figure into banal, generalised, and authoritative poetic discourse. Of course, this seamlessness has been made possible by the body of the poem, which, as I have argued, successfully ventriloquises canonical voices whose (representational) practices underwrote the authority of such discourse.

This is then the moment at which the Eton *Ode* achieves what I have described in the analysis of 'Ode on the Spring' as the 'primary affect' of these poems, inviting the reader to see in the represented poet-figure the poet Gray, gloomy and solitary. Again, this moment of isolation is simultaneously the moment of the poet-figure's greatest power, for his isolation is the condition of his knowledge, and everybody else's ignorance. If this is so, then, as I have suggested earlier, it must also be the moment of greatest identification between Gray and the thematised poet, and thus the moment at which the dialectical turn towards distantiation is put into place. This is exactly what happens in the poem, as the poet-figure is shown to refuse the precise opportunity that would make community available to him, by abdicating the only role that his ventriloquising of the discourse of morality and ethics had left open to him, that of teacher, of someone who can use insight in an instrumental and instructive way.[49] The effect of the last lines is not just to limit the capacity of the poet-figure however, but also to put into question the entire tradition of poetic discourse that he so clearly echoes and becomes a spokesman (an exemplar?) for. Ironically, in his recounting of the reasons for his refusal to play the didact, the poet-figure still speaks the diction that, throughout the poem, has based its claim to authority on the prior discourse of ethical didacticism:

> Yet ah! why should they know their fate?
> Since sorrow never comes too late,
> And happiness too swiftly flies.
> Thought would destroy their paradise.
> No more; where ignorance is bliss,
> 'Tis folly to be wise. (ll. 95–100)

Ironically, yet fully appropriately; for the gesture of the refusal to communicate turns out to be the inevitable extension of the distancing that the characteristic diction and representations of this discourse have constantly enacted in their conversion of the particular objects of their attention into generalised exemplars. This turn carries a moral too, but it is a deconstructive and ironising insight: he who speaks the language of Personified Abstraction is condemned to repeat its rhetorical evasions in more significant and tangible ways.

This, as I have been saying, is the fate of the poet-figure in the poem. What of the subject of the enunciation, that other position for the speaking subject in/of the poem? Unlike in the 'Ode on the Spring,' there is no third party ('the sportive kind') here to act as the voice of irony, to provide a neat distancing of the poet-moralist from the Poet who writes the poem. What we have instead is, as I have just pointed out, the figure of the poet-moralist who refuses to act upon his insights, who choses the way of isolation and non-communication, and whose presence is 'con-centric to' and contrasted with that of the subject of the enunciation, the Poet who speaks, who gives the poem its form, and who, in fact, communicates the larger context that is 'ex-centric to' and contains (both presents and limits) the discourse and positions of the subject of the enounced. Thus, as in the 'Ode on the Spring,' the double effect of the Creation of the Poet is exploited as the compensatory mechanism in the face of the loss and impoverishment of poetic authority enacted by the turning away from responsibility of the poet-figure in the poem.

Gray's early poems all contain figures of the poet whose active (yet ultimately passive) presence enables Gray to investigate various types of poetic discourse, to ventriloquise vocabulary and diction, to echo figure, topos and trope; to test, in short, the sources of the authority and power that any poetic discourse arrogates to itself. In each case, the poems locate aporias, or at least suggest the contradictions that shape particular poetic practices. In the 'Ode on the Spring,' the transience of spring acts as a quick check to its celebrant pastoralist poet, just as, at the end of the same poem, the judgmental distance sought by the discourse of morality is shown to lengthen into an isolation and loss. In the Eton *Ode,* first the conventional themes and figures of the prospect poem are set aside as Gray utilises the topos of the prospect to underwrite a nostalgic and (at least initially) purely personal retrospect. Then, as the poem goes on to ventriloquise the practice of those who contributed to the formation of the characteristic discourse of the genre, it reveals the profoundly ideological gap at the heart of its diction, suggesting that the—usually periphrastic—glossaries of exemplarity work by glossing-over, by encouraging the speaker to be less, rather than more, engaged with his subjects. Such an insight is clearly prejudicial to the authority of this discourse, with its claim to speak for and of ethical and social *utile,* especially as Gray's poems work to suggest that the characteristic poetic diction of such discourse is authorised only by convention and tradition, and is to be more accurately understood as speaking by artifice, and to Art. This understanding, of course, functions also as the ground for the recuperation of poetic power and authority, for it leads to the moment of ironic closure, producing the completed artifact which stands as witness to the power and significance of the artificer.

In his 'Poetics of the Lyric,' Jonathan Culler sees such a claim to creative significance as a key 'convention or expectation governing the lyric': 'To write a poem is to claim significance of some sort for the verbal construct one produces,'[50] and, one might add, for oneself as its producer. This claim to significance made by / for the Poet can be usefully articulated with de Man's discussion of irony: 'The ironic, twofold self that the writer or philosopher constitutes by his language seems to come into being only at the expense of his empirical self, falling (or rising) from a state of mystified adjustment into the knowledge of his mystification. The ironic language splits the subject into an empirical self that exists in a state of inauthenticity and a self that exists only in the form of a language that asserts the knowledge of this inauthenticity. This does not, however, make it into an authentic language, for to know inauthenticity is not the same as to be authentic.'[51] The drama of two linguistically constituted subject-positions is played out in both the Gray poems we have discussed. In the West *Sonnet*, as we shall see, Gray's attempt to authenticate the language that ironises the empirical, or the previous self, is based upon a paradoxical (though ingenious) direct address to the authentic figure of loss, the dead West, and to the cultural and ideological consensus he represented for Gray.

SONNET [ON THE DEATH OF MR RICHARD WEST]

Gray's insights into the way rhetorical tropes present as natural and permanent what is in fact constructed and transient extends to what is clearly also a topos—the Poet as Artificer. Gray's 'Sonnet [on the Death of Mr Richard West],' is the poem which most explicitly examines the poetic and cultural consensus that is required for this topos to be rendered credible and naturalised, as it is also the poem that enacts the fragility of such naturalisation. Before we get to that, though, it is necessary to recount the circumstances that determined some of the discursive particulars of Gray's *Sonnet*.

On July 4, 1737, West wrote to Gray, and included in his letter a long poem, 'Ad Amicos,' that he had written during a recent illness. 'Do you remember,' he asked Gray, 'Elegy 5th, Book the 3rd, of Tibullus, Vos tenet &c. and do you remember a letter of Mr Steele?[52] This melancholy elegy and this melancholy letter I turned into a more melancholy epistle of my own, during my sickness, in the way of imitation.'[53] Following upon Pope, West ends his poem thus:

I care not tho' this face be seen no more,
The world will pass as chearful as before;
Bright as before the Day-Star will appear
The fields as verdant, and the skies as clear:
Nor storms, nor comets will my doom declare,
Nor signs on earth, nor portents in the air;
Unknown and silent will depart my breath,
Nor Nature e'er take notice of my death.
Yet some there are (ere sunk in endless night)
Within whose breasts my monument I'd write:
Loved in my life, lamented in my end,
Their praise would crown me, as their precepts mend:
To them may these fond lines my name indear,
Not from the Author but the Friend sincere. (ll. 73–86)

Neither Tibullus's elegy nor Pope's letter express the sentiment and the desire West's poem ends with, that is, to write 'within' the breasts of friends his monument. This writing, this memorial, will be the only trace left of the poet's existence, for Nature's perpetual rhythms will not halt in order to mark a death. Inscription poems and epitaphs are engraved on materials which are occasionally less-than-marmoreal in their resistance to the ravages of time,[54] but it is still significant that West choses as his slate the corpora of his friends, who are like him subject to a similar traumatic mortality. We will tease out the implications of this irony later, in our analysis of the re-working of this idea in the *Sonnet*, but it is important here to notice another moment of delicate tension in West's lines that Gray's poem plays on too. West's 'fond lines' are to 'indear' him to his friends (l. 85), whose praise will crown him, the crown being the traditional symbol of the succesful poet. However, the last line attempts to abdicate the role of poet ('Author'), replacing it with that of 'Friend,' as if there is some special consolation to be drawn from writing as the latter rather than as the former. If this is simply a variation on the humility topos, it is one that taps, quite acutely, into an anxiety symptomatic not only of the West-Gray relationship (as readers, annotators, and critics of each other's work), but also into the psycho-social grid that contained the practice and the reception of mid-eighteenth century poets. But for all that, on to Gray.

As in the 'Ode on the Spring,' the diction of the West *Sonnet* is remarkable for its conventionality. Remarkable, and thoroughly remarked upon. Wordsworth's is the exemplary voice of condemnation: Gray's sonnet consists of little else than a diction that thrusts 'out of sight the plain humanities of nature by a motley masquerade of tricks, quaintnesses, hieroglyphics, and enigmas.'[55] Twentieth-century critics who have been more sympathetic range from Tillotson, who sees the '"poetic diction" as dramatic,' and ultimately rejected by Gray as being unequal to the expression of his more 'sincere grief,'[56] to Lonsdale, who believes that a Tillotson-like 'defence of the diction used to describe nature on the grounds that it is ironic is over-ingenious and distracting,' and is willing to take literally Gray's organisation of his poem 'around the contrast of a joyful, thriving nature and a poet's grief.'[57]

The poems's allusiveness is pronounced, and the discourse of pastoralism systematically invoked:[58]

> In vain to me the smiling mornings shine,
> And reddening Phoebus lifts his golden fire:
> The birds in vain their amorous descant join,
> Or cheerful fields assume their green attire: (ll. 1–4)
> . . . .
> Yet morning smiles the busy race to cheer,
> And new-born pleasure brings to happier men:
> The fields to all their wonted tribute bear;
> To warm their little loves the birds complain. (ll. 9–12)

The contrast between the absence that is death and the active, continuing presence of Nature follows the central sentiment of the lines quoted from both West's poem and from Pope's letter. There is, however, a significant shift. In both Pope and West, the contrast is predicated upon the absence of the poet himself, and made particularly poignant by the fact that it is only in such a case that the unceasing and perpetual rhythms of Nature cannot be converted into consolatio motifs. For all except the absent one, the discourse of pastoralism, of the eclogic elegy, offers the regenerative powers and permanence of Nature as consolation and support.[59]

To notice this is to begin to understand why the mourner in Gray's sonnet starts by ventriloquising the diction and vocabulary of the poetic discourse that offers tropes of the regenerative continuities of Nature as hope and consolation. This mourner-poet (the subject of the enounced), dramatises these tropes as offered to him by the voices of a poetic tradition that created in them rhetorical and psychological mechanisms for coming to terms with death and loss. In this case, however, such a reenactment of the tradition is futile[60]—these echoes cannot substitute for the one voice that he, impossibly, longs to hear:

> These ears, alas! for other notes repine,
> A different object do these eyes require.
> My lonely anguish melts no heart but mine;
> And in my breast the imperfect joys expire. (ll. 5–8)

Paradoxically, in these four lines the mourner does not hear West because he can hear only West; hear, that is, West's lines in 'Ad Amicos' that sing of the continuities of Nature not as markers of consolation but as the final evidence of absence and loss (ll. 73–80). Based upon this insight, West had sought to 'write' his 'monument' in the breasts of his friends (l. 82), hoping that the name of 'Friend' could ensure a perpetuity that the name of 'Author' could not (l. 86). Now, the full irony and elusiveness of this hope is brought home to the friend who mourns West, in whose 'breast the imperfect joys expire' (l. 8). In 1742, both Gray and West were authors only to their friends; the death of the 'friend' then, threatened powerfully the tenuous existence of the 'author.'

As we have learnt to expect in Gray's poems, the moment of the poet-figure's greatest insight is also the moment of his greatest isolation. The mourner, unable to see in the discourse of pastoralism the consolation it has long offered, unable, that is, to believe in the continuities of Nature or of eclogic-elegiac poetic diction, is confronted by the isolation that results from his refusal to speak a shared cultural language[61]: 'My lonely anguish melts no heart but mine' (l. 7). Here again (ll. 7–8), we have the figure of sorrowful isolation, and we have seen how, in Gray's poems, such a figure, though thematised with sympathy and great affective power, must quickly be distanced. Lest a threatening identification between the mourner (the figure of the enounced) and the poet (the subject of the enunciation) be effected, the sonnet switches, in line 9, away from the more direct discourse of the mourner to the ventriloquised discourse of pastoralism.[62] The full closure of the octet also serves to contain the affective speech of the mourner, and lines 9–12, which repeat, in a ritual, refrain-like fashion, the conventional observations of the first four lines of the sonnet, repress the sense of intense personal utterance that characterises lines 5–8. The echoes of tradition, as it were, are invoked to speak over the voice of the mourner, thereby preventing the possibility that the primary affect of the sonnet—the poet as mourner—become its lasting effect.

The last two lines, however, repeat the language of personal, rather than shared, grief:

> I fruitless mourn to him that cannot hear,
> And weep the more because I weep in vain. (ll. 13–14)

The deictics of the self are prominent here, their assertion following upon, and contrasting with, the reiteration of pastoral conventionalities. For a moment this seems paradoxical; in earlier lines the discourse of pastoralism serves to mute the affective power of similarly inflected utterance. Once again, the moving repetition of 'I' in these lines encourages a conflation of subject-positions, threatens an identification between the mourner of the narrative and the artificer of the *Sonnet*. In the 'Ode on the Spring' and the Eton *Ode*, an ironic turn had enforced proper distance between these subject-positions—here, in addition to the workings of a larger, more cultural irony (which I will discuss shortly), the form of the poem itself suggests the grounds for differentiation. After all, these two lines bring the poem to a close (a formally predetermined end, these being lines 13 and 14 of a sonnet), and thus complete the poetic artifact whose successful production is the mark of the poet-artificer. Thus, even though the 'I' mourns 'fruitless'[63] and 'in vain,' its isolation is not as total as that of the figure of the mourner in lines 5–8, as it is compensated for by the completion of the sonnet itself, the creation of the poem being consolatory fruit. (To that extent these last two lines extend the discursive tension that is played out in the sonnet form of this elegy. Tight rhymes and strong closures work to maintain and emphasise the continuity of the narration—the enounced—while the over-determined diction of most of the poem and the obvious fact of its being a fourteen-line, conventional formal unit draw attention to its artifice, to the speech act—the enunciation).

But there is another, more important sense in which the poet understands his mourning to be 'in vain.' This is the reason that he mourns not *for* West, as we might expect, but *to* him (l. 13). The poet mourns not simply the loss of a friend (that is, 'for' him), but sees in this absence the loss also of choice audience, of precisely that person who would be able to best ratify his sense of his own authority as artficer. Hence, the form of mourning, the ritual-sonnet, must be presented not just for, but *to,* the absent West. What this final gesture of the sonnet does is enact Gray's ambivalence about his own status as (unpublished) poet, and about the larger project he was involved in. Losing West was losing the one friend who constantly understood and encouraged Gray's methods and concerns. As Joseph Foladare puts it, the concluding lines of the West *Sonnet* mourn not only the potential threat to Gray's poetic creativeness, but also 'all the conscious, joyous activities of mind and heart which West called into being.'[64]

Another way to understand the full import of the last lines is to see them as registering the recognition that the status and authority of the artificer is ultimately contingent upon someone else's appreciation of the successful artistry of the finished artifact. A gloss is required here, one that is provided by Thomas McFarland's account of the two traditional conceptions of poetry, conceptions that we will see mark Gray's career profoundly:

> The divergence in conception between unconsciously or carelessly voiced 'Platonic' poetry and carefully wrought 'Aristotelian' poem is further indicated by the simultaneous currency, in both antiquity and the Renaissance, of a dual conception of the poet as reflected in the Greek *poietes*, on the one hand, and the Latin *vates* on the other. 'What is a poet?' asks Jonson. 'A Poet is that which by the Greeks is called . . . ὁ ποιητής, a maker, or a fainer . . . according to *Aristotle* from the word ποιεῖν, which signifies to make or fain.' Sidney, however, notes that 'Among the Romans a Poet was called *Vates*, which is as much as a Diviner, Fore-seer, or Prophet.' *Poietes*, in other words, refers to the maker of 'Aristotelian' poems; *vates* to the communicant of 'Platonic' poetry.[65]

I have briefly mentioned (pp. 53–55), Gray's sense of the poet as seer, as prophet, but this was not as yet (in 1742), a developed poetic persona or method for him. As my examination of the earlier poems shows, Gray was still centrally concerned with the techniques and materials of the *art* and the *craft* of the poet, with what might be described as professional perspiration rather than vatic inspiration.

The close attention Gray paid to past practice and his clear insight into the consensual basis of the reception and creation of the poetic tradition made it clear that to see the poet as *poietes*, as maker or artificer, is to require a responsive other, necessarily one equally steeped in the traditions of high culture that dictate the laws of taste, discrimination, and understanding. Vatic utterance claims for itself a transcendent inspiration (though this claim is always grounded in recognisably historical tropes) and bases its authority upon itself, or rather, upon the larger authority of the discourse of divinity it acts as a mouthpiece for. It is less easy to claim such transcendence for the authority of poetic craftsmanship, less easy to validate the finished artifact in other than situationally, culturally, and historically specific terms.

And yet to use the word 'professional' to describe Gray, the consummate eighteenth-century gentleman-scholar, one who never wrote for any market, may seem misguided. However, it is precisely his socio-economic distance from the frenzied and largely meretricious literary exchange that was Grub Street that enabled Gray to examine, at his leisure, some of the key premises, assumptions, and pretensions of the 'profession' of the poet. In doing this, he was living out what the *O.E.D.* describes as one sense of 'professional:' 'That is trained and skilled in the theoretic or scientific parts of a trade or occupation, as distinct from its merely mechanical parts; that raises his trade to the dignity of a learned profession.' Part of Gray's attempt to examine the sources of 'literary' power and authority stemmed from a vocational anxiety brought on by the increasing professionalisation of poetry, a development that threatened the cherished 'independence' of the gentleman-poet. One of Gray's compelling needs seems to have been to refine a language of poetry untainted by any kind of historical or ideological instrumentality, and thus to free the practices of poetry from the contingency of cultural values. However, insofar as poetic conventions are the reified forms of literary and cultural practices, Gray's search was doomed by his own acute literary awareness. His engagement with poetry was sharp enough to refuse his own poems the comfort of stable discursive positions; his engagement with culture incisive enough to turn the *Sonnet* to West into an elegy for a dying consensual culture.[66]

Before we examine what such a consensual culture might have meant in the mid-eighteenth century, we still need to answer some questions about the West *Sonnet* and about the 'Ode to Adversity,' the one other complete poem Gray wrote in 1742. I have argued that all of Gray's poems written in this year foreground the problems and strategies of poetry, inevitably locating, via the thematised poet-figure and the ironic dissolution common to the end of all three poems, the problematic of literary authority, and I have suggested that the West *Sonnet* occupies a special place in the attempted resolution of this problematic. Whereas the 'Ode on the Spring' and the Eton *Ode* close in a rhetorical twist that both limits and distances the poet-figure, and offers the completion of the poem and the establishment of the superior voice of the Poet as compensatory values, the West *Sonnet* ends in the recognition that such values, being constructed and literary rather than intrinsic, can only be realised within a particular cultural community. What, we might ask, allowed the *Sonnet* to be the privileged place of such a recognition? Donald Mell sees the answer in the history of a genre: 'The elegist's self-consciousness about the nature of art is implicit in the nature of elegy itself, whose genesis is peculiarly the poet's personal response to loss and time.' Hence, in the 'Augustan elegy,' the '*real* subject, transcending all others, is ultimately the question of its own significance in a world of time and death.' Mell's historicising gesture is based upon what he sees as 'the highly "professional" character of most Augustan writers from Dryden to Johnson . . . as a professional, a writer constantly analyzes and evaluates the significance and the limitations of his art as valid representation of reality, and in the process formally orders his experiences of time and loss which call into question these intimations of order and the idea of permanence through art.'[67]

Mell's discussion of the (Augustan) poet's response to loss, and our sense of the fundamentally allegorical method of Gray's poems (they are always also about the languages and the writing of poetry[68]) suggest that we might fruitfully see the West *Sonnet*, and in fact most of Gray's poetry, as special cases of what de Man describes as 'the rhetoric of temporality.' In such a rhetoric, both allegorical diction and ironic language figure predominantly, being 'linked in their common discovery of a truly temporal predicament . . . [and] in their common demystification of an organic world postulated in a symbolic mode of analogical correspondences or in a mimetic world of representation in which fiction and reality could coincide.'[69] Importantly, such a rhetoric does not signal only a demystifying discovery of temporality, but is generated by the 'conflict between a conception of the self seen in its authentically temporal predicament and a defensive strategy that hides from this negative self-knowledge.'[70] Our discussions of Gray's early poems have shown us how, in their ambiguous thematisation of a surrogate poet-figure and in their subversive ventriloquising of various poetic discourses, they enact this dialectic of insight and blindness.

This dialectic of identification and distantiation, of ventriloquising and silencing, of the enactment of temporality, is, for de Man, paradigmatic of more than the linguistic constitution of subjectivity. Temporality is also a name for the agonistic relationship between a latecomer poet and his precursors, for the gap that separates him from any possibly originary moment, for the (literary) history that defines the conditions and conventions of contemporary poetic discourse. In his 'Review of Harold Bloom's *Anxiety of Influence*,' de Man writes: 'to say that literature is based on influence is to say that it is intratextual. And intratextual relationships necessarily contain a moment that is interpretive.' In this interpretive moment, the latecomer poet will attempt 'to achieve a reversal in which lateness will become associated with strength instead of with weakness. This aim is achieved by means of a play of substitutions . . . from the moment we begin to deal with substitutive systems, we are governed by linguistic rather than natural or psychological models: one can always substitute one word for another, but one cannot, by mere act of the will, substitute night for day or bliss for gloom. However, the very ease with which the linguistic substitution, or trope, can be carried out hides the fact that it is epistemologically unreliable.'[71]

Hides, but not well enough, as the West *Sonnet* shows. In the poem, several motifs and motives come together. The elegy, as the form dedicated to the thematisation, and attempted exorcism, of loss, foregrounds the distinct temporality of (the poet's) life. Gray's repetitions and echoes of West's sentiments and language in 'Ad Amicos' and elsewhere register the revisionary encounter between texts. The constantly ventriloquised discourse of pastoralism functions as a reminder of the precursor tradition that threatens to over-write the voice of the latecomer poet, especially as its oppressive authority is masked in the ostensibly timely sentiments of *consolatio*. All these elements unravel in the *Sonnet*. The poem repudiates the discourse of eclogic-elegy, seeing through its epistemologically impossible attempt to substitute the tropes of a regenerative presence (Nature) for a manifest absence (the dead West). West's figuration, in 'Ad Amicos,' of the unchanging renewal of nature as precisely the (non-)mark of absence made this repudiation imperative and inevitable, but Gray also rewrites West's own wishful trope, the fond hope of the permanence of that memory which is inscribed in the breasts of friends. This memory too is perishable, for its monument is itself subject to the laws of temporality. All this insight is debilitating, and I have suggested that the completed form of the sonnet is, at least provisionally, asserted as the compensation that renders such insight manageable. However, as we have already seen, to attempt to compensate for loss by offering the constructs of artistry brings the poet back full circle (this attempt is clearly as epistemologically unreliable as the rhetorical substitutions of the eclogic-elegy), to a point where the last, crucial, insight of the poem is recorded: the absence it mourns (to) is the death of a shared, enabling and validating discourse, poetic tradition, culture.[72]

ODE TO ADVERSITY

After such knowledge, what forgiveness? None, perhaps, but that based upon a denial of insight, a denial that acts as a censoring and distancing mechanism, and that allows the reassertion of the conventional and the consensual, the tried and the tested. So far we have read the formal and rhetorical construction of Gray's early poems as suggesting a critique of some conventional methods of empowering the poetic voice. I have also argued that this exploration of a poetics is best understood in its location within eighteenth-century cultural politics. This location—Gray's sense of a problematic marginality—would also explain the need, in these poems, for gestures of resolution and closure to calm the dissonance set up by the poems themselves. In 'Ode to Adversity,' the last poem Gray wrote in 1742, we find exactly such a gesture of reconciliation and retreat, one that works by denying the stresses and ambivalences that characterise the 'Ode on the Spring,' the Eton *Ode*, and the West *Sonnet*.

Gray was unsure whether to call this poem a hymn or an ode. He finally chose the latter, and Lonsdale's understands his decision as follows: 'though *Hymn* was more appropriate for a poem addressed to a goddess, G. must have later decided that the distinction was immaterial.'[73] Perhaps so, but the fact that Gray thought of his poem as a hymn suggests his overall conception of its mode and affect.[74] The 'Ode to Adversity' is meant to exhibit the virtues of a hymn—affirmation and allegiance, acceptance and obeisance — and, within the trajectory of Gray's four poems of 1742, to be the poem that asserts and accepts the foundational tropes of its tradition and culture. In contrast to the West *Sonnet*, the poem that enacts most fully the personal, poetical, and cultural crises that Gray experienced, the 'Ode to Adversity' invokes the ritual forms and old goddesses of poetry in their most benign, most protective aspects, hoping to see in them figures that will sustain and authorise the vocation of poet.[75]

In order to effect this shift, the 'Ode to Adversity' rewrites precisely those images and forms of the Eton *Ode* which were witness to the agonistic relationship between the poet and the strong precursor tradition of moral-didactic verse. The opening address to Adversity, 'Daughter of Jove, relentless power' (l. 1), establishes, in the structure of apostrophe, the fully interconnected and dependant relationship between the poet and (a figure representative of) this tradition. As Jonathan Culler has shown, apostrophe tropes on 'the circuit or situation of communication itself,' the vocative of the apostrophe being 'a device which the poetic voice uses to establish with an object a relationship which helps to constitute him.'[76] Not only is invocation a way to authorise the poetic voice, but it is 'a figure of vocation,' and of the 'pure embodiment of poetic pretension: of the subject's claim that in his verse he is not merely an empirical poet, a writer of verse, but the embodiment of poetic tradition and of the spirit of poesy.'[77] Thus, the opening apostrophe to Adversity not only signals the rhetorically constitutive relationship between this invoked figure and the subjectivity of the poet, but also categorically reveals the authoritative nature of the relationship between the larger discourse of moral-didacticism that Adversity is representative of and the poetic voice.

In the opening lines, Adversity is seen as the

> tamer of the human breast,
> Whose iron scourge and torturing hour,
> The bad affright, afflict the best! (ll. 2–4)

For a moment, Adversity seems another name for the 'human fate' (l. 56) of the Eton *Ode* that all 'little victims' (l. 52) are inevitably to suffer. However, such moral indiscriminateness would clearly be inimical to the non-agonistic conception of Adversity that the 'Ode to Adversity' must establish. Accordingly, the next lines clarify the differences between the 'bad' being affrighted—'The proud are taught to taste of pain/ And purple tyrants vainly groan' (ll. 6–7)—and the 'best' being afflicted. The latter is worked out by indirection, lines 9–16 reminding us that Adversity played 'Stern rugged nurse!' (l. 13) to Virtue, Jove's 'darling child,' when she was sent to earth:

> What sorrow was, thou bads't her know,
> And from her own she learned to melt at others' woe.
> (ll. 15–16)

Thus, the stage is set for a reconstitution of the 'murtherous band,' the 'ministers of human fate,' that lay in ambush for all men in the Eton *Ode* (ll. 55–59). Here, Adversity's 'frown terrific' (l. 17) scares away only 'Self-pleasing Folly's idle brood,/ Wild Laughter, Noise, and thoughtless Joy' (ll. 18–19), the 'summer friend, the flattering foe' (l. 22), leaving 'us leisure to be good' (l. 20). In these lines, and in the next stanza (ll. 25–32), the parade of personified abstractions, of 'allegorical ideograms,' betrays none of the frenzied, hysterical quality of the diction of the equivalent lines in the Eton *Ode* (ll. 61–90). The change in tone and temper is the change from the description, in the Eton *Ode*, of the darkest exemplars of moral discourse—the 'fury Passions' that tear (l. 61)—to an elaboration of the nurturing and didactic possibilities of such discourse. Accordingly, it is 'Wisdom,' 'Melancholy,' 'Warm Charity,' 'Justice,' and 'Pity' (ll. 25–32) that attend on Adversity's 'solemn steps' (l. 29), a far cry from the 'vultures of the mind' (l. 62) that are 'black Misfortune's baleful train' (l. 57) in the Eton *Ode*. The blind inevitability of Misfortune is refigured as the purposive, discriminating activity of Adversity, the impossible, potentially anarchic pessimism of the former converted into the controlled, ethically unambiguous status of the latter. The chilling horrors of gothic figuration are tamed into the sensible sorrow that accompanies meditative 'thought profound' (l. 26)—the rewriting, in domesticated and foundational tropes, of the traumatic, subversive figures of the Eton *Ode* seems complete.

Or so we might believe, as the next two lines supplicate Adversity's influence:

> Oh! gently on thy suppliant's head,
> Dread goddess, lay thy chastening hand! (ll. 33–34)

This apostrophic gesture of ritual submission, of complete obeisance, however, is problematic enough to reawaken all the threatening visionary possibilities that had been described in the Eton *Ode* and which had, so far, almost been exorcised:

> Not in thy Gorgon terrors clad,
> Not circled with the vengeful band
> (As by the impious thou art seen)
> With thundering voice and thundering mein,
> With screaming Horror's funeral cry,
> Despair and fell Disease and ghastly Poverty. (ll. 35–40)

Though there is the parenthetical reference to the impious as being the targets of Adversity in her Gorgon-aspect, this return of the repressed figures of the Eton *Ode* suggests the threatened confidence of the poet. There is a lingering nervousness about the terrifying exemplary figures of moral-didactic discourse (and even an implicit retrospective validation of the critique, in the Eton *Ode*, of precisely such rhetorical and ideological formulae).

The ambivalence generated by the refiguration of the central figure of moral-didactic discourse—Misfortune into Adversity—might be accounted for more fully if we examine its particular manifestation, in line 35 of the 'Ode to Adversity,' as a Gorgon, seen as such, of course, only by 'the impious' (l. 37). In a 1922 note, 'Medusa's Head,' Freud suggested that the terror of the Medusa is 'a terror of castration that is linked to the sight of something.' He goes on to speculate on 'a remarkable fact,' that apotropaic reversal is central to any representation of this horror. For example, the 'sight of Medusa's head makes the spectator stiff with terror, turns him into stone. Observe that we have here . . . the same origin from the castration complex and the same transformation of affect! For becoming stiff means an erection. Thus in the original situation it offers consolation to the spectator: he is still in possession of a penis, and the stiffening reassures him of the fact.'[78] Is this then the circuit of hysterical specularity, with its component compensatory, apotropaic moment, that the poet is implicated in when he supplicates Adversity not to appear to him in her 'Gorgon terrors clad'?[79]

For in the 'Ode to Adversity,' Adversity is the figure for the precursor poetic and ideological discourse with which, as the Eton *Ode* demonstrated, Gray co-existed so uneasily. Any attempt at a seamless and anxiety-free refiguration of this relationship would thus be difficult, because an acceptance of the poetic tradition as other than Gorgon-like would also surrender the reactive poetic power that is engendered in resisting its seductions. In the Eton *Ode*, where this discourse appeared to the poet in all its castrating horror (witness the hysterical figuration of lines 61–90) as the voices of the fathers that would overwhelm the son, it was possible for the poet to, as it were, stiffen in reaction, the apotropaic moment engendering and authorising the conception of an oppositional poetic self. In the 'Ode to Adversity,' there is the attempt to avoid the burden of the agonistic moment by displacing it onto the 'impious,' but the price of this dissipation of anxiety is the blind, willed acceptance of the power and authority of moral-didactic poetic discourse. The pressure of making this gesture, of giving up the search for a separate space and a distinct voice, then, generates the last hysterical vision of the Gorgon.

Thus, lines 31–40 of the 'Ode to Adversity' provide evidence (symptomatic rather than positive, to be sure), of Gray's great need to retreat from the epistemological, vocational and personal crises enacted by the West *Sonnet*. There is no dialectical or ironic reversal that distances the subject of the enounced from the subject of enunciation in the 'Ode to Adversity.' In fact, there is a profound identification effected between the two, the deictics of self being firmly in place, especially in the last stanza. There, the poet begs Adversity to 'soften, not to wound my heart' (l. 44), and to

> The generous spark extinct revive,
> Teach me to love and to forgive,
> Exact my own defects to scan,
> What others are to feel, and know myself a man.
>
> (ll. 45–48)

This is indeed a thorough rewriting of the last stanza of the Eton *Ode*. There, the poet's insight into the inevitability of human suffering had led to his hubristic and isolating turn away from engagement with the consequences of such insight; here, the experience of adversity is exactly the learning road to an acceptance of moral and discursive community. In keeping with this search for peaceful coexistence within the tradition, lines 47–48 allude deferentially to the central sentiment of Alexander Pope's *Essay on Man*: 'Know then thyself, presume not God to scan' (ii. 1). The last stanza of the 'Ode to Adversity' then, offers no questioning of the poem's uneasy progress, and is primarily a literalising and elaboration of the epigraph from Aeschylus's *Agamemnon*: 'Zeus, who leadeth mortals in the way of understanding, Zeus, who hath established as a fixed ordinance that wisdom comes by suffering.' After the ironic distance and critical awareness manifest in the 'Ode on the Spring,' the Eton *Ode*, and the West *Sonnet*, such a quiescence comes, to say the least, as a strange capitulation.

NOTES

1. Johnston, 'Thomas Gray: Our Daring Bard,' p. 54.
2. The lines that Gray translates here are:

    Mentre essi stan sospesi, a lor d' aspetto
    venerabile appare un vecchio onesto,
    coronato di faggio, in lungo e schietto
    vestir, che di lin candido e contesto.
    Scote questi una verga, e'l fiume calca
    co' piedi asciutti, e contra il corso il valca.

    Torquato Tasso, *Gerusalemme Liberata*, ed. Mario Sansone (Bari: Adriatica Editrice, 1963), p. 273.

    Tasso's hermit is an old man of venerable aspect, whose honest and sincere appearance is emphasised. Gray, however, describes a 'wondrous sage' of 'awful ... mein' who materialises almost magically, thus translating Tasso's unadorned pastoral figure into a powerful, vatic presence. (I am grateful to Susan Bruce for help with translation.)
3. Letter to West, May 8, 1742. *Correspondence*, i. 201.
4. Lonsdale, *Gray*, p. 48. Lonsdale's annotations are, of course, more than adequate to allow us to see exactly how self-concious Gray was being in this 'richness of allusion.' Geoffrey Tillotson describes the first four lines of the poem as 'the equivalent of a bow to the ode form.' For a fine discussion of the ('borrowed) diction of these lines, see Tillotson's 'Gray's "Ode on the Spring",' in *Augustan Studies* (London: The Athlone Press, 1961), pp. 204–09.
5. See A. Johnston, '"The Purple Year" in Pope and Gray,' *RES* 14 (1963), pp. 389–93.
6. For an account of the formation and continuing fortunes of the group of friends who styled themselves the Quadruple Alliance, see *The Correspondence of Gray, Walpole, West and Ashton*, ed. Paget Toynbee, 2 vols. (Oxford: Clarendon Press, 1915). In their correspondence, as in their poetry, displays of literary erudition were accompanied by disclaimers of effort or intent: for instance, Walpole claimed that he wrote his letters 'rapidly and carelessly' (*Correspondence*, i. 373). How-

ever, as Ian Jack correctly suggests, such a claim is an affectation representative of letter-writers in this age. Similarly, he points out that in 'Gray's early letters to Walpole ... we are less likely to be struck by artlessness than by artifice.' 'Gray in his Letters,' *Fearful Joy*, eds. Downey and Jones, p. 22.

7. Lonsdale's annotations assure us about, and give us examples of, the convention of the recumbent *poeta*: 'The description of the poet reclining in the heat of mid-day beneath a tree and beside a stream occurs frequently in classical poetry ... Such passages were widely imitated in Augustan poetry.' Lonsdale refers to Horace, Virgil, Lucretius and then to Gay, Mallet and Thomson. *Gray*, p. 50.
8. These translations are from Paul Alpers, *The Singer of the Eclogues* (Berkeley: University of California Press, 1979), p. 11.
9. Gray, in his Commonplace book, did entitle this poem 'Noon-Tide, an Ode,' but apart from a mention of 'panting herds' (l.22), and the cessation of work (l.21), he doesn't feel the need to develop a particularly detailed account of the specific time of day. Compare, for example, Mallet's account of heat and shade:

   Exalted to his noon the fervent sun,
   Full-blazing o'er the blue immense, burns out
   With full effulgence. Now th' embowring maze
   Of vale sequester'd, or the fir-crown'd side
   Of airy mountain, whence with lucid lapse
   Falls many a dew-fed stream, invites the step
   Of musing poet, ... (ll. 130–36)

   David Mallet, *Excursion*, ed. Robert B. Pearsall (Cornell University Thesis, 1953).
10. Lonsdale, *Gray*, pp. 52–53.
11. Samuel Johnson, 'Thomas Gray' in *Lives of the English Poets*, p. 466.
12. Anthony Easthope, *Poetry as Discourse* (London: Methuen, 1983); especially pp. 3–47.
13. Easthope, *Poetry as Discourse* , pp. 30, 31.
14. In a somewhat similar vein, Norman Maclean uses the ending of this poem and that of the Eton *Ode* to suggest that Gray's 'descriptive Odes' could well be 'objects of his own satire,' satire that is directed at the generic expectation that the 'descriptive ode' should involve 'a progression from a highly selected description of natural objects to some great concept supposedly inhering in the objects selected' (p.

444). 'From Action to Image: Theories of the Lyric in the Eighteenth Century,' in *Critics and Criticism*, ed. R.S. Crane (Chicago: Chicago University Press, 1952), pp. 408–460.

15. Easthope, *Poetry as Discourse*, pp. 42–44; also cf. p. 46.
16. That this has been the strongest argument of both those who would apologise for or celebrate the role of poetry in the history of Western culture hardly needs documentation. In the poetic practice of the first half of eighteenth century, for instance, *dulce* was clearly meant to follow upon, and stem from, *utile*, the ascendancy of both (urban) satire and (country) georgic being predicated on the poets' acclaimed desire to be read as arbiters of social and moral codes.
17. Michael Riffaterre, in an analysis of the overdetermination of poetic discourse, says: 'The functions of overdetermination are three: to make mimesis possible; to make literary discourse exemplary by lending it the authority of multiple motivations for each word used; and to compensate for the catachresis [that is the poem itself].' *Semiotics of Poetry* (Bloomington: Indiana University Press, 1978), p. 21. In this schema then, Gray's poetic practices can be seen as enacting the contradictory values of the second and third functions Riffaterre mentions, as playing out the desire for conventional poetic authority against a sharp sense that such literary conventions can no longer invest poetic performance with cultural or even linguistic authority.
18. It is instructive to remind ourselves of the work of Harold Bloom, particularly *The Anxiety of Influence* (New York: Oxford University Press, 1973). For Bloom, 'Poetry (Romance) is Family Romance. Poetry is the enchantment of incest, disciplined by resistance to that enchantment' (p. 95), and 'A Poem is not an overcoming of anxiety, but is that anxiety' (p. 94). Bloom's Oedipal scenario is meant to be read as a partial (though central and prescriptive) understanding: 'That even the strongest poets are subject to influences not poetical is obvious even to me, but again my concern is only with *the poet in a poet*, or the aboriginal poetic self' (p. 11). In distinction from Bloom, this book examines (in Gray) also those 'influences not poetical' that meditated the encounter between (re)reader and poetic (pre)texts, and the consequent conversion of this encounter into what is predominantly a confrontation between the poet and the vocation of poetry.
19. Rosalind Coward and John Ellis, *Language and Materialism* (London: Routledge and Kegan Paul, 1977), p. 38.
20. Lonsdale, *Gray*, p. 48.

21. Gray to West, May 27, 1742. *Correspondence,* i. 209. Gray himself provides a gloss to 'Leucocholy.' In an earlier letter to West he describes his writing and his activities in these terms: 'I am a sort of spider; and have little else to do but spin it ['my web'] over again, or creep to some other place and spin there. Alas! for one who has nothing to do but amuse himself, I believe my amusements are as little amusing as most folks. But no matter; it makes the hours pass.' Gray to West, April 8, 1742. *Correspondence,* i. 194.
22. Hagstrum, 'Gray's Sensibility,' *Fearful Joy,* eds. Downey and Jones, pp. 6–7.
23. Paul de Man, 'Review of Harold Bloom's *Anxiety of Influence,*' in *Blindness and Insight,* 2nd ed., rev., (Minneapolis: University of Minnesota Press, 1983), p. 276.
24. Eric Rothstein, *Restoration and Eighteenth-Century Poetry 1660-1780* (London: Routledge and Kegan Paul, 1981), p. 51.
25. Roger Lonsdale, 'The Poetry of Thomas Gray: Versions of the Self,' *Proceedings of the British Academy* 59 (London: Oxford University Press, 1973), pp. 17–18. Lonsdale is constantly aware of the fictive, artful and allusive language that is the 'expression' of these poems. Many critics of the eighteenth century suffer, like James Sutherland, from an occasional infection of uncritical Wordsworthitis, which leads them to formulations like: 'So little was the eighteenth-century poet habituated to the free expression of spontaneous emotions' [whatever that might mean], that it was 'therefore *natural* for Gray to write impersonally about 'the wretch who long had tossed on the thorny bed of pain.' *A Preface to Eighteenth Century Poetry* (Oxford: The Clarendon Press, 1948), p. 71.
26. Lonsdale, *Gray,* p. 55.
27. Donald Davie, *Purity of Diction in English Verse* (London: Routledge and Kegan Paul, 1967), p. 37.
28. F.W. Bateson, *English Poetry and the English Language* (Oxford: Clarendon Press, 1973), p. 52.
29. Gray to West, April 8, 1742. *Correspondence,* i. 192.
30. This is not to suggest, obviously, that there is no distinguishable difference between the language and diction of, say, Wordsworth's 'Lucy' poems and those of Gray's 'Odes.' However, once we have said so much, there seems little to be gained in maintaining further that Wordsworth's poems speak the 'language of their age' in any less problematic a manner than do those of Gray.

31. Johnson, 'Thomas Gray,' p. 467.
32. Davie, *Purity of Diction*, p. 33. Johnson's example of Gray's errors shows that he did acknowledge the force of literary precedent: 'finding in Dryden "honey redolent of spring," an expression that reaches the utmost reaches of our language, Gray drove it a little more beyond common apprehension by making 'gales' to be "redolent of joy and youth".' 'Life of Gray.' p. 467.
33. Brendan O Hehir, *Expans'd Hieroglyphics* (Berkeley: University of California Press, 1969), pp. 15, 17.
34. Cf. lines 71 ff. in John Dyer, *Grongar Hill*, ed. Richard C. Boys (Baltimore: The Johns Hopkins Press, 1941), pp. 90–93.
35. Ralph Cohen, 'On the Interrelations of Eighteenth-Century Literary Forms', in *New Approaches to Eighteenth-Century Literary* ed. Philip Harth (New York: Columbia University Press, 1974), p. 42.
36. For a stimulating analysis of the 'unerring gaze: the prospect of society' in the eighteenth-century Georgic see John Barrell, *English Literature in History, 1730–80*, pp. 51–109. Eric Rothstein describes the influence of the 'less theological traits of *The Seasons*' ('the stress on the discovery of an intuitional order, on man as observer and participant, on the senses and ideal presence') as follows: 'A rush of topographical poems in the second quarter of the century was prompted by Thomson (some, too, by the popularity of Dyer's "Grongar Hill"). In general, these followed him in the most obvious ways, such as his blank verse, his mixture of close and more abstract descriptions (invitations to ideal presence), his stating his intuitions of order, and his associative digressiveness.' *Restoration and Eighteenth-Century Poetry 1660–1780* , p. 151.
37. Ian Watt, 'Two Historical Aspects of the Augustan Tradition,' in *Studies in the Eighteenth Century*, ed. R.F. Brissenden (Canberra: Australian National University Press, 1968), p. 83.
38. Robert A. Aubin, *Topographical Poetry in XVIII-Century England* (New York: The Modern Language Association of America, 1936), p. 172.
39. Johnson, 'Thomas Gray,' p. 467.
40. Jan Mukarovsky, 'Standard Language and Poetic Language,' in *Essays on the Language of Literature*, eds. Seymour Chatman and Samuel R. Levin (Boston: Houghton Mifflin Co., 1967), pp. 142–43.
41. Geoffrey Tillotson, *Augustan Poetic Diction* (London: The Athlone Press, 1964).

42. Tillotson, *Poetic Diction*, p. 45.
43. Paul Fussell, in *The Rhetorical World of Augustan Humanism* (Oxford: The Clarendon Press, 1965), defines the nature and methods of eighteenth-century 'humanism,' and legislates Gray, because he was not prescriptive nor 'obsessed with ethical questions,' and because he found it possible 'to leave serious moral subjects alone' (p. 7), out of this tradition. (I agree with this conclusion, though the line of argument is less easy to accept.) In the opening chapter, 'What is "Humanism"?' Fussel lists as some of the characteristics of this "'orthodox" ethical tradition' the following: a belief in the permanence of human nature that sanctions a belief in the equivalent permanence of the literary genres (p. 4); an assumption that 'ethics and expression are closely linked' (p. 7) and a 'devotion . . . to received modes of metaphor as a technique of expression' (p. 10); a conviction that 'man's primary obligation is the strenuous determination of moral questions' (p. 7) and thus that 'man's relation to literature and art is primarily moral and only secondarily aesthetic' (p. 9). Fussell also usefully suggests that it is possible to sense the shaping of literary history by charting the 'contrast between humanist orthodoxy and its opposition' (p. 25).
44. Thomas Quayle, *Poetic Diction* (London: Methuen, 1924), p. 156.
45. It 'depended wholly on the compositor's putting, or not putting, a *small capital*, . . . in many . . . passages of the same poet, whether the words should be personifications, or mere abstractions.' S.T. Coleridge, *Biographia Literaria*, ed. J. Shawcross (Oxford: The Clarendon Press, 1907), p. 12.
46. Jean Hagstrum, *The Sister Arts* (Chicago: The University of Chicago Press, 1958), pp. 290–91.
47. This is also an example of Mukarovsky's theory of 'automatization,' where the reader's apprehension of the specifics of (ethical) discourse is subordinated to a prior sense of what it is that this discourage does. The rhetorical and formal individualities of the poem are glossed over till they functions as the signifier whose single signified is the authority of the discourse that articulates it—in this case, that established by the history of the moral-didactic tradition of ethical humanism. This making sense of by stressing context and reading conventions rather than the text itself has been commented upon by William Empson, who suggests that the reader, once confronted by any one of several contextual signals, will work to 'invent' a variety of reasons

why the text at hand should be seen as representative of that context. *Seven Types of Ambiguity* (London: Chatto and Windus, 1949), pp. 23–25.

48. Lonsdale, *Gray*, pp. 60–61. It is clear here, as elsewhere, that Gray is interested not only in the poetic discourse of eighteenth-century humanism, but also in its classical and Renaissance literary geneology.

49. Fussell, writing about the end of the Eton *Ode*, suggests that Gray's position is a sentimentalist one, antithetical to the tough-minded 'humanist attitudes that Gray affects to be entertaining. When we reach the last stanza of Gray's poem we perceive even more clearly the trick that has been played on us, for here the speaker decides *not* to "tell them they are men" but instead to withold that liberating knowledge from them, for "Tis folly to be wise." The end of the poem thus asserts the sentimentalist position.' *Augustan Humanism*, p. 153. Rather than see this 'sentimentalist' position as that of Gray, I read it as the precise gesture that limits that 'speaker' (the subject of the enounced), and thus distances him from the subject of the enunciation. In fact, I argue that Gray sees such 'sentimentalism' as not antithetical to humanism but as one of its logical extensions—a conclusion encouraged by the fact that these ideological positions articulate, for the most part, the same discursive formations.

50. Jonathan Culler, *Structuralist Poetics*, p. 175. Culler's analysis, of course, is more interested in the reading conventions and expectations generated by such a claim to significance.

51. Paul de Man, 'The Rhetoric of Temporality,' in *Blindness and Insight*, p. 214.

52. Pope wrote to Steele on July 15, 1712, a letter Steele printed in *The Guardian* 132. In this letter, the passage of interest to us here is: 'The morning after my exist, the sun will rise as bright as ever, the flowers smell as sweet, the plants spring as green, the world will proceed in its old course, people will laugh as heartily, and marry as fast, as they were us'd to do.' *The Correspondence of Richard Steele*, ed. Rae Blanchard (London: Oxford University Press, 1941), p. 59.

53. This letter is printed in its original form in *Gray and His Friends*, ed. Duncan C. Tovey (Cambridge: Cambridge University Press, 1890), pp. 95–98.

54. Geoffrey Hartman, in 'Wordsworth, Inscriptions and Romantic Nature Poetry,' says that 'the inscription was anything conscious of the

place in which it was written, and this could be tree, rock, statue, gravestone, sand, window, sundial, dog's collar, back of fan, back of painting.' Lest this catalogue trivialise what was a largely contemplative genre, Hartman reminds us that 'Inscribing, naming, and writing are types of a commemorative and inherently elegiac act.' *Beyond Formalism* (New Haven: Yale University Press, 1970), pp. 207, 233.

55. William Wordsworth, 'Appendix to the Preface (1802)' in *Literary Criticism of William Wordsworth*, ed. Paul M. Zall (Lincoln: University of Nebraska Press, 1966), p. 65.
56. Tillotson, *Augustan Studies*, p. 88.
57. Lonsdale, *Gray*, p. 66.
58. Joseph Foladare, 'Gray's "Frail Memorial" to West,' *PMLA* 75 (1960), pp. 61–65, and Donald C. Mell, *A Poetics of Augustan Elegy* (Amsterdam: Rodopi N.V., 1974), pp. 63–76, examine the West *Sonnet*'s relationship to such discourse.
59. Peter M. Sacks offers a fine account of the psychological and mythopoeic bases of the work of mourning in *The English Elegy* (Baltimore: The Johns Hopkins Press, 1985), pp. 1–37. He reminds us that 'the elegy, as a poem of mourning and consolation, has its roots in a dense matrix of rites and ceremonies, in the light of which many elegiac conventions should be recognized as being not only aesthetically interesting forms but also the literary versions of specific social and psychological practices' (p. 2).
60. By 'confessing its repetitive nature at large, the elegy takes comfort from its self-insertion into a longstanding convention of grief. And by repeating the form of the vegetation rites, for example, an individual elegy may borrow the ritual *context* of consolation. The particular lament is assimilated to a comforting commonality of grief, and the object of sorrow becomes identified with the oft-sung deity who returns each year.' Sacks, *English Elegy*, pp. 23–24. Sacks also shows how 'the echo might represent the elegist's particular sensitivity to the fact that the language he uses is and is not his own. Here again we touch on the ecologic nature of elegies, and we anticipate the numerous moments in which elegists seem to submit, by quotation or translation, to the somehow echoing language of dead poets' (p. 25).
61. Donald Mell speaks of 'the hint that the speaker has in mind not only the loss of a friend but, in his references to Milton, perhaps the loss of a great age of poetry.' *Augustan Elegy*, p. 75.
62. Wordsworth thought lines 6–8 and 13–14 the only ones 'of any value,'

their language 'in no respect differ[ent] from that of prose.' 'Preface to *Lyrical Ballads*' (1800), in *Literary Criticism*, ed. Zall, p. 24. Wordsworth's accurate registering of shifts in discourse did not, however, help him make particular sense of Gray's sonnet.

63. Gray's use of the word 'fruitless' here resonates from an earlier context. West, responding to a self-denigrating tone in Gray's account of his own work (the relevant passage has been quoted in footnote 21), wrote: 'I desire that you will quarrel no more with your manner of passing your time. In my opinion it is irreprochable, especially as it produces such excellent fruit; and if I, like a saucy bird, must be pecking at it, you ought to consider that it is because I like it. No una litura [Gray had been arguing about corrections in style and diction] I beg you, no unravelling of your web, dear Sir! only pursue it a little further, and then one shall be able to judge of it [*Agrippina*] a little better.' *Correspondence*, i. 194.

64. Foladare, 'Gray's "Frail Memorial",' p. 63. Book II of 'De Principiis Cogitandi' is another elegy to West that begins its lament for him in terms that make explicit the literary and cultural support West was for Gray:

    So far had I, interpreter of the Muses, assiduously uncovered the secrets of Nature and first led a lucid stream from the Roman river through British fields. But now you, the inspiration and the cause of so great a task, have deserted me in the midst of it and have hidden yourself in the eternal shadow of Death!'

    (Lines 1–5, translated by Lonsdale in *Gray*, p. 332).

    The formality of tone and language locates this lament in the larger classical 'river' from which Gray claimed to be leading out 'a lucid stream'.

65. Thomas McFarland, 'Poetry and the Poem: The Structure of Poetic Content,' in *Literary Theory and Structure*, eds. Frank Brady et al. (New Haven: Yale University Press, 1973), p. 83. McFarland's argument reminds us that the *Phaedrus* sees *poetry* as a 'current of feeling,' at once 'a mania and a philosophical glimpse of ultimate reality' (p. 81), as opposed to the Aristotelian emphasis on *the poem* as 'artifact, as consciously formed verbal structure' (p. 83).

66. Joshua Scodel makes a similar point in his survey of the epitaphic tradition in English verse: 'Poets such as Thomas Gray and Johnson voice a desperate need for highly sensitive readers who alone can truly appreciate and mourn the deceased in his or her vulnerable uniqueness . . . . Such calls for ideal readers came at the same time as

the growth and social diversification of the reading public made the responses of readers all the more unpredictable. In the face of a larger, more heterogeneous readership, epitaphs beg the feeling few to reverence the dead.' *The English Poetic Epitaph* (Ithaca: Cornell University Press, 1991), pp. 9–10.

67. Mell, *Augustan Elegy*, pp. 10–11.

68. This discussion of Gray's diction can be usefully compared to de Man's analysis of Rousseau's description of the Elysium garden in *Julie*: 'Rousseau does not even pretend to be observing. The language is purely figural, not based on perception, less still on an experienced dialectic between nature and consciousness.' 'The Rhetoric of Temporality,' in *Blindness and Insight*, p. 203. De Man examines this both as an example of intertextuality and of 'allegorical diction.'

69. De Man, 'Rhetoric of Temporality,' p. 222.

70. De Man, 'Rhetoric of Temporality,' p. 208.

71. De Man, 'Review of Harold Bloom's *Anxiety of Influence*,' in *Blindness and Insight*, pp. 273–74.

72. Linda Zionkowski offers a similar reading of the 'problem' of Gray's poems: 'Gray's uncertainty about addressing his readers and his pessimism about the future of literature signal his disillusion over the loss of an intimate elite community—an idealized union of writers and their audiences that seemed a better alternative to the present literary system.' Zionkowski is clear also that Gray 'located the source of his problem in the culture that commodified print fostered.' 'Bridging the Gulf Between,' p. 339.

73. Lonsdale, *Gray*, p. 69.

74. A good example of a mid-eighteenth-century hymn is that which ends James Thomson's *The Seasons*. *The Seasons* itself constantly struggles to resolve all the ideological contradictions that its encyclopedic account of nature and society engenders. 'Winter,' for example, closes with a gesture that is at once optative and imperative: 'The Storms of WINTRY TIME will quickly pass,/And one unbounded SPRING encircle All' (ll. 1068–69). In contrast, 'A Hymn' is purely affirmative and celebrational, ending in a vision of divine communion, and, appropriately, in a cessation of the poetic voice: '... But I lose/Myself in HIM, in LIGHT INEFFABLE!/ Come then, expressive Silence, muse HIS Praise' (ll. 116–18). *The Seasons*, ed. James Sambrook (Oxford: The Clarendon Press, 1981), pp. 157, 162.

75. The shift from the *Sonnet* to the *Hymn/Ode* is, in de Manian terms, a

shift from the meaning constituted by the allegorical sign (which can 'consist only in the *repetition* . . . of a previous sign with which it can never coincide, since it is of the essence of this previous sign to be pure anteriority'), to the re-mystifying creation of 'an organic world postulated in a symbolic mode of analogical correspondences.' De Man, 'Rhetoric of Temporality,' pp. 207, 222.

76. Jonathan Culler, 'Apostrophe,' in *The Pursuit of Signs* (Ithaca: Cornell University Press, 1980), pp. 135, 142.

77. Culler, 'Apostrophe,' pp. 142–43. This invocatory appropriation of vocation and tradition is one way the poetic voice refuses and mystifies the insight that apostrophe, as Culler puts it, 'which seems to establish relations between the self and the other can in fact be read as an act of radical interiorization and solipsism' (p. 146).

78. Sigmund Freud, 'Medusa's Head,' in *Sexuality and the Psychology of Love*, ed. Philip Rieff (New York: Collier Books, 1963), p. 212.

79. There is a certain (hysterical) logic to the fact that Adversity is represented as a Gorgon immediately after the poet represents himself at the feet of the goddess (11. 33–34). In a 1927 essay on 'Fetishism,' Freud had speculated that fetish-objects were often determined by the visual trajectory resulting from the 'circumstance that the inquisitive boy used to peer up the woman's legs towards her genitals.' In *Sexuality*, ed. Rieff, p. 217. It is, of course, castration anxiety that underlies both fetishism and the representation of the Medusa.

III

Contesting Value(s)

> Man is a creature not capable of cultivating his mind but in society, and in that only where he is not a slave to the necessities of life.
>
> Want is the mother of the inferior arts, but ease is that of the finer; as eloquence, policy, morality, poetry, sculpture, painting, architecture, which are the improvements of the former.
>
> Commerce changes intirely the fate and genius of nations, by communicating arts and opinions, circulating money, and introducing the materials of luxury; she first opens and polishes the mind, then corrupts and enervates both that and the body.
>
> —Thomas Gray[1]

In Chapter Two, my analysis of the four poems that Gray completed in 1742 concentrated on charting the shifting, unstable presentation of the poetic self. The analysis was based on a consideration of the thematic representation of poet-figures (the 'subject of the enounced'), of the position of the narrative or lyrical voice (the 'subject of the enunciation'), and, in particular, of the peculiar, almost dialectical, dynamic that is set up between these two subject positions. I also described how these complex articulations of the authorial self exist in a structurally and formally reciprocal relationship with an internal, dialogic interrogation of the methods and efficacity with which particular discursive traditions empower the (poetically) speaking subject. That is to say, Gray's early poems enact, and evaluate, the genre-specific deployment of tropes, topoi, and themata which, in different historical moments, provide the formal unity and ideological continuity upon which is predicated the Authority of the Poet.

These poems (with the qualified exception of the 'Ode to Adversity') exist in an agonistic relationship with the aesthetic power of the ideology now known as Augustan or civic humanism. The 'Ode on the Spring' translates the 'timeless' celebrations of the Pastoral and of the pastoralist into transient, isolated murmurs. The Eton *Ode* emphasises the allegorical form of the Prospect poem, and goes on to deconstruct the language of moral exemplarity that lies at the heart of both the genre and its corresponding vision of history. The West *Sonnet* rejects the epistemologically unreliable pieties of elegiac and *consolatio* motifs, which seek to substitute tropes of a regenerative presence (usually 'Nature') for a manifest absence (the lost one), and ends with the insight that the loss it mourns is actually the passing of a shared, enabling poetic credo, cultural discourse, social tradition. Of course, in each case, and especially in the 'Ode to Adversity,' these poems close in gestures of consolatory creation, reading themselves (their completion, their existence) as fragments that shore up crumbling authorial and cultural ruins.

In Chapter One, via our reading of Pope and Young on authors and cultural authority, we saw that the tremors that Gray's poems register originate in a larger social and ideological convulsion whose epicenter lay in London, in the rapid, overwhelming commodification of the social relations of cultural production. I have argued that all these poets experience, and articulate, this crisis as more than simply personal, indeed as social and vocational. For Gray particularly, the problem is expressed in the urgent questions of poetics—how (with what generic, rhetorical and formal practices) best to maintain the constellation of values, discourses, and socio-economic allegiances that described the culture of the aristocracy (and of its client groups) against the dilutive, and ultimately, dissolutive, energies of a increasingly hegemonic bourgeois- entrepreneurial ideology?

My phrasing here follows John Brewer's distinction between the 'two types—the client of the aristocracy and the entrepreneur in the free market—[who] are important expressions of a tension or duality that can be found within the eighteenth century middling lot of people.' In his analysis of the contemporary 'commercialization' of English life and culture, Brewer elaborates on the larger phenomenon of which the change in the economic and social relations of literary production was a sub-set: 'The broadening of the market involved a change in social and economic values; a transformation of the relationship between producers, distributors and consumers. Of course the patricians were still a vital part of the clientele . . . but, increasingly, the aristocracy constituted the top end of a large market rather than the market *tout court*. They could no longer exercise such complete control or command through their purchasing power and patronage.'[2] Reactions to these changes, as literary and social historians have documented, ranged from celebration to denunciation, and it is within such reaction that I wish to read Gray.

Nothing less than a palpable socio-cultural transformation was underway. Discontinuities were marked. By the mid-eighteenth century, the commodity relations that characterise widespread commercialism were unalterably dominant within English society. The economic values of mercantile capitalism, now symbolised by the energy and transformative financial power of London, forced structural changes in social and cultural relations, both within and without the city. As Neil McKendrick notes, 'to speak merely of the continued *development* of a consumer society in the eighteenth century would not acknowledge sufficiently the sharp break in trend between Stuart England and Georgian England. To speak of the further *growth* of a consumer society would be even more banal—far too flat a description of an event which excited such a positive reaction, such an excited response from contemporary observers, and which introduced such marked changes into so many people's lives.'[3] While McKendrick's sense of the 'sharp break' is correct, his categoric assertion of a 'positive reaction' is somewhat misguided in its inability to hear the voices of (high-cultural) contestation, one of which speaks in the maxim from Gray which is the third epigraph to this chapter.

This maxim is particularly interesting because its resistance is articulated in historically specific and ideologically representative terms. Augustan humanism did not offer an unqualified, radical critique of the new commodification, but rather sought to shape it in its own image, further it to its own ends. As the representational and discursive form of the aristocratic, high-cultural reaction, Augustan humanism sought to harness the unbridled energies of market-capitalism, and thus to retain its own precarious power. Thus, it consistently levelled criticisms of final (moral) *effects*, rather than engaging in more fundamental critiques of *process*.[4] In Young and Pope, this double move stems directly from their need to exploit the economic mechanisms of the cultural market, even as they legislated against its socially subversive character. Similarly, Gray's maxim has a space for the celebration (and hoped-for eventual recuperation) of the role of 'Commerce,' but also a condemnation of what will happen (has already happened?) if this powerful agent is not contained: Commerce 'first opens and polishes the mind, then corrupts and enervates both that and the body.'[5]

In this same series of maxims, Gray linked an attack on what he perceived as the moral and doctrinal evils attendant upon the contemporary commodification of social and economic relations with another, more curious critique, that this age is contemptuous of fame:

'The doctrine of Epicurus is ever ruinous to society: It had its rise when Greece was declining, and perhaps hastened its dissolution, as also that of Rome; it is now propagated in France and in England, and seems likely to produce the same effect in both.'

'One principal characteristic of vice in the present age is the contempt of fame.'

'Many are the uses of good fame to a generous mind: it extends our existence and example into future ages; continues and propagates virtue, which otherwise would be as short-lived as our frame; and prevents the prevalence of vice in a generation more corrupt than our own. It is impossible to conquer that natural desire we have of being remembered; even criminal ambition and avarice, the most selfish of all passions, would wish to leave a name behind them.'[6]

Gray invokes, in alarmed resistance against the commodification of values, the public machinery of cultural memory, or, more precisely, the continuity of social and moral exemplarity that is manifested in, and canonised by, the discourse of civic humanism. In this view, the vast power of that which is seen as 'impossible to conquer,' the 'natural desire we have of being remembered,' can be usefully directed against a particular social pathology. That is, even 'criminal ambition and avarice, the most selfish of all passions,' can possibly be curbed if they are confronted with the certainty of their being monumentalised as negative exemplars. The continuity of cultural memory, where the 'immortal' is a trope of the 'ahistorical' (that which never changes or loses its exemplary status) is thus both the critique of, and the defence against, the contemporary hegemony of the commodity relation.

Interestingly, it is possible to trace, in greater detail, the fruition (if not the genesis) of Gray's ideas in these maxims. On March 9, 1749, Gray wrote enthusiastically to Wharton about Montesquieu's 'L'Esprit des Loix' (1748), in which, Gray said, the author

lays down the Principles on wch are founded the three Sorts of Government, Despotism, the limited Monarchic & the Republican, & shews how from thence are deduced the Laws and Customs, by wch they are guided and maintained; the Education proper to each Form, the influences of Climate, Situation, Religion, &c: on the Minds of particular Nations, & on their Policy. the Subject (you see) is as extensive as Mankind; the Thoughts perfectly new, generally admirable, as they are just, sometimes a little too refined: in short there are Faults, but such as an ordinary Man could never have commited.[7]

Gray's regard for Montesquieu's work is corroborated by his friend and editor William Mason, who said that Gray had stopped writing his own poem on 'The Alliance of Education and Government' only because he believed that 'the Baron had forestalled some of his best thoughts.'[8]

For the eighteenth century, Montesquieu was, in the words of a recent commentator, 'the most influential exponent of the doctrine of the *doux commerce*,' in whose discourse the *douceur* induced by commerce conveyed 'sweetness, softness, calm, and gentleness and [was] the antonym of violence.'[9] Montesquieu did have some reservations about the effects of commerce, but for the most part he held that 'Commerce is a cure for the most destructive prejudices; for it is almost a general rule that wherever we find agreeable manners, there commerce flourishes; and that wherever there is commerce, there we meet with agreeable manners.'[10] At another point, Montesquieu's praise was even more fulsome: 'the spirit of commerce is naturally attended with that of frugality, economy, moderation, labour, prudence, tranquillity, order, and rule. So long as this spirit subsists, the riches it produces have no bad effect.'[11]

Gray's maxims echo such language: 'Commerce changes intirely the fate and genius of nations, by communicating arts and opinions, circulating money, and introducing the materials of luxury; she first opens and polishes the mind. . . .' The parallels are clear and sharp; it is thus even more startling to note the way in which Gray refuses Montesquieu's optimism, rewriting the *douceur* of his language and thought, forcing his narrative to reveal an ugly telos. Gray's sentence continues: '. . . then corrupts and enervates both that and the body.' The abruptness of the turn emphasises a finality and an inevitability—the record of history, Gray's categoric closure seems to say, bears no other interpretation.

If Montesquieu had 'forestalled' some of Gray's 'best thoughts,' he certainly had not converted Gray to an unqualified belief in the social and political progress that followed upon the spread of commercial activity. For Montesquieu, the very nature of the commercial instinct ensured the historical development of the system of checks and balances that he believed characterised modern European civilisation. In a chapter entitled 'How Commerce broke through the Barbarism of Europe,' he wrote a schematic history that ends in the conclusion that 'it is fortunate for men that they are in a situation in which, though their passions may prompt them to be wicked, they have nevertheless an interest in not being so.' As Hirschman shows, in this formulation Montesquieu deploys the terms of contemporary theories of the 'passions,' in which the proper regulation of avarice, the passion of acquisition, was most central to the political and economic debate. A 'Principle of the Countervailing Passion' had emerged from this debate,[13] and for Montesquieu, this balancing act of the human passions is axiomatic of the natural development of commerce, contained within its dialectic and revealed clearly by its history.[14]

Gray, on the other hand, does not share in this vision of a self-corrective, self-regulative commerce, in which the individual interest is converted (sublated?) into a functional social ethic by the ineluctable workings of an inner necessity. For Gray, the control of the passions demanded cultural and social mechanisms more specific than the Invisible Hand of the state or the market, and it is as such a regulatory ideal that he thinks of 'fame': 'Many are the uses of good fame . . . it extends our existence and example into future ages; continues and propagates virtue . . . and prevents the prevalence of vice . . . It is impossible to conquer that natural desire we have of being remembered; *even criminal ambition and avarice, the most selfish of all passions, would wish to leave a name behind them*' (my italics).[15] Responsible cultural practice, that is, must constantly intervene to guide social and economic progress. Gray suggests a contemporary urgency to this discussion—the ruinous spread of what he saw as the 'doctrine of Epicurus' in England and France is linked directly with his understanding that 'one principal characteristic of vice in the present age is the contempt of fame.'

This too is a version of the 'Principle of the Countervailing Passion,' but Gray is less sanguine about the intrinsic, systemic efficacy of such a principle than is Montesquieu. For the latter, the passion for 'honour' is just one more cultural and psychological mechanism which ensures socially bountiful effects: 'Honour sets all parts of the body politic in motion, and by its very action connects them; thus each individual advances the public good, while he only thinks of promoting his own interest.' Even Montesquieu, though, believed that 'Honour' was an efficacious ideal only within monarchical governments and aristocratic cultures; within a 'republic,' it took the form of a morally and psychologically dubious desire: 'Ambition is pernicious in a republic.'[16] For Gray, this suspicion of Ambition—the degraded republican form of Honour—spills over into his belief that its socially responsible form—'good fame'—must be invoked and put to specific, ideological use in the present time.

This of course begs the question—what might Gray have had in mind when he wished to invoke the unconquerable love 'of being remembered' as a check against 'criminal ambition and avarice; the most selfish of all passions?' In the context of eighteenth-century England, Gray obviously wished to separate the desire for fame from the 'criminal ambition' that Montesquieu too had seen as 'pernicious in a republic.' Still, it is difficult to see how Gray would wish to convert a moral and psychological ideal—the love of good fame—into a force strong enough to be deployed against the perceived larger problem, the rampant commodification of social and cultural relations and values. Rather than attempt to answer this question abstractly here, I will instead shift the discussion to the long and important poem that Gray wrote between 1742 and 1750,[17] one which is informed by many of the same concerns that we have been elaborating—'Elegy Written in a Country Churchyard.'

Central to the 'Elegy' is a displaced engagement with the transformative power of Commerce (which 'changes intirely the fate and genius of nations'), played out as the literary fable of the country versus the city. The binary argument of the fable itself is mediated and stabilised by the affective power and the iconology of pastoral elegy, which are also brought to bear against some of the social and cultural machinery of Commerce (which works 'by communicating arts and opinions, circulating money, and introducing the arts of luxury'). In what follows, I will read key images, formal elements, and historical references in the *Elegy* as (over)- determined by the ideological imperatives of a high-cultural poet reacting to a transformative commercial culture. I will suggest that the poem's continuing prestige stems not from its success at seamlessly coordinating poetic forms and ideological positions but precisely from its inability to do so. Indeed, its power derives from the resolution of socio-cultural contradictions through and into affect (pathos, melancholy). In that, it provides a fine example of how an appropriate display of empathy and sentiment can seem psychologically and culturally uplifting, socially conscious, and politically legitimate.

ELEGY WRITTEN IN A COUNTRY CHURCHYARD

When William Empson wrote of Gray's *Elegy* as 'an odd case of poetry with latent political ideas' he chose to comment on one stanza:

> Full many a gem of purest ray serene
> The dark unfathomed caves of ocean bear:
> Full many a flower is born to blush unseen
> And waste its sweetness on the desert air. (ll. 53–56)

'What this means,' says Empson in his inimitable manner, 'as the context makes clear, is that eighteenth-century England had no scholarship system . . . This is stated as pathetic, but the reader is put into a mood in which one would not try to alter it . . . By comparing the social arrangement to Nature [Gray] makes it seem inevitable, which it was not, and gives it a dignity which was undeserved.'

Empson's analysis continues to unravel the rhetorical moves made in this stanza:

> Furthermore, a gem does not mind being in a cave and a flower prefers not to be picked; we feel like the man is like the flower, as short-lived, natural, and valuable, and this tricks us into feeling that he is better off without opportunities. The sexual suggestion of *blush* brings in the Christian idea that virginity is good in itself, and so that any renuncia-

tion is good; this may trick us into feeling that it is lucky for the poor man that society keeps him unspotted from the World. The tone of melancholy claims that the poet understands the considerations opposed to aristocracy, though he judges against them; the truism of the reflections in the churchyard, the universality and impersonality it gives to the style, claim as if by comparison that we ought to accept the injustice of society as we do the inevitability of death.[18]

The point of this extended quotation from Empson is not to show that he got it all right (in fact, as my analysis will go on to show, the specific details of this stanza, and the larger rhetorical and ideological shifts in the poem, are far more complicated in their articulation than he suggests). Empson's analysis was, however, the first to foreground sharply an irritation 'by the complacence in the massive calm of the poem;' a recognition that this seemingly innocuous and (hence) largely celebrated stanza might be central to an understanding of the political and ideological project of the poem; and a sense of the constitutive importance of 'feeling' and 'tone' (of melancholy) in both the writing and the literary-historical reception of the poem. Empson also shrewdly noticed that though the poet's discourse seemed to emphasise the opposition between the poor and the aristocracy, the poem's ultimate values were most easily assimilable to bourgeois ideologies.[19]

Empson correctly reads this stanza as encoding a socially motivated allegory, which works its ideological craft through the manipulation of affect and mood. I wish here to ask more literal questions of this stanza: what kind of value (economic, social, poetic) does a gem have if it indeed rests, presumably unseen, in the 'dark unfathomed caves of ocean?' Why should a flower be thought 'born to blush' and 'to waste its sweetness' because its organic, natural cycle of desert life and death makes it inaccessible to human eyes? Is this stanza simply a testament to the anthropocentric structure of poetic, or indeed of all language, or is there a more mediated, historically reflexive way in which we can understand the particular linguistic forms of its will to nominative and descriptive power?

I will argue that lines 53–56 represent, microstructurally, the larger attempt in Gray's poem to designate and sanctify emblems or locations of value that could stand in opposition to the contemporary forms of reified social relations. This results in a quasi-utopian, modified-pastoral vision of a pre-commodified system of value. In that, this stanza also stages in miniature the poignant drama of the poem's attempt to roll back the effects of the passage of time, to rewrite History. The analysis that follows documents this attempt and its failure, and suggests why such failure was inevitable for both textual (literary-historical) and contextual (historical) reasons.

Romancing the stone : In his desire to wrest a symbol of intrinsic worth, of non-commodified value, from the hegemonic system of exchange values, Gray chooses to reinscribe the very nature of an emblem of the processes of contemporary commodification: the 'gem.' The specific existence of the gem as 'a measure of value' and a 'medium of circulation' is structurally representative of the strange process by which an object of minimal use-value is transformed into a commodity of great exchange-value.[20] Also, at this moment in English history, the gem is a sharply overdetermined signifier of the potential riches of the English overseas trade, of the accumulated 'surplus' of colonial territories, of the easy transportability (circulation) of capital. In Gray's alternative scenario, however, the gem is meant to signify none of these, only to *be* itself; not to be a (commodified) measure of value, but (natural) value itself.

Gray's choice of the gem is astute—the gem, like gold or silver, is what Marx called a 'money-form of commodities,' and an equally powerful signifier of the international circulation of commodities. However, precisely for such historically overdetermined reasons, ascribing to it a different value must overcome much resistance. Also, the gulf between 'the palpable and real bodily form' (use-value) of the gem and its 'purely ideal or notional form' (exchange-value) makes it impossible to claim the former as the basis of a 'natural' value even remotely commensurate with its value as a commodity. Thus, in his desire to reinscribe the gem in a context other than that which gives it its contemporary significance, Gray has to resort to the language of unqualified assertion, insisting that a gem has a value even outside of the circuit of commodity exchange:

> Full many a gem of purest ray serene
> The dark unfathomed caves of ocean bear.

Even if we were only briefly to notice and then to bracket the questionable epistemological basis of such a claim, and to allow it to stand on the grounds of statistical probability, we read several evasions and displacements at work here. The 'caves of ocean' are 'dark' and 'unfathomed,' but this lack of light does not interfere with what Gray can 'see', the 'gem of purest ray serene.'[21] These caves are, in fact, not simple locations of chance value, but are meant to provide, in the sublimity of their 'dark unfathomed' underseascape, an affectively powerful context for the ascription of 'natural' value. They are meant to produce, that is, a power that will displace what Marx called the equally mystifying, supra-sensible character of the commodity form.

For Marx, the 'mysterious character of the commodity-form consists . . . in the fact that the commodity reflects the social characteristics of men's own labour as objective characteristics of the products of labour themselves, as the socio-natural properties of these things . . . Through this substitution, the products of labour become commodities, sensuous things that are at the same time suprasensible or social.'[22] That is, the creation of the commodity requires the simultaneous appropriation and effacement of the labour that gives it value, such that the commodity seems to possess *natural* value. From this perspective, then, the ascription of any (other than use-) value is predicated upon a mystery, whose rhetorical form is the catachrestic substitution of social labour by the 'socio-natural.'

The *Elegy* claims the gem has value without being commodity, without coming into contact with the social labour that creates value. In this couplet, the language of assertion ('Full many . . . ') claims such value, a claim whose credibility and psychological force also come from a mystifying catachresis. That is, Gray's location of the gem in 'dark unfathomed caves of ocean' allows for the displacement of the most affectively powerful characteristic of the latter, the 'natural' sublimity of their unknown depths,[23] onto the gem, and thus endows the gem with what Gray claims as its preeminent property, its natural value. In Marx's discussion of the representation of the commodity-form, we see how catachresis functions to efface the source of value; in Gray's representation of the gem, it is a similar substitution that makes the apprehension of value credible in the first place.

The categoric assertion of natural value, then, turns out to be contingent on a rhetorical effect, that of dark natural sublimity. The power of (poetic and psychological) affect, that is, is meant not only to counter the history of the gem, to erase its socio-historical character as commodity-form, but also, paradoxically, to reveal its pristine and immanent *natural* value. What seems to begin as the simple affirmation of the natural or originary value of the gem actually turns out to be an aestheticization of the entire question of value. The political economy of the determination of commodity value is not, as at first it seemed, discarded in favour of a totally other 'natural' determination, but is actually displaced into the aesthetic economy of the rhetorical sublime. Natural value, in fact, turns out to be an unstable, perhaps impossible, category.

In this stanza, the primary denominator of the value of the natural object is its '*purest* ray serene,' which is meant to signal a metonymic triumph over the tainted lustre of the commodity-form. Gems, of course, do not emit light, they only reflect it. In the darkness of its cave, the gem shines by rhetorical fiat, Gray's description of the comparative superiority of its rays ('purest') necessitated by his need to demonstrate not only the existence of pre-commodified natural value, but also the superiority, as it were, of this value. However, the only vocabulary he possesses is itself derived from the evaluative discourse of the market determination of commodity value, and is hence contaminated irreparably by the social history of the commodity. History, manifested in the specific effects of linguistic overdetermination, thus denies what Gray's attempted shift in the ground for determining value sought to reveal, that the gem possesses an essential, pre-commodified value. Its essence is no more (and no less) than the history of (its) commodification; it can be a signifier for little else.

Gilding the lily: In this reading of the image of the gem, then, the attempt to re-determine the 'natural' worth of the gem mines, as it were, the rhetorical economy of the aesthetic. What Paul de Man has called 'a nostalgia for the natural object'[24] informs this attempted reinscription, and, even more strongly, structures the image that follows immediately after, that of the flower:

> Full many a flower is born to blush unseen
> And waste its sweetness on the desert air. (ll. 55–56)

De Man suggests that the repeated presence and power of the image of the flower in the language of poetry is due to a particular perception of the origination of flowers:

> They rise out of the earth without the assistance of imitation or analogy. They do not follow a model other than themselves which they copy from or from which they derive the pattern of their growth. By calling them *natural* objects, we mean that their origin is determined by nothing but their own being. Their becoming corresponds at all times with the mode of their origination: it is as flowers that their history is what it is, totally defined by their identity. There is no wavering in the status of their existence: existence and essence coincide in them at all times.[25]

Is this not Gray's project too: to reinstate a context of pure, untarnished origin, to rediscover the possibility of value based on being and essence, to reassert the existence of a natural object whose history is its ontology. All this, of course, against the contexts of commodified value, where an incommensurable gap exists between the origins of the object and its mode of existence, where its primary value is other than its alienated essence, where its history is the record of its conversion from natural object to exchange value. In de Man's schema, poetic language in its Romantic usage problematises the ontological priority of the natural object; in Gray, equally surely, the 'natural' turns out to be a fiction of the aesthetic. The flower wears a human face: it 'is born to blush unseen.' However, it is not only the general logic of poetic or literary language that we see at work in this deconstruction of the natural into the anthropomorphic. In this case, as our detour through Pope's *The Rape of the Lock* will show, there is a more specific tropology operating, one that is generated out of the contemporary encounter of poetic language and practice with the prior texts of commodification.

Of the 'sources' of this image that commentators have enumerated, one brings together a blush and the idea of flowers blooming and dying unseen. In Canto IV of *The Rape of the Lock*, Belinda mourns the cutting of her lock, and wishes she had 'un-admir'd remain'd'

> Where the gilt *Chariot* never marks the Way,
> Where none learn *Ombre*, none e'er taste *Bohea*!
> There keep my Charms conceal'd from mortal Eye,
> Like Roses that in Desarts bloom and die. (ll. 155–58)[26]

Belinda's expressed desire is clear: she wishes she had stayed clear of the circuit of reified social relations signified by the 'gilt *Chariot*,' '*Ombre*,' and '*Bohea*.' But here too, she cannot think of a feasible alternative mode of existence. Her world is such that for her to be away from the values of Hampton Court she must live 'conceal'd from mortal Eye.' Topography provides the negative metaphor here for the hegemony of commodification—only 'Desarts' are free.

The mention of her 'Charms' in line 157, in opposition to the world of the commodity, suggests the naturalness that is, of course, embodied in the 'Roses' of line 158. The unsettling irony of this simile is brought home to us when we remember that Belinda's charms had earlier been explicitly delineated as the product of commodities. In fact, in Canto I, lines 121–44 (Belinda at her *Toilet*), her image, her very nature, are shown as constructed out of commodities, till it is impossible to tell one from the other:

Unnumber'd Treasures ope at once, and here
The various Off'rings of the World appear;
From each she nicely culls with curious Toil,
And decks the Goddess with the glitt'ring Spoil.
This Casket *India*'s glowing Gems unlocks,
And all *Arabia* breathes from yonder Box.
The Tortoise here and Elephant unite,
Transform'd to *Combs*, the speckled and the white.
. . . .
Now awful Beauty puts on all its Arms;
The Fair each moment rises in her Charms,
Repairs her Smiles, awakens ev'ry Grace,
And calls forth all the Wonders of her Face;
Sees by Degrees a purer Blush arise,
And keener Lightnings quicken in her Eyes. (ll. 129–44)[27]

This entire process of the reinscription of Nature as Commodity is perhaps most sharply focused in line 143: it is a '*purer* Blush' that is *painted* on to Belinda's face.[28]

What Pope's Belinda so aptly demonstrates is that 'Nature' or 'the natural' is not a viable ontological category in a world of commodity fetishism. Even at its most reduced, as an enervated, brief vision of a desert utopia, the desire for a genesis, fruition, and death untouched by commodity is unrealisable. In *The Rape of the Lock*, Canto IV, lines 157–58 record this desire, and Canto I, lines 121–44 list the material reasons that both refuse it and explain why it can only be manifested as defensive dream. It is Belinda's history then, that shapes Gray's language in lines 55–56 in the *Elegy*.[29] Gray's vocabulary too records the oppositional nostalgia for (the ontological and originary status of) the natural object, but also, more importantly, encodes a story of powerful prior textual encounters with the rhetorical and phenomenal logic of commodification.[30] De Man's deconstructive itinerary of poetic language is, in Gray, the rhetorical path dictated by the eighteenth-century English experience of social history.[31]

Perhaps what the *Elegy* really mourns, as this analysis of lines 53–56 suggests, is that poetic practice uninflected by the logic of commodity is not possible. But such insight is of course not the explicit theme of the *Elegy*. The poem sets itself up as a structure of antitheses: the country versus the city, nature versus culture, the organic versus the reified, those left outside History versus those who would appear to make it, appropriate forms of cultural memory versus inappropriate memorials. It is also about the place of the poet, whose attempt to mediate between these oppositions is at once an attempt to articulate a role for himself as a culturally-vital mediator of such social oppositions. If these are indeed the poem's concerns, a question about genre suggests itself: what kind of ideological and discursive anxieties does the choice of graveyard meditation, of pastoral Elegy, as the form of intervention into a cultural, social and historical problematic reveal? What functions do the melancholy and pathos that centrally constitute these genres perform in the case that Gray wishes to make?

In *The Country and the City*, Williams briefly traces the literary-historical shift between poems that celebrate 'humble and worthy characters, in a country setting, in a more or less conscious contrast with the wealth and ambition of the city and the court,' and poems 'which develop this ethical contrast, in which the contrast of country and city is as it were an atmosphere or determining climate, into a historical contrast, in which the virtues are seen as unmistakably past, in an earlier and lost period of country life.' He says this shift is 'marked by a radical change of tone,' which he describes as 'a sense of ineradicable melancholy.'[32] The tone of the *Elegy* certainly places it in the latter group of poems that mourn the irretrievable passing of a way of life, but it also contains rhetorically assertive sections that incline it towards Williams's first, less enervated, category of poems. That is, Gray's poem shifts uneasily between two poetic paradigms, one in which representations of the country and the city primarily facilitate ethical contrast and the other in which such representations are inflected in more historically sensitive ways.

By the time Gray wrote the *Elegy*, the literary coordination of the topographical with the ethical and the political had taken many well defined forms. Pope, in some of his Horatian satires, and in almost all of his poems written in 'retirement' at Twickenham, had shown how the aristocratic retreat into the 'country' was in fact a powerful strategy of attack on the city bourgeoisie. Even Johnson's Juvenalian satire 'London' (1738) is made more pointed by the fact that Thales is going into patrician self-exile away from the corrupt city. For these writers of the aristocratic reaction, the 'country' was never more than a rhetorical staging place for attacks on their chosen targets. These could have been the coordinates of the *Elegy* too, except for Gray's desire to locate oppositional value in some configuration of the 'natural'—the village community, that is, rather than the patrician (Horatian) estate.

Most eighteenth-century poets acknowledged (even if they objected to) the fact that the village community had been assimilated into, and restructured by, the circuit of production and exchange dominated by 'city' mercantilism.[33] The *Elegy*, however, resists such an explicit admission and theme. Unlike (for instance) Thomson, who could see the 'simple scene' of country labour as being the first step in Britain's mercantile and imperial progress, Gray can only emphasise the unequal divide that exists between the country and the city. Accordingly, the first twenty-eight lines of the poem rework the poetic convention of the pastoral prospect, in which the spectator-poet's view of the landscape from on high allows him to construct a particular socio-political allegory.

John Barrell has formulated the problematic of eighteenth-century 'spectating' authors in terms especially useful for contextualising Gray's ambivalences: 'They certainly believed that the society of eighteenth-century Britain was "really", fundamentally coherent; but their preoccupation was with the problem of the viewpoint, the intellectual or social position, from which the coherence could be observed, and of the language in which it could be described; for from any but the "right" position, social experience, social events, will appear random, and society will seem a loose and unorganized collection of individuals each pursuing selfish and separate ends.'[34] Gray certainly shared this preoccupation, but because he did not share equally the foundational belief in social coherence, his search for viewpoints, languages, and self-representational possibilities was more anxious, and perhaps more interesting.

In the opening lines of the *Elegy*, Gray refuses the contemporary trend to celebrate the smiling features and topography of a powerful and ever-expanding mercantilist 'Happy Brittania' precisely by *reversing* its use of the central topos of the prospect, thus (in a move analogous to his reinscription of the idea of the gem) rewriting, rather than ignoring, the forms and practices of *literary* history.[35] When the figure of the poet in the opening lines of the *Elegy* looks at the landscape, he sees little to celebrate.[36] Rather, he converts the sounds and images of an average country evening into a catalogue of loss—the curfew that tolls the knell of parting day, the herds that wind slowly away, the ploughman who 'homeward plods his weary way' (l. 3). The landscape, instead of being populated by the signs of plenty and prosperity, is emptied, depopulated, and, by line 4, darkened. The ironies of Gray's rewriting of the prospect are manifest: the 'vision' of the poet-figure is circumscribed by the absence of light, and, when the act of appropriation central to the writing of the prospect poem takes place, it is a pathetic shadow of its usual self. That is, the poet-figure no longer commands the landscape; it is *left* to him, his sovereignty and authority both undercut by his solitude and shared with the 'darkness': 'And leaves the world to darkness and to me' (l. 4).

In keeping with the spirit of this revisionist staging, the next eight lines show the poet-figure first losing contact with (and control of?) the landscape: 'Now fades the glimmering landscape on the sight' (l. 5); and then reasserting a saving *aural* contact (though diminution is stressed here too):

> *Save where* the beetle wheels his droning flight,
> And drowsy tinklings lull the distant folds;

> *Save that* from yonder ivy-mantled tower
> The moping owl does to the moon complain.
> (ll. 7–10, my italics)

In the West *Sonnet,* we had seen how the moment of greatest isolation and loss was figured in terms of aural and visual deprivation:

> These ears, alas! for other notes repine,
> A different object do these eyes require. (ll. 5–6)

In the *Elegy,* such total isolation is always guarded against, for, as the end of the poem shows us, the other name for such isolation is death.

In the West *Sonnet,* the themes of loss and death were ultimately located within the specific problematic of the 'life' and 'death' of the Poet or Author, whose authority was seen as dependent on the existence of a particular cultural constituency. Similarly, in the *Elegy,* the overt conventional contrast between two kinds of life (that of the country and that of the city) and two kinds of death is restructured by different, though obviously related, concerns. Here too we find questions about the authority of the poet and the search for an appropriate audience or cultural community; here too are overt questions about the nature and functions of the various (monumental, poetic, natural) representations of (life and) death; and here, as the epitaph, is the despairing assertion of the continuing presence of the inscription as the final example of the power of letters to recuperate the absence that is death.

A refusal to celebrate need not be an invitation to mourn, but in the *Elegy,* from the outset, pathos is constitutive of the representation of the countryside. Of the several reasons for this, one may be noted here. If Gray took at all seriously the connection between socio-economic realities and cultural and moral possibility (as in his maxims above), he could hardly have claimed that village life retained the values and virtues that the life of the city had lost: enslavement to 'the necessities of life' denies 'eloquence, policy, morality, poetry, sculpture, painting, architecture,' and it is 'Commerce' that 'first opens and polishes the mind.' Culturally and ideologically, Gray speaks from, and to, the 'city,' but here wishes to speak *for* the 'country.' In Elegy, pathos is, as it were, the poetic language that allows the poet to speak across the existential chasm between life and death; Gray's *Elegy*, however, enshrines the failure of this language to bridge the gulf between cultures. The poet's art that would speak for the villagers, discover value in them, cannot speak to them or be valued by them, a contradiction that the poem enacts in its woeful conclusion (ll. 98–115).

Such a contradiction might have driven a poet to silence; it drives Gray to mourning and death. When the poet-figure in the *Elegy* looks at the rural countryside he claims to champion, he sees a graveyard, a record of the death of the community (which he reads in immediately existential rather than historical terms, of course). The disturbing knowledge that death might also be a figure for the historical passing of rural communities is repressed when the graveyard is framed within the familiar iconology and rhetoric of existential loss. This sense of loss itself is partially recuperated, as the vision of communal death actually generates a picture of community life: when the poet-figure 'sees' the graveyard where

> Each in his narrow cell for ever laid,
> The rude forefathers of the hamlet sleep (ll. 15–16),

he discerns not only markers of death but also monuments to community and continuity. He speaks of the 'forefathers of the hamlet,' and his portrayal of their absence is in fact a way of painting a warm, communal, organic country life (ll. 17–28):

> For them no more the blazing hearth shall burn,
> Or busy housewife ply her evening care:
> No children run to lisp their sire's return,
> Or climb his knee the envied kiss to share.
>
> Oft did the harvest to the sickle yield,
> Their furrow oft the stubborn glebe has broke;

How jocund did they drive their team afield!
How bowed the woods beneath their sturdy stroke!
(ll. 21–28)

Although these lines are supposed to be reflective and mournful, and inspite of the 'no more' of line 21, they actually achieve the local effect of rural felicity and ease. What begins as a graveyard meditation slides smoothly into the comforting imagery of pastoral, as the memorials of death become, in the vision of the poet, reminders of the rituals of life.[37]

That effect alone should alert us to the great need Gray seems to have here for images of community. Both the 'Ode on the Spring' and the West *Sonnet* show how qualified (even dismissive) Gray's use of the pastoral idiom—the idiom of rural felicity and ease—was. In those early poems, writing, as it were, both in and against the languages of the pastoral, Gray was able to problematise, ironise, even reject. But in the 'Ode to Adversity,' after the recognition of the cultural and social loss that the last two lines of the West *Sonnet* record, Gray begins to write in a more traditional idiom, one of accommodation with, and even homage to, central figures of poetic convention. Now, in the *Elegy,* after his experience of political marginalisation (his quarrel with Walpole), personal and cultural trauma (the death of West), social loss (the fear that 'Epicurean' values had restructured the sphere of culture and discrimination), Gray's depiction of the life of the country as pastoral and communal is defensive, a return into a vocabulary that offers both political and poetic retreat.

This series of poetic displacements and elegaic compensations in the opening of the poem, then, allows us to see Gray's socio-historical anxiety both surfacing and being assuaged. The elegaic tone and structure serve a more impersonal poetic and cultural purpose too, because they also ensure that the signifiers of the life of nature, of 'homely joys and destiny obscure,' can be credibly invested with values lost to, and of greater significance than, the life of 'Ambition' and 'Grandeur.' The 'ineradicable melancholy' of the poem is here no passive, necessary product of the poet's meditation on the country churchyard, but is a far more active rhetorical principle, deployed to foreclose particular arguments, structure observation and engagement and effect appropriate ideological closure.

Thus, the power and valence of the representation of the 'country' (as the particular manifestation of the 'natural') in the *Elegy*, emerges fully only in its opposition to the representation of the city.[38] The (lost) community of the villagers (ll. 21–28) is designed to offset the values of the city, here personified in the terms of moral allegory: 'Ambition,' 'Grandeur,' 'ye Proud,' empty 'Honour,' 'Flattery.' Represented as unfeeling and unthinking, 'Ambition' and 'Grandeur' are enjoined not to mock, 'nor . . . hear, with a disdainful smile,/ The short and simple annals of the poor' (ll. 29–32). They are asked to respect the 'useful toil,' 'homely joys and destiny obscure' of the rural folk, but the stress of the quatrain is on its last line, on the 'short and simple annals of the poor.' This is important, for we are at once within the problematic of the representations of life and death ('the uses of good fame') mentioned earlier. If 'Ambition' and 'Grandeur' are to 'hear' these annals, then they must also recognise the annalist, who, in this particular instance, and in the larger discourse of pastoral poetry, is the poet. But it is not enough that that should happen. The *Elegy* is not a plea for patronage, and the poet-annalist is not simply asking to be incorporated into the values and power structures of the 'city.' As the analysis of the gem and flower stanza showed, Gray insists on an idea of value that exists outside of, and in opposition to, the commodified value systems of the city.

Accordingly, the *Elegy* does not emphasise the fact that death is the great leveller (ll. 33–36), and that the 'paths of glory lead but to the grave' (l. 36), but rather what cultures do with the fact of death. Annals, gravestones, monuments are necessary as markers of lives and deaths, as emblems of the 'good fame' that Gray wrote about when he thought about preventing the spread of the 'doctrine of Epicurus.'[39] The poem represents as objectionable the 'trophies' (l. 38), 'long-drawn aisle and fretted vault' (l. 39), the 'storied urn or animated bust' (l. 41) that exceed their proper memorial, hence moral, purpose. They are attacked as tokens of personal or public extravagance, as signifiers of empty 'Honour' (l. 43) and 'Flattery' (l. 38). Like the 'frail memorial' (l. 77) that they contrast with, these monuments ought to be 'a holy text' that teaches the 'moralist to die' (ll. 83–84). In the absence of a proper interpretive, indeed didactic, frame, they become mementoes only of pride and power, an unholy text that communicates wholly pernicious social, cultural and moral meanings. This argument, of course, also implies an especially significant role for the poet as the creator of proper cultural narratives, as necessary guardian of the 'place of fame and elegy' (l. 82).

Before we go on to examine further the status of this claim to poetic authority in the *Elegy*, the poem invites us to consider the literary and historical context of the crisis in contemporary culture. Lines 45–51 deal with the lack of social opportunity that Empson refers to when he says that 'eighteenth-century England had no scholarship system or *carrière ouverte aux talents*:'

> Perhaps in this neglected spot is laid
> Some heart once pregnant with celestial fire;
> Hands that the rod of empire might have swayed,
> Or waked to ecstasy the living lyre.
>
> But knowledge to their eyes her ample page
> Rich with the spoils of time did ne'er unroll;
> Chill Penury repressed their noble rage,
> And froze the genial current of their soul.

As Lonsdale's editorial notes show, such a claim to a 'natural' talent or genius that perished unfulfilled because undiscovered is not uncommon. What the footnotes do not show, however, is that in each case, such a claim is part of a larger, more elaborate argumentative and ideological structure.

For instance, Addison, in *The Spectator* 215, writes that 'the philosopher, the saint, or the hero, the wise, the good, or the great man, very often lie hid and concealed in a plebeian, which a proper education might have disinterred, and have brought to light.' Within the essay, however, the egalitarian scope of this sentiment is necessary only to enable Addison to construct a myth of the noble savage. The essay is actually more about those who *cannot* be redeemed by education: 'negroes,' or 'those men whose passions are not regulated by virtue, and disciplined by reason.' Its final argument is informed by ideological imperatives that speak to both imperial and domestic considerations: 'It is, therefore, an unspeakable blessing to be born in those parts of the world where wisdom and knowledge flourish; though it must be confessed, there are, even in these parts, several poor uninstructed persons, who are but little above the inhabitants of those nations of which I have been here speaking.'[40] Addison's little genuflection towards undiscovered plebeian or native genius is then only a pretext for his exclusionary celebration of English 'wisdom and knowledge' and imperial 'civilisation.'

While Addison specifies a lack of education as keeping the 'plebeian' from being some version of 'the great man,' the more usual culprit was considered to be Poverty. In Johnson's 'London,' Thales attacks an England where 'All Crimes are safe, but hated Poverty' (l. 159), and wonders

> Has Heaven reserv'd in Pity to the Poor
> No pathless Waste, or undiscover'd Shore?
> No secret Island in the boundless main?
> No peaceful Desart yet unclaim'd by SPAIN?
> Quick let us rise, the happy Seats explore,
> And bear Oppression's Insolence no more.
> This mournful Truth is ev'ry where confest,
> SLOW RISES WORTH, BY POVERTY DEPREST:
> But here more slow, where all are Slaves to Gold,
> Where Looks are Merchandise, and Smiles are Sold.
> (ll. 170–79)[41]

These are strange lines—Thales wishes for a 'pathless Waste' or 'peaceful Desart' as yet uncolonised by any imperial power, which will turn into 'happy Seats' for those who would escape 'Oppression's Insolence.' Worth, 'BY POVERTY DEPREST,' would presumably be slow to rise there too, but not so slow as in a *nouveau riche*, mercantilist London. Perhaps nothing offers evidence of the shock of the contemporary as strongly as visions of cankered utopias—the pastoral space is here the uncolonised desert, and value ('worth') must seek a viable context far from the circuits of the 'city.'

Gray's lines must be read in the context of such contradictions. In the *Elegy*, even though 'Knowledge' is what the rural folk lack, it is also ambiguously represented as plunderer, 'Rich with the spoils of time' (l. 49).[42] For Addison, education is civilisation, a seamless correlation. For Gray, however, knowledge is problematic precisely because it is available in its social incarnation ('Rich with the spoils of time'), and is thus implicated inextricably in the values associated with the 'rod of empire.' On the one hand, a lack of knowledge prevents the country poor from becoming the great; on the other, 'Knowledge' itself is figured in the precise terms that make the Great suspect. This ambiguous personification of knowledge as conqueror, within a pastoral parable of corrupt culture, is a formal symptom of the larger ideological contradiction within which Gray operates.

The *Elegy* is, for the most part, a masterful appropriation of formal, generic, and cultural signifiers to suit a particular purpose, but, as this example suggests, it is not seamless in its appropriations. Gray's choice of poetic convention encouraged a contrast between 'country' and 'city' which forced him to claim an unlikely alliance with the unlettered and the uncultured. This logic of genre works in a manner similar to the intertextual imperatives we examined in our analysis of the gem and flower stanza (ll. 53–56). That is, the literary history of the contrast between the country and the city enables the quick and emphatic construction of an arena of 'natural' value, but also encodes the moment when the natural will be revealed as the tropological. More specifically, it reveals the natural as a *reactive* fiction of pure origin; which does not exist before, but is only deployed after, and in critique of, the particular un-natural condition (the 'Fall,' the 'city,' 'Knowledge,') under attack.

Similarly, the syntax of lines 45–72 describes socially negative values and historically suspect actions in terms of all that is denied to those belonging to the village community. The effect is to confirm the passivity of the villagers, and the sense that they are left out of a corrupt history, but also to emphasise that the 'country' can only be known via an account of all that it is not, and can not be. (The priority of the representation is here reversed in the same way that the full depiction of the warm community of the village reverses the priority of the markers of absence and death in lines 15–28). Thus, the 'country' in the *Elegy* exists more as a structure of feeling, a utopian fiction strategically deployed, rather than as a portrait of a way of life Gray identified himself with and whose everyday virtues he championed. Such an understanding, in fact, enables us to chart better the shifting and problematic relation between the village community and the poet-figure who describes them, a relation whose tensions play out some of the same contradictions that bedevil Gray's use of pastoral conventions to mount an attack on the contemporary forms of power and wealth.

We have seen how the (lost) community of the villagers (ll. 21–28) is designed to offset the values of the city, here personified in the terms of moral allegory: 'Ambition,' 'Grandeur,' 'ye Proud,' empty 'Honour,' 'Flattery.' It is in continuity with this opposition that we are to read the pathos of those whose 'celestial fire' (l. 46) remained dormant. At first, the powerful role this pathos plays in the *Elegy* is not obvious, especially as the signifiers of the what-might-have-been ('the rod of empire,' 'the living lyre,' ll. 47–48) themselves lack particularity, and are in any case weakened by their being contained by two strong qualifiers: 'Perhaps' (l. 45) and 'might have' (l. 47). If the pathos is hypothetical, it is because the occasion for it is only potential. However, as lines 57–76 make clear, the 'rod of empire' and 'the living lyre' are meant to have a pointed reference, one that moves out of the domains of moral allegory and of existential speculation, and into a specific engagement with three makers of the political history of the English revolution—Hampden, Cromwell, and Milton:

Some village-Hampden that with dauntless breast
The little tyrant of his fields withstood;
Some mute inglorious Milton here may rest,
Some Cromwell guiltless of his country's blood.
(ll. 57–60)

These lines help us realise the politics of the pathos that is central to the representation of the country in the *Elegy*. For this pathos of the unfulfilled turns out to be another form of the pure, the untainted; only in this case, purity is contingent upon being left out of history. While such an ahistorical condition was usually posited as the world of the pastoral, here it is a *particular* history that is labelled contaminated and contaminating. This is the history of the radical English parliamentarians, in which Cromwell's political and military rise to the position of Lord Protector is emblematic of those who acted

Th' applause of listening senates to command,
The threats of pain and ruin to despise,
To scatter plenty o'er a smiling land,
And read their history in a nation's eyes (ll. 61–64)

and who 'wade[d] through slaughter to a throne,/ And shut the gates of mercy on mankind' (ll. 67–68).

Lonsdale offers the following gloss on these lines: Gray needed 'examples of greatness which had proved dangerous to society (as opposed to the innocence of the villagers) and the Civil War, 100 years earlier, provided him with three convenient examples. For all their individual qualities, these three men had been responsible in one way or another for bringing turmoil to their country.'[43] The supposed 'convenience' of these examples should not get in the way of our recognising the politics of this historical allusion. Gray's examples of a socially ambiguous greatness come from an era in English history whose politics (especially Cromwell's foreign policy) created the basis for the mercantile and imperial state with which Gray coexisted so uneasily. Furthermore, Gray rewrote the poem to replace Cato, Tully, and Caesar (his earlier examples), with Hampden, Milton, and Cromwell, names that carried a politically and ideologically polarising charge.

Yet, even though Hampden, Milton, and Cromwell are mentioned, as it were, in one breath, Gray's version of a turbulent Commonwealth English history can be credible only as a critique of Cromwell, and can scarcely be construed as a legitimate attack on the careers of Hampden or Milton. Hampden was best known for his work in Parliamentary committees, and his early death in a skirmish on June 18, 1643 suggests that he is not one who gained from the misery of others. In any case, the *Elegy* speaks of him as a man who 'with dauntless breast/ The little tyrant of his fields withstood' (ll. 57–58), not as a self-aggrandising 'great' man. Milton, whatever else can be said of his political and poetical presence, certainly did not participate in the narrative of bloody history Gray writes. Can Hampden then be thought of as one who suppressed the struggles of 'conscious truth' (l. 68)? Is Milton a poet who worshipped 'Luxury and Pride' (l. 70)? In fact, in these lines the names Cromwell, Hampden, and Milton funtion as historical shorthand, their individual specificity subordinated to the evocation of a particular period of English history whose transformative politics are seen as socially divisive and morally dubious.

At this point, then, the *Elegy* establishes a fuzzy continuity between the specific historical references and the moral-allegorical discourse in the poem by the repetition of 'some,' a word that dilutes the particularity of historical names into the typological generality of ethical paradigms: 'Some Village-*Hampden*' (l. 57), 'Some mute inglorious *Milton*' (l. 59), 'Some *Cromwell*' (l. 60). The historical name becomes the moral type; upon comparison, the marginal situation of the villagers saves them from both historical and ethical impropriety:

> Their lot forbade: nor circumscribed alone
> Their growing virtues, but their crimes confined;
> Forbade to wade through slaughter to a throne,
> And shut the gates of mercy on mankind,

The struggling pangs of conscious truth to hide,
To quench the blushes of ingenuous shame,
Or heap the shrine of Luxury and Pride
With incense kindled at the Muse's flame. (ll. 67–72)

This discussion of lines 45–72 suggests that they are a mess of the specific and the allegorical, of the historical and the ethical, where continuity is generated inspite of incoherent reference or argumentation. The continuity here is a function largely of literary assumptions, that is, of the conventions of the pastoral fable of the country versus the city. The poem's rhetorical and referential individualities—the contradictory meanings of historical reference, moral allegory, and contested values—can be reconciled only in their dissolution into the system of meaning and emotion constituted by the poetic convention itself. That is, key to the power of the *Elegy* is its reproduction of a certain kind of morally and politically unobjectionable pathos—it is, after all, such pathos which guarantees the authority of pastoral elegy.

In the *Elegy*, then, the power to move—the power of pathos, that is—is deployed precisely to proceed beyond those moments in the poem where its ideological contradictions become most obvious, when the contradictions between its structuring tropes render the argument immovable. In the poem, the power of pathos is a function of the perceived power of overwhelming historical and socio-cultural transformation—the 'country' is a credible fiction only if the 'city' is unavoidable and all-powerful. Thus, in a fine reversal, the country no longer surrounds the city, but appears rather as the besieged space, hemmed in by a dubious political and ethical reality:

Far from the madding crowd's ignoble strife
Their sober wishes never learned to stray;
Along the cool sequestered vale of life
They kept the noiseless tenor of their way. (ll. 73–76)

This then is the full scope of the politics of pathos in the *Elegy*: in the poem, Gray relies overwhelmingly on the development of an ethically normative pathos to structure the opposition between the country and the city. Appropriate literary sentiment, that is, allows the foreclosure of questions of political and ideological affiliation, the dissolution of contradictions, the resolution of meanings. To read the *Elegy* on its own terms, to read it as an exercise in Pastoral, is to discover both the literary strategy, and the ideological contradiction, of the poem. It is also, most importantly, to discover a strong source of the ease with which the structures of feeling incarnated in the *Elegy* were appropriated to bourgeois humanist ideologies.

If, as Johnson thought it did, the *Elegy* 'abounds with images which find a mirror in every mind, and with sentiments to which every bosom returns an echo,'[44] it is because the poem offers itself both as political, and as the resolution of the political, or, more accurately, as the enervation and recuperation of the political into the morally correct emotion, all under the legitimising aegis of the literary. Literary history teaches us that the techniques for such recuperation came to their full ideological flower as later eighteenth-century Sentimentalism, which has been well described as the ideology of unpurposive pity. The continued popularity of the *Elegy* is not separate from that development. Indeed, it is a compelling possibility that the literary contours of the Sentimental took the shape they did in implicit acknowledgement of the ideological power of the politics of pathos in the *Elegy*. The *Elegy*, by making pity seem both political and purposive, legitimated the literary and ideological project of the tradition within which it was co-opted and canonised. Such a literary and critical reception also ensured that the contradictions of the *Elegy* were gradually repressed and allowed to disappear.

In the *Elegy*, however, the pressure of these contradictions leads to the abandoning of the country and the city as a structuring opposition. This antithesis does not altogether disappear, and in fact resurfaces in the distinction between the literate and the illiterate, between those who can read (l. 115) and those who only participate in an oral culture. However, from line 77 to the end of the poem, the *Elegy* shifts its concerns to the problematic that structures much of Gray's poetry: the Authority of the Poet. These lines are concerned, once again, with the search of the poet for an enabling community; with questions about the nature and status of representation; and thus, ultimately with the historically specific sense of social and cultural loss experienced by the high-cultural poet in the period of ascendant bourgeois culture.

Lines 77–84 go back to the 'mouldering heap' of village graves described in lines 14–16, but now these graves are not simply the 'narrow cell[s]' in which 'the rude forefathers of the hamlet sleep.' In these lines they are distinguished by their being recognisable monuments with an important community purpose:

> Yet even these bones from insult to protect
> Some frail memorial still erected nigh,
> With uncouth rhymes and shapeless sculpture decked,
> Implores the passing tribute of a sigh.
>
> Their name, their years, spelt by the unlettered muse,
> The place of fame and elegy supply:
> And many a holy text around she strews,
> That teach the rustic moralist to die. (ll. 77–84)

The threat of the 'city' still lingers in line 77, in the fear of 'insult,' but these lines are actually a tribute to the village community, which, though 'unlettered,' knows well how to respond to these 'frail monuments' with their 'uncouth rhymes' and basic inscriptions ('Their name, their years'). These gravestones are sermons in stones—'a holy text'—because they can elicit 'the passing tribute of a sigh,' and in the appropriateness of this reaction, 'teach the rustic moralist to die.' They can do, that is, what good 'fame and elegy' are meant to do in other, more literate contexts: provide texts of the continuity and permanence of human community.

The West *Sonnet* had shown us that such concerns had long been with Gray. The questions were the same as in the *Elegy*:

For who to dumb Forgetfulness a prey,
This pleasing anxious being e'er resigned,
Left the warm precincts of the cheerful day,
Nor cast one longing lingering look behind? (ll. 85–88)

What preserves memory? the *Sonnet* had asked, as the *Elegy* now wonders; only community, the *Sonnet* had answered, and the *Elegy* now echoes:

On some fond breast the parting soul relies,
Some pious drops the closing eye requires;
Ev'n from the tomb the voice of nature cries,
Ev'n in our ashes live their wonted fires. (ll. 89–92)

In 'Ad Amicos,' West had hoped to counter the fact that 'Nature' would take no notice of his death by writing his monument in the 'breasts' of his friends (ll. 80–82).[45] In the West *Sonnet*, Gray had shown this hope to be elusive, rewriting the 'breast' as the site not of the continuity of fraternal memory, but of the disruptions of absence and loss: 'And in my breast the imperfect joys expire' (l. 8). In the *Sonnet*, the irony of this repetition (of 'breast') was too strong to be recuperated, and in fact had broadened to include the loss of an enabling, empowering cultural community.

In the *Elegy*, however, it is precisely the existence of a responsive, 'uncultured' community that is shown to guard against final loss. The sound and sight of expressed emotions—the 'sigh' of line 80, the 'pious drops' of line 90—are all taken as signs that the 'fond breast' indeed bears witness to the 'voice of nature' that cries from the tomb. In the West *Sonnet*, the opposite had been true; the continuity of life could offer no compensation for the absence caused by death:

The birds in vain their amorous descant join,
Or cheerful fields resume their green attire:
These ears, alas! for other notes repine. (ll. 3–5)

The *Elegy* reverses this position—death is here less than an obliteration of life: 'Ev'n in our ashes live their wonted fires' (l. 92). The suggestion of tenacious self-regeneration emphasises the force of the desire to, as it were, live beyond death. Closing off the quatrain, this image of phoenix-like continuity validates the memorialising power of the 'fond breast.'

Ironically, it is just this unqualified assertion of the saving powers of the village community that reminds the poet-figure of his own ambiguous position vis-a-vis that community. Even though he sings of this community, he is not part of it. He does 'mindful of the unhonoured dead,/ . . . in these lines their artless tale relate' (l. 93–94), but precisely because he is other than 'artless,' precisely because he does not worship 'the unlettered muse' (l. 81), he is condemned to remain an outsider, marked by the stigma of his 'city' art. Once again, it is the poet-figure's enactment of the collapse of conventional pastoral alliances into alienation that reveal the ideological dichotomies of Gray's attempted strategic solidarity with the unlettered, the artless, the 'country.'

From this point on, the *Elegy* stages a drama of several poetic figures and voices, whose interaction, if anything, renders even more ironic the poet-figure's tentative claim to cultural and moral authority. In fact, the poet-figure now seems to lose his voice, and is presented as the subject of a pathetic (and not quite artless) tale told by one of those who were his subjects, a 'hoary-headed swain' (l. 97). The literate celebration of the pathos of an oral culture turns upon itself here, as an exemplar of the older oral tradition speaks a sentimental tale about the sad figure of the perhaps-too-literate young poet. The only way the poet-figure survives, it seems, is as a character in a village tale, a tale of an alienated life and an isolated death.

Yet if this very survival as the subject of a tale be taken as (ambiguous) proof of the entry of the poet-figure into communal memory, and as a kind of memorialisation, we must remember that the tale is called forth by the explicit enquiry of a 'kindred spirit' (l. 96). The swain's response to this new figure emphasises his cultural difference, and the mark of this difference is the latter's literacy: 'For thou cans't read' (l. 115). The entire exchange between the 'swain' and the enquiring 'spirit' (ll. 96–116) serves to individuate them, but also to obscure the fact that they are both projections of the poet-figure's fantasy of death and community-in-death:

> *If chance*, by lonely Contemplation led,
> Some kindred spirit shall inquire thy fate,
>
> *Haply* some hoary-headed swain *may* say.
>
> (ll. 95–97; my italics)

All this might happen; should happen, in fact, if the poet-figure's ideal scenario of the communal recuperation of death is to be put into place.

This shift into the world of fantasy and wish-fulfillment is triggered by the poet-figure's recounting of the recuperative, even regenerative, powers of the village community in lines 77–92, a recounting that reminds him of his lack of a similar community. It is then that he conjures up this 'kindred spirit' as a figure for the literate community that he is missing, and whose ability to read (as we shall see) is of particular importance here. The fantastic appearance of this spirit is not, however, the only trace of the poet-figure's anxious thoughts of isolation and death. The very deictics of the self register a shift—no more do we have the integrated, first person 'me' of line 4. Instead, in line 93, the poet-figure switches to a dissociated, second-person address to himself: 'For thee,' he says, and then in line 96, talks of 'thy fate.' But most striking of all, and most revelatory of the fact that the swain and the wandering spirit are figures in the psychic drama of the poet-figure, is the nature of the swain's voice. The lines he speaks (ll. 98–116) are clearly a speech not his, because they are distinctly identifiable as the conventional 'literate' idiom and language of pastoral poetry. In the dialogic interplay of these lines with the rest of the poem, a play marked by quotation marks, it becomes obvious that this is not the voice of the unlettered swain, but is in fact the ventriloquised discourse of the poet-figure.

And not only this poet-figure, but the repeated poet-figures who are thematised in so many of Gray's major poems. Specifically, the *Elegy* here looks back to the 'Ode on the Spring,' and the poet-moralist who had discovered his isolation in that poem. The same muse—Contemplation ('Spring,' l. 31; *Elegy*, l. 95)—is company for the poet-figures in both poems, and this repetition should remind us that in the earlier poem, Contemplation had turned out to be a figure for isolation. As we have seen, the same disillusioning discovery obtains in the *Elegy* also. That, though, is not the only repetition in these poems. The swain's representation of the poet in the *Elegy*:

> 'There at the foot of yonder nodding beech
> 'That wreathes its old fantastic roots so high,
> 'His listless length at noontide would he stretch,
> 'And pore upon the brook that babbles by (ll. 101–04)

echoes that of 'Ode on the Spring:'

> Where'er the rude and moss-grown beech
> O'er canopies the glade,
> Beside some water's rushy brink
> With me the Muse shall sit, and think. (ll. 13–16)

Most significant about this repetition is, of course, the fact that the poet-figure in 'Ode on the Spring' himself repeats, enacts, a conventional poetic topos, that of the recumbent *poeta*.[46] In the *Elegy*, then, re-presentation is vertiginous: the pre-figuration of the pre-figuration is, as it were, an entire poetic, discursive tradition.

There is this repetition, but it is not repetition without change. Whereas in 'Ode on the Spring' the poet-figure's discovery of his isolation had comprised the moment of peripeteia that closed the poem, in the *Elegy*, this figure daily enacts the anxieties of a similar predicament:

> 'Hard by yon wood, now smiling as in scorn,
> 'Muttering his wayward fancies he would rove,

> 'Now drooping, woeful wan, like one forlorn,
> 'Or crazed with care, or crossed in hopeless love.
>
> (ll. 105–08)

The contemplative air of the 'Ode on the Spring' is gone, and the neuroses of isolation are on display. Something has clearly been lost, or else the awareness of loss has been brought home firmly.

Again, as so often in Gray, it is the language of his poems that gestures towards the contexts of significance within which this loss must be read. In the early part of the 'Ode on the Spring,' the contemplative assurance of the poet-figure ('With me the Muse shall sit, and *think*;' my italics) had been predicated upon his comfortable location within a powerful discursive tradition, that of ethical humanism. This provided the poet-figure with an authoritative designation—Moralist—and a calm, if pietistic and dull, voice and language. All this, of course, unravels in the poem, but there is no gainsaying its initial enabling power. In lines 105–08 in the *Elegy*, the diction shifts radically, making its representation of the poet a precursor, in both figure and idiom, of the literary-historical tradition we know as Romanticism. More important for our purposes here, lines 107–08 speak a language soon to be enshrined as the literary convention that celebrated the social utility and virtue of (individual examples of) pathos—Sentimentalism. With one difference: here it is the poet who is 'drooping, woeful wan, like one forlorn/ 'Or crazed with care, or crossed in hopeless love.' This is pity made self-purposive, pathos turned in upon itself, so that the object of pathos is in fact the Subject(ivity) of the Poet.

This debilitating slide from the assurances of the ethical-humanistic to the pathetic postures of the sentimental involves, as we have seen, a reversal of most of the central tropes of poetic power and authority. The prospect, the contemplative distance, the detached view of the object, the sense that the discursive tradition contained a formal and a linguistic vocabulary adequate to the representation of this scrutiny of 'man' and 'nature,' all gave way to an (at least partial) understanding that the social configurations that had supported such representations were themselves now unreliable. No more, for instance, does the prospect work as a formal consolidation of the patrician values and power of the 'country house' tradition. By the middle of the eighteenth century, the prospect took for its text not only the topography of rural England and the country seat, but looked outwards onto a globe being mapped even then by an imperial and mercantile cartography. This 'world-view,' in turn, signalled a different configuration of domestic power, in which the country aristocracy were giving way to the mercantile bourgeoisie. The poet of the prospect 'saw' these socio-historical transitions—Gray's poems offer symptomatic evidence of such disruption, as also, of course, of inconsistencies in the high-cultural reaction to changes in the private and public culture of England.

The *Elegy* is complicated further by the fact that even though it is the swain who speaks lines 98–116, he is as a ventriloquist's dummy mouthing a part in the solipsistic, tragic psychic drama of the poet-figure. The contradiction between this 'crazed' (self-)representation of the poet-figure, and the far more collected and composed figure of the contemplative poet who meditates on the country churchyard (the protagonist of the enunciation, as it were) is obvious, and can easily be mapped onto the divide between the pathetic-sentimental and contemplative-humanist modes. That is, the *Elegy* plays out internally the repetition with difference that we have analysed in comparing the 'Ode on the Spring' and the *Elegy*. Rather than being a poem that simply subsides into the ahistorical, static ('timeless') format and formulae characteristic of most eighteenth-century 'melancholy' verse, the *Elegy* enacts, in its representations of the poet and of the languages of poetry, the social and discursive history of the changing status and authority of the high-cultural poet. When within, as also between, these poems, (humanistic) assurance devolves into (pathetic) neurosis, we recognise that an accurate diagnosis of this pathology will inevitably be a prognosis of eighteenth-century literary history, and also ultimately a personal history of the social and ideological position occupied by Gray.

The *Elegy,* in this reading, thus controverts John Sitter's description of 'The Flight from History in Mid-Century.' While the *Elegy* does not have the 'allegiance to the specific' that Sitter correctly says distinguishes Pope and Swift, it is far more ideologically contestatory than he would allow poems of its kind to be: 'We have seen how the conflict and violence of public history as it is conceived metonymically by many of the poets leads to images of Retreat, images of shepherds fleeing as they sing, for example, hurrying towards the shelter of shady groves or the protection of caves, and we have seen that these images of seclusion are also metaphors for the solitary poetic imagination itself.'[47] What the *Elegy,* and contemporary poems like it, show us is not the Poet in retreat from History, but poets coming to terms with particular versions of English history. If 'public history' emerges as especially conflicted and violent in the poetry of some high-cultural poets, it is because the public sphere itself was then being reconstituted by the ideologies, cultures, and politics of the bourgeoisie, a reconstitution that effectively challenged and marginalised such poets. Such a marginalisation lies behind the rewriting of the very 'poetic imagination' as solitary, as not-social; but even such a defensive refiguration, as the *Elegy* illustrates, was simultaneously an offensive strategy. These poems thus record not a Flight from History, but an insistent engagement with its contemporary discursive, cultural, and social forms.

The *Elegy* ends not with the discovery of the death of the poet-figure (as recounted by the swain in lines 113–14), but with a reading of 'The Epitaph' that is 'Graved on the stone' (l. 116) that marks his grave. This conclusion is appropriate for more than one reason. It returns us to our awareness that the poem is concerned not so much with the absolute loss that is death as with the social and historical loss of the 'proper' culture of life and death. That is, the end of the poem mourns the passing of those community values and traditions that make the proper monumentalisation of individual deaths possible. In the 'city,' monuments are mis-read or disregarded; here, in the country churchyard, kindred spirits can read, and be reminded:

Here rests his head upon the lap of earth
A youth to fortune and to fame unknown.
Fair Science frowned not on his humble birth,
And Melancholy marked him for her own.

Large was his bounty and his soul sincere,
Heaven did a recompense as largely send:
He gave to Misery all he had, a tear,
He gained from Heaven ('twas all he wished) a friend.
(ll. 117–24)

'The Epitaph' also reminds us that to monumentalise thus is also to textualise—an (auto)biographical narrative is to be read in these eight lines. The entire epitaph, but especially these lines, are engaged in authorial self-construction. This is the chosen persona of the poet-figure in the *Elegy*: a youth who claims a social, political, and economic sameness with the villagers ('to fortune and to fame unknown'); but a difference in temperament ('Melancholy marked him for her own'), and in education ('Fair Science frowned not on his humble birth'). The poet-as-sentimentalist also finds a place here. His soul being 'sincere,' he 'gave to Misery all he had, a tear,' and 'gained from Heaven ('twas all he wished) a friend.'

However, the invitation to read ('for thou cans't read') the epitaph, to acknowledge its narrative, is, as we might expect, fraught with its own complications. Even though the epitaph is written in what Wordsworth would call 'the general language of humanity as connected with the subject of Death,'[48] it is impossible to control both the ironies internal to the epitaph and those that are generated in its dialogic (though ostensibly purely referential) relation to the rest of the poem. The play of identity and difference that marks the epitaphic version of the relationship between the deceased poet and the villagers echoes, and is scarred by, the larger formal and ideological disjunction that we have examined in the body of the *Elegy*. The dispossession of authorial capacity (l. 123) that is masked by the topos of sentimental bounty and the claim of heavenly recompense (ll. 121–24) is doubly emphasised in that the compensatory language of sentimentality reminds us of the enervation and loss that it marks in the *Elegy*. The status accorded the unnamed, single 'friend' (possibly meant to be, in this ventriloquised drama of the poet-figure's death, the person who composed 'The Epitaph') is undercut by the fact that it is not he, but a comparative stranger, the swain, who now introduces the epitaph.

These dissonances threaten the ostensible assonance and ease of the proper language of epitaphs that Wordsworth called 'truth hallowed by love—the joint offspring of the worth of the Dead and the affections of the Living.'[49] Truth hallowed is here truth hollowed, and before the full consequences of these internally antithetical readings can emerge, a closure is mandated:

> *No farther seek his merits to disclose,*
> *Or draw his frailties from their dread abode,*
> *(There they alike in trembling hope repose)*
> *The bosom of his Father and his God.* (ll. 125–28)

The rhetorical pattern, as de Man's analyses have often shown us, is clear. Tropes are converted into anthropomorphisms, the threatening interchangeability of tropes and propositions is frozen by transforming them—grammatically, syntactically—into the foreclosed space that is the (epistemological) authority of the proper name.[50] In a moment of perfect literary irony, the (name of the) Father, 'God' (l. 128), provides the 'bosom'[51] to contain the fame of the poet; but the price of this immortality is high. Voice, narrative, reading—all these tropes for poetic power and authority must be silenced, and the circuit of communication closed. The closure of the epitaph, then, is also the belated foreclosure of the problematic of the Authority of the Poet, the moment that denies the very need to have written / mourned at all.

And yet not quite. For we must not let the injunction to read the epitaph (l. 115) obscure the fact that it is the gravestone which speaks. This prosopopeia, 'which, as the trope of address, is the very figure of the reader and of reading,'[52] ensures that the tropological frame of the epitaph will remain in tension with its content, its final message. (In the bosom of God, the reward for the death of speech is eternal life; in the epitaphic prosopopeia, the compensation for the cessation of life is eternal speech.) That is, the introductory trope of the activated voice, which is also the figure of the lyric, will keep alive the kinds of questions that the last four lines of the epitaph attempt to lay to rest.

This tension between the formal and the semantic, the figural and the literal, is further complicated by the fact that the epitaph, 'Graved on the stone' (l. 116), suggests a materiality different from the rest of the *Elegy*. The inscription, like prosopopeia, makes the invisible visible, creates a text where nothing of the kind existed before, but does so in a wholly different register. It seems literal (rather than figural) because it claims to exist, as prosopopeia does not, in a medium other than the mind. As prosopopeia is a figure of speech, inscription is a figure for writing, for that insistent desire to create a marker of the here and now that will resist mutability and allow for its satisfactory recovery in later moments of reading. It is this which makes the grave(d)stone both the emblem of transience and the promise of escape from transience, both a sign of mortality and a trope of immortality. In this way, inscription too is structured around the tension between the injunction to silence that is the last four lines of the epitaph and the tropological activation of voice that is prosopopeia.

How are we to understand the play of these figurations and significations that are unleashed by the (imagined) death of the poet-figure in the *Elegy*? To answer this question, we must return to the dynamic interrelation between the subject of the enounced and the subject of enunciation that we had charted at length in the discussion of Gray's early poems in Chapter II. In the *Elegy*, the primary subject of the enounced is the poet-figure indicated by the 'me' of line 4, and the 'thee' and 'thy' of lines 93 and 96. In the analysis of the 'Ode on the Spring,' we noticed that the deictics of the self could be read as a record of the dialectic of identification and distancing that characterised the relationship between the subject(s) of the enounced and the subject of the enunciation, especially as regards the seductive and threatening power the figure of the gloomy, sensitive solitary has for Gray. Thus, the early 'me' in the *Elegy* encourages an identification between the subject of the enounced and the subject of the enunciation, encouraging the (auto) biographical reading of the melancholy poet as Gray. This loneliness is not yet threatening, for it is contained by the discursive authority granted by the topos of Contemplation—social isolation is compensated for by the promise of philosophical or moral insight. However, by the time we get to line 93, the question of poetic insight and authority is reduced to a subset of the more vexed problem of the loss of cultural and social authority, and the poet-figure's local isolation is recognised as a marginalisation consequent upon the changed social relations of (cultural) production. Thus, lines 93 and 96 effect a distance between the subject of the enounced and the subject of the enunciation, revealing the subject of the enounced as fissured and traumatised, refusing the moment of identification by deploying second person pronouns: 'thee,' 'thy.'

The psycho-drama of the poet-figure's imagined death also begins here, this final isolation being enacted as the loss of voice. The subjects of the enounced are now the 'hoary-headed swain' who speaks and the 'kindred spirit' who reads: this naming of the speaking subject as other than a / the poet-figure asserts the distance between the subject of the enunciation and the subject of the enounced that is imperative to Gray's attempts to rescue poetic authority from the several enactments of precisely the loss of that poetic authority in his poems. That such a rescue does not come easily (if it comes at all) is evident from the fact that even as the new name of the subject of the enounced—'hoary-headed swain'—is meant to preclude identification, the language that he speaks is so conventionally that of a 'poet' that it threatens the entire effort to effect distance. Furthermore, the pathos of the swain's representation of the poet-figure reinforces the identification-through-affect that structures the relationship between the subject of the enunciation and the subject of the enounced. That is, in the *Elegy,* the subject of the enunciation is represented as both identifying with, and resisting, the thematised poet-figure, in each case doing so because the poet-figure of the enounced is a seductive emblem of gloom, melancholy, and loss.

Finally, however, we get to the signifier of absolute loss in the poem: the epitaph on the gravestone (itself, of course, a proleptic fantasy of death and remembrance). At this point, the entire *Elegy* seems to have been a long detour—a kind of tmesis—to avoid arriving at what can only be read as the last words on the subject of the Poet, that he can no longer speak, and can only be spoken of. Even as the injunction to read, and the prosopopeia that begins, the epitaph enact the phenomenalisation of the poetic voice[53] that signifies life and power, the materiality of the inscription of death insistently signifies the final loss of such life and power. The anthropomorphism at the end of the epitaph (the resting place that is the bosom of the Father, God) is then to be read as an admission that not even prosopopeia can override the effect of the epitaphic inscription—that the only way to avoid recognising the full implications of the epitaph is to close off all questions by invoking the non-negotiable, intractable power of the divine proper name. The *Elegy,* does not end with the rhetorical flourish that we read in Gray's early poems as the gesture of self-assertion by which the subject of the enunciation finally distances himself from the thematised poet-figure and announces his specific and separate power as the enunciator of the entire poem. Instead it closes with a rather despairing attempt to claim a heavenly solution / reconciliation for the irreconcilable earthly problems of poetic, cultural, social marginalisation.

Gray wrote at a time when the circuits of commercial literary production and circulation existed in an uneasy relation with the still culturally powerful rituals of manuscript circulation within a miniscule, select company. In a letter to Thomas Wharton, Gray wrote about his hesitations regarding an unplanned expansion in the circle of his chosen readers for the *Elegy*:

the Stanza's wch I now enclose to you, have had the Misfortune by Mr W[alpole]:s Fault to be made still more publick, for wch they certainly were never meant, but it is too late to complain. they have been so applauded, it is quite a Shame to repeat it. I mean not to be modest; but I mean, it is a Shame for those, who have said such superlative Things about them, that I can't repeat them. I should have been glad, that you & two or three more People had liked them, wch would have satisfied my ambition on this Head amply.[54]

We might of course choose to dismiss this as another overworked variation of the topos of authorial humility and lack of ambition, but such a dismissal is made more complicated when we set this passage against another from a letter he wrote to Walpole at the same time.

'My dear Sr,' Gray wrote from Cambridge on February 11, 1751,

As you have brought me into a little Sort of Distress, you must assist me, I believe, to get out of it, as well as I can. yesterday I had the misfortune of receiving a Letter from certain Gentlemen (as their Bookseller expresses it) who have taken the *Magazine of Magazines* into their Hands. they tell me, that an *ingenious* Poem, call'd *Reflections* in a Country Churchyard, had been communicated to them, wch they are printing forthwith: that they are inform'd, that the *excellent* Author of it is I by name, & that they beg not only his *Indulgence*, but the *Honour of his Correspondence*, &c: as I am not at all disposed to be either so indulgent, or so correspondent, as they desire; I have but one bad Way left to escape the Honour they would inflict upon me. & therefore am obliged to desire you would make Dodsley print it immediately (wch may be done in less than a Week's time) from your Copy, but without my Name, in what Form is most convenient for him, but in his best Paper & Character . . . if he would add a line or two to say it came into his Hands by Accident, I should like it better.

If you behold the Mag: of Mag:s in the Light that I do, you will not refuse to give yourself this Trouble on my Account, wch you have taken of your own accord before now.[55]

The snobbery and cultural elitism in Gray's tone, as he ventriloquises and parodies the language and manner of the 'certain Gentlemen' compiling the *Magazine of Magazines*, is transparent. The esteem in which he held this magazine may be surmised from some prefatory editorial material that introduced the aims and methods of that periodical:

The public may, perhaps, be surpriz'd that a society *of gentlemen should engage in a work of this kind, when the very name of Magazine carries ridicule with it: yet object what they will, a design like this must be own'd very necessary. The variety of Magazines is so great, every one is in doubt where to fix for the best; and, fix where he will, equally disappointed: we are far from presuming to say* ours is *or* will be *the* best; *but thus much we may be bold to say, our design is more elegant, more spirited, and better adapted to please, than any yet attempted . . . Everything that deserves public notice, in any of the periodical pamphlets, will be met with in this: and as we shall find it difficult from all of them to complete our work with such pieces as are really good, we propose giving from our own private stock such originals (and such only) as appear to be truly curious . . .*

We promise ourselves that those of our own class will not fail of being our friends: and as there is always something that truly distinguishes the compositions of gentlemen, we should be greatly oblig'd to them for any useful and entertaining originals, which we shall always particularly esteem.[56]

This is the discourse not of the 'society *of gentlemen,*' but of those who would be so; these are gentlemen *manque*, members of the bourgeoisie who are using their control of various modes of literary production to *create* themselves. The very idea of a miscellany compiled from excerpts of the 'best' writing in other periodicals, which tries hard to distinguish itself from other similar miscellanies ('*our design is more elegant, more spirited, and better adapted to please, than any yet attempted*') and which is designed to provide an easy guide to the right reading—such a development itself represents perfectly the historical shift from the literary circle of writers and readers to the market mechanism of compilers, publishers, and mass consumers.

Little wonder then that Gray wished so ardently for the 'one bad Way left to escape the Honour they would inflict on me.' He did get his wish, as Dodsley printed the *Elegy* before the *Magazine of Magazines* did,[57] but when the latter appeared, it framed the *Elegy* within a pseudo-pastoral, 'intellectual' dialogue starring characters by the names of Hilario (who recites the poem, after attributing it to Gray), Nicander, Sir Lionel, and Politian. The ironies of such an appropriation are particularly mocking: in the *Elegy*, a version of the pastoral had provided Gray with a poetic strategy of attack against the commodification of literary and cultural values. Here, in the names and 'cultured' activity of these would-be gentlemen who emphasise and cherish what they speak of as the existential questions and the melancholy mood of the *Elegy*, a different set of pastoral values surfaces. Only this time, the framework of pastoral dialogue sanctifies the contemporary bourgeois accession to cultural and ideological significance, an accession based in part on the successful recuperation and appropriation of complex literary documents like the *Elegy*.

NOTES

1. These maxims were printed by William Mason in his Memoirs of Gray prefixed to *The Poems of Mr. Gray*. They are quoted by Lonsdale in *Gray*, pp. 90–91.
2. John Brewer, 'Commercialization and Politics,' in *Birth of a Consumer Society: The Commercialization of Eighteenth-Century England*, eds. Neil McKendrick, John Brewer, and J.H. Plumb (Bloomington: Indiana University Press, 1985), pp. 197–98.
3. McKendrick, 'Commercialization and Politics,' p. 5. My use of the term 'commodification' is of course based on Marx's analyses of the psycho-structural basis of the same historical phenomena that McKendrick describes as the birth of a 'consumer' society or as the 'commercialization' of England. See Karl Marx, *Capital: A Critique of Political Economy, Vol. I*, tr. Ben Fowkes, (New York: Random House, 1977), pp. 163–77.
4. This offers us one way to think about the predominance of Satire in the early eighteenth century. Marx's critique of the fetishism of the commodity reminds us that the economic generalisation of the market-processes of capitalism threatens to collapse distinct and different traditional relations between people into the single equivalence and

exchangeability dictated by the sign of exchange value. Satire, with its scapegoating rituals, and its formal and rhetorical methods of defining and enforcing distance and distinction, is thus an appropriate cultural response to such a threat.

5. These maxims, it should be pointed out, were meant as notes for an unfinished poem by Gray on 'the Alliance of Education and Government,' which he worked on in late 1748 and early 1749. I will return to this poem in the next chapter.
6. Quoted by Lonsdale in *Gray*, p. 91.
7. *Correspondence*, i. 317.
8. *The Poems of Mr. Gray*, p. 192. Lonsdale finds Mason's statement 'convincing.' Lonsdale, *Gray*, p. 86.
9. Albert O. Hirschman, *The Passions and the Interests: Political Arguments for Capitalism before Its Triumph* (Princeton: Princeton University Press, 1977), pp. 59–60. Hirschman's discussion alerted me to the specific politico-economic context of Gray's maxims, and I draw from them accordingly. Hirschman notes that Bolingbroke and the Tory attack on Walpole and Company notwithstanding, 'during much of the century, in both England and France, the dominant appraisal of the 'love of gain' was positive, if somewhat disdainful' (p. 57).
10. Charles de Secondat, Baron de Montesquieu, *The Spirit of Laws*, trans. Thomas Nugent, rev. J.V. Prichard (Chicago: Encyclopedia Brittanica, 1955), xx. 1. For Montesquieu's reservations, see Hirshman, *Passions and Interests*, p. 80.
11. Montesquieu, *Spirit of Laws*, v. 7. On either side of this statement, the whole comprising a single paragraph, Montesquieu has these two sentences: 'True it is that when a democracy is founded on commerce, private people may acquire vast riches without a corruption of morals.' And 'The mischief is, when excessive wealth destroys the spirit of commerce, then it is that the inconveniences of inequality begin to be felt.' It is 'the spirit of commerce,' then, that holds these incompatible claims together in a strange and powerful tension, a tension whose symptoms and pathology mark many documents of the eighteenth century.
12. Montesquieu, *Spirit of Laws*, xxi. 20.
13. For this discussion see Hirschman, *Passions and Interests*, pp. 7–66. Hirschman charts the history of the 'Principle of the Countervailing Passion,' in which, at different times, human 'Interests' were seen as tamers of the 'Passions,' or vice versa, such that '*one set of passions,*

hitherto known variously as greed, avarice, or love of lucre, could be usefully employed to oppose and bridle such other passions as ambition, lust for power, or sexual lust' (p. 41). Helvetius reminded moralists that 'only a passion can triumph over a passion; that ... [they] might succeed in having their maxims observed if they substituted in this manner the language of interest for that of injury.' *De l'espirit* (1758), quoted by Hirschman, p. 28.

14. Hirschman, quoting a sentence from Hume's 'Of Interest' ('It is an infallible consequence of all industrious professions, to ... make the love of gain prevail over the love of pleasure'), says: 'Hume's statement can stand as the culmination of the movement of ideas that has been traced: capitalism is here hailed by a leading philosopher of the age because it would activate some benign human proclivities at the expense of some malignant ones—because of the expectation that, in this way, it would repress and perhaps atrophy the more destructive and disastrous components of human nature.' *Passions and Interests*, p. 66. As I will go on to show, Gray's was not quite as warm a welcome, because it was based, in part, on a less unproblematic faith in the 'love of gain.'
15. Quoted by Lonsdale in *Gray*, p. 91.
16. Montesquieu, *Spirit of Laws*, iv. 7.
17. Lonsdale's editorial discussion of the dating of this poem is exhaustive. He makes clear 'that all of the evidence is ambiguous and nothing more confident than an assertion of likelihood can be achieved,' but tends to believe that most of the poem was written between 1746 and 1750, possibly even in 1746. *Gray*, pp. 103–10. For my purpose, it is enough that these are the years in which Gray should have been thinking so systematically about issues like the alliance of education and government, for instance, to feel that Montesquieu's work had forestalled some of his best ideas.
18. William Empson, *Some Versions of Pastoral*. All passages quoted are from pp. 4–5.
19. I should point out that Empson does not see anything contradictory in that–for him all statements which suggest 'that for the poor man things cannot be improved even in degree' are 'in a way "bourgeois".' *Some Versions of Pastoral*, p. 5. My analysis will differ from his in that I believe Gray to be conscious of the historically specific distinctions between the values of the aristocracy and those of the eighteenth-century English bourgeoisie, particularly as the *Elegy* traces some of the oppositional (though shifting) contact between these ideologies.

20. Marx's analysis of the 'money commodity' provides the context for the discussion here: 'The commodity which functions as a measure of value and therefore also as the medium of circulation, either in its own body or through a representative, is money. Gold (or silver) is therefore money.' Further, the 'money-form of commodities is like their form of value generally, quite distinct from their palpable and real bodily form; it is therefore a purely ideal or notional form,' and that 'in its function as a measure of value, money . . . serves only in an imaginary or ideal capacity.' 'Money, or the Circulation of Commodities,' in *Capital*, pp. 227, 190–191.
21. These two lines also condense the play of darkness and insight, of loss and recuperation, that structure the beginning stanzas of the poem, in which the falling of night engenders the vision of the poet.
22. Marx, *Capital*, pp. 164–65.
23. Gray's sublime here would be a version of Burke's later (1757) empiricist and psychologistic definition of the natural sublime in his discussion of 'Obscurity.' See *A Philosophical Enquiry into the Origin of our Ideas of the Sublime and Beautiful*, ed. J.T. Boulton (London, 1958), pp. 58–64.
24. Paul de Man, 'Intentional Structure of the Romantic Image,' in *The Rhetoric of Romanticism* (New York: Columbia University Press, 1984), p. 6. In this essay, de Man shows how the early romantics were 'the first modern writers to have put into question, in the language of poetry, the ontological priority of the sensory object' (p. 16). My use of this essay represents a part, or even mis-reading, of de Man's purposes, but that too was his method.
25. De Man, 'Intentional Structure,' p. 4. De Man generalises from this to suggest that 'this type of imagery is grounded in the intrinsic ontological primacy of the natural object. Poetic language seems to originate in the desire to draw closer and closer to the ontological status of the object' (p. 7). Of course, he goes on to show (as I quote in the previous note), precisely how this ontological primacy is put into question.
26. Alexander Pope, *The Rape of the Lock*, ed. Geoffrey Tillotson, 2nd ed. (New Haven: Yale University Press, 1954), p. 193. Martin Wechselblatt reminded me of the place of the blush in Pope.
27. See Laura Brown: 'Belinda is adorned with the spoils of mercantile expansion . . . these are the means by which her natural beauty is "awakened." In other words, imperialism dresses nature to advantage here.' *Pope*, p. 9.

28. There is a logic behind this inscription. In the semiotics of public sexual response, the blush is taken to be the most accurate (because grounded in physiology) signifier of the woman's acknowledgement that she is the *object* of the interested male gaze. Belinda's status as commodity thus (over) invests her with the signifiers of social objectification.
29. Not only this history, of course. For instance, Belinda's roses 'bloom and die' 'naturally' in the desert, whereas Gray's flower '*waste[s]* its sweetness' there. Gray's trope adds to Pope's language the (inorganic) idea of 'waste,' another powerful signifier of the transformation of the natural into the commodified.
30. In *Poet Without a Name* (Carbondale: Southern Illinois University Press, 1991), Henry Weinfield suggests that Edmund Waller's lyric, 'Go, lovely rose,' is the 'clearest "source" in the English tradition' for this stanza of the *Elegy* (p. 85). Waller's poem contains the words 'wastes,' 'sweet,' 'deserts,' and 'blush,' and is thus a credible precursor for Gray's images. Indeed Waller's third stanza sets in play the themes of sexual objectification and the cultural estimation of value which structure Pope's poem too:

    Small is the worth
    Of beauty from the light retired;
    Bid her come forth,
    Suffer herself to be desired,
    And not blush so to be admired. (ll. 11–15)

    However, the *carpe diem* theme of Waller's lyric insulates it from a sustained engagement with such socio-cultural issues. For Gray, as for most eighteenth-century poets, Pope's Belinda would have been the prime product of the contemporary commodity culture, and *The Rape of the Lock* the primary text of the nostalgic (if constantly satirised) gap between the 'natural' and the commodified.
31. The general literary-theoretical point is made by Terry Eagleton: '"Textuality" is to be understood not . . . as a privileging of the discursive or the "literary", but as the resituating of otherwise idealistic perceived entities within the "weave of differential relations, institutions, conventions, histories, practices" of which they are always the internally conflictual effects.' 'Frére Jacques: The Politics of Deconstruction,' *Semiotica* 63 (1987), p. 352.
32. Raymond Williams, *The Country and the City* (New York: Oxford University Press, 1973), p. 72.

33. James Thomson's enthusiastic comment on hay-making and sheep shearing ('A simple Scene!'), bears witness to the assimilating imperatives of such mercantilism:

> A simple Scene! yet hence BRITTANIA sees
> Her solid grandeur rise: hence she commands
> Th' exalted Stores of every brighter Clime,
> The Treasures of the Sun without his Rage:
> Hence, fervent all, with Culture, Toil, and Arts,
> Wide grows her Land: her dreadful Thunder hence
> Rides o'er the Waves sublime, and now, even now,
> Impending hangs o'er *Gallia's* humbled Coast,
> Hence rules the circling Deep, and awes the World.

'Summer' (ll. 423–31), *The Seasons*, p. 80.

34. Barrell, *English Literature in History, 1730–80*, p. 177.

35. In emphasizing that the opening of the poem should be read as Gray's troping on the prospect, and in claiming that the melancholy mood of the *Elegy* is a specific literary response to developments in eighteenth-century English social history, I am arguing against critical readings like those of Amy L. Reed, who sees the *Elegy* as one more example of the pensive pastoral, those poems in which there is a well-established association 'between the description of nature and either pensive or gloomy reflection.' *The Background of Gray's Elegy* (New York: Columbia University Press, 1924), p. 196. Reed's book is a useful survey of 'The Taste for Melancholy Poetry 1700–1751,' but is limited in its understanding of the *Elegy*: 'In its essence, the poem combines the assertion of the right to individual tastes and feelings–to the choice of a way of life different from the prevailing one–with the benevolent attitude of Shaftesbury's school of philosophy' (p. 247). In a related issue, Eleanor M. Sickels is right to point out that the *Elegy* must not be read as one of the poems about 'mortuary landscapes' that constitute the 'graveyard school' or poetry, if only because it lacks the paraphernalia of the horrible that distinguishes the latter. *The Gloomy Egoist* (New York: Columbia University Press, 1932), pp. 27–28.

36. Thomson can conveniently supply us with another passage for comparison. In 'Spring,' the poet is led by his theme

> to the Mountain-brow
> Where sits the Shepherd on the grassy Turf,
> Inhaling, healthful, the descending sun.

Around him feed his many-bleating Flock,
. . . .
They start away, and sweep the massy Mound
That runs around the Hill; the Rampart once
Of iron War, in ancient barbarous Times,
When disunited BRITAIN ever bled,
Lost in eternal Broil: ere yet she grew
To this deep-laid indissoluble State,
Where *Wealth* and *Commerce* lift the golden Head;
And o'er our Labours, *Liberty* and *Law*,
Impartial, watch, the Wonder of a World. (ll. 832–48).

The Seasons, p. 42.

37. John Barrell points to the contrast between the 'jocund' dead ploughmen and the 'singular, plodding and weary' ploughman of the opening lines. For Barrell, the poet of the *Elegy* has no connection with the present peasant community, and 'if he thinks he could have had [any connection] with that in the past, this is because he is at liberty to recreate that community on his own terms, just as he wants it to be.' *The Dark Side of the Landscape: The Rural Poor in English Painting 1730–1840* (Cambridge: Cambridge University Press, 1980), p. 158. Most poets who wrote on rural affairs forged imagined communities, past or present, in their poems—the important detail is the role alienation, historical or existential, played in the construction of these fond communities.

38. Joshua Scodel offers a parallel observation on eighteenth-century 'paternalistic epitaphs' which commemorate 'the simple, generic virtues of such lowly creatures as contented labourers and devoted servants': 'Though they celebrate a realm of supposedly uncontested social values, such epitaphs are in fact nostalgic responses to, and participants in, vast and unsetting social change. In the face of the mounting tension between classes that accompanied the onset of capitalist relations, epitaphs upon exemplary members of the lower orders, or upon animals such as faithful dogs that could represent the lower orders, attempt to demonstrate in a radically new way the enduring mutual affection of high and low.' *The English Poetic Epitaph*, p. 10. Scodel's fine survey is particularly sensitive to literary-historical shifts in epitaphic forms of 'defining, in credible fashion, the social role of the dead' (p. 10).

39. Thomas Edwards suggests, similarly, that an 'elegy is of course a poem about death itself, but it is also a demonstration of how death

is best observed and commemorated—no literary elegy is ever without a certain reflexive consciousness of its own status as memorial object.' However, when he goes on to claim that in the *Elegy* the 'country churchyard, like the ruined castles and abbeys that dot the landscape in so many eighteenth-century poems and paintings, is a sign of cultural amnesia, so to speak, the loss of one's particular awareness of a particular past,' my reading differs from his. Rather than being a sign of 'cultural amnesia,' I see the country churchyard as a signifier for community memory, wherein the loss of the particular is constantly recuperated in its merging with the organic, the communal, the social. As Edwards himself realises, 'storied urns and animated busts' ('ruined castles and abbeys') are different because they represent 'the bewildering *surprise* death is to a world intent on power and achievement.' *Imagination and Power: A Study of Poetry on Public Themes* (London: Chatto & Windus, 1971), pp. 126–27.

40. Addison, *Works,* ii. 96–98.
41. Samuel Johnson, *Poems,* ed. David N. Smith and Edward L. McAdam (Oxford: The Clarendon Press, 1974), pp. 76–77.
42. Lonsdale compares this line with 'Rich with the spoils of nature' (Browne, *Religio Medici,* i. xiii) and 'For, rich with Spoils of many a conquer'd Land' (Dryden, *Palamon and Arcite,* ii. 452). *Gray,* p. 126.
43. Lonsdale, *Gray,* p. 128.
44. Johnson, 'Thomas Gray,' p. 470.
45. In the *Elegy* too, the discovery of the death of the poet-figure is enacted within an account of the daily, unceasing cycles of nature:

> '*One morn* I missed him on the customed hill,
> 'Along the heath and near his favourite tree;
> '*Another came*; nor yet beside the rill,
> 'Nor up the lawn, nor at the wood was he;
>
> '*The next* with dirges due in sad array
> 'Slow through the church-way path we saw him borne.
> (ll. 109–14; my italics)

46. See Chapter II, n. 7.
47. John Sitter, *Literary Loneliness in Mid-Eighteenth Century England* (Ithaca: Cornell University Press, 1982), p. 102.
48. Wordsworth, 'Essay on Epitaphs,' in *Literary Criticism,* p. 100.
49. 'Essay on Epitaphs,' p. 102. Wordsworth does warn against such 'readings' of epitaphs: 'But an epitaph is not a proud Writing shut up

for the studious; it is exposed to all, to the wise and the most ignorant, it is condescending, perspicuous, and lovingly solicits regard; it's story and admonitions are brief, that the thoughtless, the busy and indolent, may not be deterred, nor the impatient tired . . . it is concerning all, and for all' (p. 103). For Wordsworth, an epitaph must both be read and foreclosed to reading, a double move that the *Elegy* also thematises as the injunctions to read (l. 115), and not to read (ll. 125–26) the epitaph. For a discussion of the general cognitive and tropological constitution of this double move in Wordsworth, see Paul de Man, 'Autobiography as De-Facement,' in *Rhetoric of Romanticism*, esp. pp. 72–81.

50. De Man, 'Anthropomorphism and Trope in the Lyric,' in *Rhetoric of Romanticism*, esp. pp. 239–43, 260–62.
51. The word 'bosom' here signals to us that this is the final stage of the problematic of poetic power and responsive audience that the word 'breast' brought into play in the West *Sonnet*, and earlier in the *Elegy*.
52. Paul de Man, 'Hypogram and Inscription: Michael Riffaterre's Poetics of Reading,' *Diacritics* 11 (1981), p. 31.
53. De Man sees such a phenomenalisation as central to the intelligibility of the lyric. See his 'Lyrical Voice in Contemporary Theory,' in *Lyric Poetry: Beyond New Criticism*, eds. Patricia Parker and Chavira Hosek (Ithaca: Cornell University Press, 1985), p. 55.
54. December 18, 1750, *Correspondence*, i. 335. Walpole had circulated the *Elegy*, in manuscript, to some of his friends.
55. *Correspondence*, i. 341–42. Gray parodies, in part, the letter he received from the publishers of the *Magazine of Magazines*. In discussion, Judy Frank pointed out that Gray's mimicry of their over-wrought language reveals, among other sensitivities, a genteel horror prompted by his cultural and class values.
56. 'The Preface,' *Magazine of Magazines* (London: William Owen, 1751), i. ii. Walter Graham, in *English Literary Periodicals* (New York: Thomas Nelson & Sons, 1930), describes the *Magazine of Magazine* as one of many 'parasites among magazines [which] have little to recommend them and may be easily dismissed' (p. 171).
57. For dates and details see Lonsdale, *Gray*, pp. 110–12.

IV

What Daring Spirit . . . ?

But I will not be silent about those praises which are mine by right, nor the deeds already predestined, prophesies of our country's reknown. The time will come when you will see whole crowds hastening aloft in a great procession, and the first colonists emigrating to the moon, giving up their familiar hearths; meanwhile, the old inhabitant gazes in astonished silence and from afar descries strange new birds, a flying fleet.

As once Columbus sailed across the watery plains of an unknown sea to see the lands of Zephyr, new realms; so the shores around and the waves look on in wonder at the iron-clad ranks, the regiment of monsters, and gigantic beasts full of armed men, and the inimitable lightning. Soon I see treaties made and traffic between the two worlds, and troops of men gathered under a sky with which they have grown familiar. England, which for so long has held sway over the sea and so often set the winds to work and ruled the waves, will assume the symbols of power in the sky, will bring her wonted triumphs even here and have dominion over the conquered air.

—Thomas Gray, 'Luna Habitabilis' (1737)

Yet might your glassy prison seem
A place where joy is known,

Where golden flash and silver gleam
Have meanings of their own.
—William Wordsworth,
'Gold and Silver Fishes in a Vase' (1829)

ODE ON THE DEATH OF A FAVOURITE CAT, DROWNED IN A TUB OF GOLD FISHES

In February 1747, Gray wrote a short 'memorial' poem in response to a request from Walpole, one of whose cats had drowned in a goldfish bowl. This poem, which Gray thought 'rather too long for an Epitaph,'[1] was 'Ode on the Death of a Favourite Cat, Drowned in a Tub of Gold Fishes.' Walpole's request, and Gray's witty, mock-elegaic ode, are paradigmatic of the conventions of the literary culture of eighteenth-century English gentlemen: we have here a familiar scenario of literary production as cultured exchange. However, our concern has been to broaden the enquiry into Gray's poetics to notice the ways in which his poems tap into larger socio-cultural discourses, and to pay particular attention to the rhetorical mechanisms by which these discursive positions empower the poetically-speaking subject. In that context, this *Ode* provides a fine example of how even such incidental verse often draws strength from, and facilitates, contemporary socio-political discourses of mercantile and imperial expansion. Further, Gray's deployment of a historically characteristic imagery of woman as fallen, avaricious consumer, makes possible an assurance of tone and authority that is missing from most of his other poems.

The literary contours of the discourses of mercantilism and empire, and literature's shaping role in the contemporary definition of a British 'national' identity, have been traced by those critics and historians who have surveyed the many 'patriotic' or 'panegyric' poems of the period.[2] A few critics have noticed the fact that many of these poems also function as imaginative apologias for commerce, or as deliberate and consistent mystifications of the imperial process.[3] While we would expect to (and do) see continuities of images, themes, and world-views in late seventeenth-and eighteenth-century poems on public themes,[4] such continuities also extend into, and structure, the most 'occasional' private poems, which turn into palimpsestic records of the influence of empire on the poetic imagination.

If there is a single recurrent imperative in what might be described as the ideological project of such poems, it can be characterized as the impulse towards domestication (a getting ready for by getting used to), towards repeated and varied enactments of certain cultural, political, and economic themes such that they are assimilated and consolidated as the hegemonic outlook of the nation-state. Of the ensemble of motifs that make up this repetition and variation, (negative) representations of 'femaleness' and female desires function especially effectively as ideological surrogates for the playing out of the more anxious scenarios of imperial desire. Gray's ode, which takes the overt form of the animal fable, is also an allegorical satire on women and a displaced account of the eighteenth-century British domestication of the imperial ideal. The point will be to unravel the representational, literary, and socio-historical codes that enable it to perform equally and effectively at all these levels.

The *Ode* has usually been read as one of the many eighteenth-century moralizing tales that take women as their satiric or ironic subjects. This reading of course recognises the appropriate formal or generic context for the *Ode,* but we must remember that such sub-genres served a particular historical and ideological purpose. As recent, especially feminist, criticism is making us increasingly aware, the 'late seventeenth and early eighteenth centuries mark a critical point in the codification of modern strategies for conceptualizing women,'[5] and moralizing tales on ('characters' of) women are centrally representative of such codification. When poets of this period wrote about women, Ellen Pollack points out, 'they were inescapably confronted with the necessity of establishing some relation to what were becoming, to what to some extent already had become, the representational codes of modern sexual ideology.'[6]

The maxims that constitute the last stanza of Gray's allegorical *Ode* make quite clear that the poem is addressed to the figure (representational code) of woman as excessive, mindless, amoral consumer:

> From hence, ye beauties, undeceived,
> Know, one false step is ne'er retrieved,
> And be with caution bold.
> Not all that tempts your wandering eyes
> And heedless hearts is lawful prize;
> Nor all that glisters gold (ll. 37–42)

Addison, in *The Spectator* 15, draws a parallel moral from a similar set of cautionary tales: 'I have often reflected with myself on this unaccountable humour in womankind, of being smitten with everything that is showy and superficial; and on the numberless evils that befall the sex, from this light fantastical disposition.' In this *Spectator*, Addison also recounts details of the death of Camilla in Book 11 of Virgil's *Aeneid* (a passage that lines 16–24 of Gray's *Ode* allude to as well) and concludes on this note: 'This heedless pursuit after these glittering trifles, the poet (by a nice concealed moral) represents to have been the destruction of his female hero.'[7]

Both Gray and Addison mean the connection they make between women's desire for the 'showy and superficial' and an inevitable moral downfall to be normative and paradigmatic. To that extent, Gray's and Addison's efforts are of a piece with what John Sekora has described as the larger contemporary attack on 'luxury.' As Sekora demonstrates, such moral criticism expresses not only 'a theory of value, an ethic for both individuals and nations,' but also 'a theory of history, an explanation of both personal and collective decline in the past.'[8]

For some of Gray's contemporaries, history offered compelling evidence that the presence of moral corruption caused the social and historical decay of nation-states and civilizations. Such evidence was seen as having more than just a retrospective explanatory power—read appropriately, signs of contemporary moral laxity could prefigure and foretell decline and fall. This predictive capacity gave such 'theories of history' a particular and partisan urgency in the eighteenth century. In this age of mercantile expansion and nascent empire, the warnings of history were constantly invoked by those who were made uneasy, or rendered marginal, by such commercial and imperial 'progress.' Gray's response too was based on the connectedness of moral and national decline: 'The doctrine of Epicurus is ruinous to society: It had its rise when Greece was declining, and perhaps hastened its dissolution, as also that of Rome; it is now propagated in France and in England, and seems likely to produce the same effect in both.'[9]

Perhaps the best example of the contemporary use of theories of 'collective decline in the past' is John Dyer's *The Ruins of Rome* (1740), which concludes with a diagnostic warning:

> Vain end of human strength, of human skill,
> Conquest, and triumph, and domain, and pomp,
> And ease and luxury! O luxury,
> Bane of elated life, of affluent states,
> What dreary change, what ruin is not thine?
> . . . .
> Dreadful attraction! while behind thee gapes
> The unfathomable gulf where Asshur lies
> O'erwhelmed, forgotten; and high-boasting Cham;
> And Elam's mighty pomp; and beauteous Greece;
> And the great queen of earth, imperial Rome.
>
> (ll. 533–45)[10]

Laurence Goldstein's reading of Dyer emphasizes the tightrope that eighteenth-century ideologues of imperial power had to walk in their efforts to both propagate, and warn against, the doctrine of empire: 'Rome, according to Dyer, became the victim of her own success; she perished by the surfeit of goods accumulated as her due reward for strength and skill. So long as empire is motivated by 'proud desire/ Of boundless sway, and feverish thirst of gold' (ll. 454–55) so long will it remain virile, orderly, and the possessor of 'proud security.' But the quest of gold must remain pure; when it degenerates into a quest for ease, when gold is alchemised into the leaden riots of hedonism, then the national will becomes soft, a prey for vandals.'[11]

The eighteenth century is full of texts like Dyer's, generated by poets responding to the possibilities and the anxieties attendant on the prospect of a British empire. These texts, as Laura Brown says of Pope's (construction of) Virgil, 'serve as a nationalist and expansionist ideal, and yet sustain an anti-materialist moral standard'; it is thus that they are 'the supreme exemplar[s] of Augustan humanism.'[12] One feature of this humanism, one important way in which these texts of caution and warning serve to perpetuate a 'nationalist and expansionist' ideology, is that they deflect, or reinflect, general arguments against 'luxury' and moral corruption by retelling these arguments as tales of errant female figures. Two complementary effects are registered: social anxieties are focused —displaced onto, and contained by, a thematically appropriate negative construction of the female. Simultaneously, the functional mythology and discursive strategies of contemporary sexual ideology are further consolidated.

As Louis Landa writes, Pope's Belinda 'and others like her, were [represented as] the beginning and the end, the stimulus to 'the adventurous merchant' whose ships roamed 'securely o'er the boundless main' from Lapland to 'the sultry line'; and they were the final recipients of the exotic products, 'the glitt'ring Spoil' from Indian grottoes, from the frozen north and the southern seas.'[13] Landa goes on to quote from James Ralph's *Clarinda, Or the Fair Libertine* (1729):

> For them the Gold is dug on Guinea's Coast,
> And sparkling Gems the farthest Indies boast,
> For them Arabia breathes its spicy Gale,
> And fearless Seamen kill the Greenland Whale.
> For them the Murex yields its purple Dye,

And orient Pearls in sea-bred Oisters lye;
For them, in clouded Shell, the Tortoise shines,
And huge *Behemoth* his vast Trunk resigns;
For them, in various Plumes, the Birds are gay,
And *Sables* bleed, the savage Hunter's Prey!
For them the *Merchant*, wide to ev'ry Gale,
Trusts all his Hopes and stretches ev'ry Sail,
For them, O'er all the World, he dares to roam,
And safe conveys its gather'd Riches home.[14]

In this construction, women are seen as requiring, justifying, and legitimizing the expansion of the British overseas trade. In Laura Brown's formulation, 'Mercantile capitalism itself, with all its attractions as well as its ambiguous consequences, is attributed to women, whose marginality allows them to serve, in the writings of celebrants and satirists alike, as a proxy for male desires, male anxieties.'[15] This double displacement not only conceals the real acquisitive agency but also deflects onto women ('For them . . .') the ultimate authority for the violence that accompanied mercantile and imperial expansion. The poet can thus be appropriately moral, sympathetically enumerating the victims of this search for riches—whales, Murex, oysters, tortoises, elephants, birds, sables—even as his verse celebrates the daring merchant's safe conveyance of the world's 'gather'd Riches *home*' (emphasis added).

At this historical moment, the en-gendering of figures of female vanity, luxury, and consumerism is often explicitly tied up with the creation of structural alibis that will validate and affirm overseas expansion.[16] It is in such a context that Gray's drowned-cat ode must be read.

'Twas on a lofty vase's side,
Where China's gayest art had dyed
  The azure flowers, that blow;
Demurest of the tabby kind,
The pensive Selima reclined,
  Gazed on the lake below. (ll. 1–6)

This opening stanza resonates with two specific pre-texts, John Gay's *The Toilette* (1716, 1720) and Pope's *The Rape of the Lock* (1714). In Gay's poem, Lydia, a London belle past her prime, mourns her faithless beau (who has left her for a younger woman, Chloe) as she is at her morning 'toilette.' In compensation for his absence, she thinks she might

> dress, and take my wonted range
> Through ev'ry *Indian* shop, through all the *Change;*
> Where the tall jarr erects his costly pride,
> With antic shapes in *China's* azure dy'd;
> There careless lies the rich brocade unroll'd,
> Here shines a cabinet with burnish'd gold. (ll. 51–56)[17]

Appropriately, it is there, in the '*Change,*' that Lydia's faithless Damon 'first convers'd with *Chloe's* eyes' (l. 60). The site of the celebration of mercantile commodities is, as we might expect, also the location of the inevitable moral downfall of the female consumer.

Selima, like Belinda, and perhaps even more immediately than Lydia, is juxtaposed with an object whose repetition functions as an index of the literary nexus between the figuration of women and the mercantile and imperial process: the 'lofty Chinese vase' (ll. 1–5).[18] Pope's *Rape of the Lock,* in a memorable zeugma, had firmly established an ironic cultural equivalence between women's honor and imported commodities. In the poem, Belinda's guardian-spirit Ariel wonders uneasily about the catastrophe to come:

> Whether the Nymph shall break Diana's Law,
> Or some frail *China* Jar receive a Flaw,
> Or stain her Honour, or her new Brocade. (ii. 105–108)[19]

In lines 1–5 of the *Ode,* Gray's strategic placing of the reclining Selima 'on a lofty vase' of Chinese design insinuates a similar connection, one whose implications become obvious only later, once the sexual theme is made explicit.

At this moment, Selima is 'pensive,' but lest we read her as somehow intellectual (a feline 'Thinker'!), we are quickly told that her pensiveness is a product of her narcissism; she is gazing 'on the lake below':

> Her conscious tail her joy declared;
> The fair round face, the snowy beard,
> The velvet of her paws,
> Her coat that with the tortoise vies,
> Her ears of jet and emerald eyes,
> She saw, and purred applause. (ll. 7–12)

Like Eve in *Paradise Lost*, who 'pin'd with vain desire' (iv. 466) for her own image, Selima is pleased with what she sees. Her narcissism, however, celebrates more than just natural charms. Selima's very image seems made up of the commodities that Laura Brown, writing of Pope's Belinda making herself up in her toilet mirror (i. 121–44), describes as 'the spoils of mercantile expansion . . . these are the means by which her natural beauty is "awakened." In other words, imperialism dresses nature to advantage here.'[20] Selima, made up of 'velvet,' tortoise-shell (cf. line 7 of James Ralph's *Clarinda* quoted above), 'jet' and 'emerald,' is very much the creature (the creation) of a commodity culture.

This moment is clear in its moral valence; its ideological use soon becomes obvious as well. This scenario of vanity turns out to be a specific prelude to an allegory of excessive and ultimately destructive desire for acquisition—and not only a prelude, but, strangely enough, almost the entire cause: it seems that Selima's narcissistic gazing into the mirror-like water surface allows further events to transpire:

> Still had she gazed; but 'midst the tide
> Two angel forms were seen to glide,
> The genii of the stream:
> Their scaly armour's Tyrian hue
> Through richest purple to the view
> Betrayed a golden gleam. (ll. 13–18)

The goldfish are invisible for the long moment of Selima's mirror stage, during, that is, the entire second-stanza articulation and pleasureful integration of reflected body parts (ll. 7–12). But underneath this surface, as it were, lurk the signifiers of the real essence of women, waiting for the moral lapse (in this case, Selima's narcissism) that will bring them to the surface. The agency of sight in stanzas two and three is deflected by the syntax. In stanza two, we are told that Selima 'saw' (l. 12) her reflection, but in stanza three, the goldfish 'were seen to glide' (l. 14). The shift from the active to the passive voice causes a momentary loss of certainty about who exactly is seeing. The implication seems to be that Selima when gazing narcissistically can clearly see her appearance, but that the moment of the emergence of her 'real' signification is less clearly visible to her.

The fish, with their 'golden gleam,' are not simply signifiers of wealth or riches.[21] Their 'Tyrian hue' aligns them with mercantile commodities; they are, at this historical juncture, living reminders of the potential of a trading empire. Louis Landa refers to homiletic literature in which 'London's resemblance to the ancient city of Tyre is a constant refrain.' He suggests that the 'mercantile zest or hunger, the feeling for material objects,' settled on representations of Tyre as a symbol of national eminence.[22] Tyre was seen as furnishing (in the words of Alexander Catcott, a clergyman):

'all the western parts [of the world] with the commodities of *Arabia, Africa, Persia,* and *India* . . . Its fleets brought in to *Tyre* all the useful and rare commodities of the then known world . . . silver, iron, tin, lead, brass, slaves, horses, mules, ivory, ebony, emeralds, purple, embroidery, fine linen, coral, wheat, pannag, honey, oil, balm, wine, white wool, bright iron, cassia, calamus, precious cloaths, lambs, rams, goats, spices, precious stones, gold, blue cloaths and rich apparel.'[23]

This enthusiastic cataloguing of commodities pays homage to the effect that mercantile capitalism had upon the imagination and rhetoric of eighteenth-century Britain, an effect condensed into the single signifier 'Tyre.' Gray's Tyrian goldfish, then, swim in overdetermined seas.

It is no surprise that the poem now makes explicit what animal fables usually keep implicit—the allegorical identification of animal characters with human figures—because from the beginning, the powerful logic of the mercantile sub-text has been establishing the structural scapegoat, avaricious woman:

> The hapless nymph with wonder saw:
> A whisker first, and then a claw,
> With many an ardent wish,
> She stretched in vain to reach the prize.
> What female heart can gold despise?
> What cat's averse to fish? (ll. 19–24)

This formal aberration was commented upon as such by Johnson: 'Selima, the cat, is called a nymph, with some violence both to language and sense; but there is [no] good use made of it when it is done; for of the two lines [ll. 23–24], the first relates merely to the nymph, and the second only to the cat.'[24] When the formal requirements of pure allegory (the animal fable) confront the peculiar logic of the mercantile imagination, it is the logic that is decisive. An inversion of formal priorities results; the allegorical sub-text emerges as text, even as dominant text: 'What female heart can gold despise?' The fabular element lingers, of course, but it is anti-climactic, even reductive and redundant: 'What cat's averse to fish?'[25]

The next two stanzas, about Selima's death by drowning, are written in a mock-heroic idiom that emphasises the parodic, heavily periphrastic and euphemistic language of the entire ode:

> Presumptuous maid! with looks intent
> Again she stretched, again she bent,
> Nor knew the gulf between.
> (Malignant fate sat by and smiled)
> The slippery verge her feet beguiled,
> She tumbled headlong in.
>
> Eight times emerging from the flood
> She mewed to every watery god,

Some speedy aid to send.
No dolphin came, no Nereid stirred:
Nor cruel Tom nor Susan heard.
A favourite has no friend! (ll. 25–36)

Earlier, in lines 16–24, the ode had alluded to the death of Camilla in book xi of Virgil's *Aeneid*, reading in the earlier text an appropriate account of a heroic woman's death because of her inability to cleanse herself of a 'woman's desire for booty and spoils' (xi. 782).[26] Such an allusion works not simply to trivialise, or trifle, with the Selima story, but also to establish a continuity of reference to women and their wondrous desire for gold.

A simultaneous trivialising and taking seriously is, of course, only made possible by the form and conventions of the mock-heroic. The mock-heroic deploys an easily recognizable ethically normative discourse (Selima is a 'Presumptuous maid' who tempts 'Malignant fate') even as the genre subverts, through an incongruous misapplication, the ponderous weight of such discourse. The overall effect though is still ideologically appropriate. 'If Selima were a woman,' the form of the fable signals, 'such language would of course be diagnostic and appropriate . . . (un)fortunately, she is only a cat!'

What the mock-heroic also allows Gray's *Ode* is the humorous elaboration of Selima's drowning, while containing, in lines 30–34, the violence of that event in a series of stylized references. This conversion of the pathetic into the bathetic is a standard feature of the mock-heroic, but here it serves an even more important, ideological purpose. The social text that shapes, and is encoded in, this allegory includes an unavoidable perception of the violence that accompanied contemporary mercantile and imperial expansion. The catalogue of victims in the lines from James Ralph's *Clarinda* quoted above demonstrates one way in which this perception surfaces, and Gray's own 'Luna Habitabilis' also gives voice to such an awareness of violence: the moon-scape wonders at 'the iron-clad ranks, the regiment of monsters, and gigantic beasts full of armed men, and the inimitable lightning' that is the first view of British colonists.[27] Even in a poem that is explicitly whimsical and fantastical, on the theme that the Moon is habitable, the violent material basis of the dream of domination surfaces. It does so by a structural displacement—the poem's speaker shifts to the perspective of the imagined 'old' inhabitants of the moon to present this vision of barbarous power. Of course, the whimsy works to divert any serious engagement with the content of the poem.

In the ode, the symptomatic figuration of such violence is the drowning death of Selima, but the proper diagnosis of this symptom is inhibited by a formal and rhetorical encouragement not to take the cat's demise seriously. Line 31 ('Eight times emerging from the flood') therefore turns Selima's struggle into a parody of the epic number three and of the popular belief in the nine lives of a cat. More importantly, line 36 introduces a theme that has previously been latent—the sexuality of female desire, which earlier lines represent as primarily acquisitive, cupidinous, is now defined in sexual terms. The innuendo in the word 'favourite' is clear: Selima is linked to the long tradition of socially transgressive figures whose threatening sexual power and misdeeds are the constant theme of commentators on culture and morality.[28] As a kept woman, a mistress, Selima can certainly have no divine guardians (ll. 32–34) or allies amongst the domestic underclass (ll. 35–36); her fallen moral status rules out the guardians, as her illegitimate social position does the allies.

The surfacing of the sexual theme does not merely add one more negative feature to the representation of the female in the ode; it also marks a strategic rhetorical shift (between generic codes) in the progress of the poem. The use of the mock-heroic to represent the drowning death of Selima allows unsettling, even subversive possibilities to disturb the surface of the allegory being constructed. The codes composing the form of the mock-heroic destabilize as much as assert meanings; as for the content, to elaborate ritually while trivialising and thus to enjoy the imagined spectacle of Selima's death seems at best unfortunately conceited and at worst unfeeling and unsavory.[29] To recuperate and fix fabular meaning, a less recalcitrant, less wittily self-indulgent genre is called for, and the homily of the fallen woman serves ideally.

Twin warnings, against rampant female cupidity and lust, close the poem off (see lines 37–42, quoted above). The generality of the homiletic idiom is perfect for Gray's purposes, allowing easy transitions between the morals of the story. Selima's stretching for the gold(fish) is like the one 'false step' that causes maidenly honor to be lost forever; women's 'wandering eyes' and 'heedless hearts' must be disciplined into learning that not all that seems attractive is 'lawful prize' for sexual conquest. For those of us who (schooled in Johnsonian ways) find the 'From hence' of line 37 an unconvincing connective, it is instructive to remember John Barrell and Harriet Guest's formulation regarding such a rhetorical move in other eighteenth-century poems: 'a successful "transition" was not one which concealed discursive shifts, but which made them appear, at least, to be appropriate and "natural".'[30]

In these stanzas then, the fable of morally and personally destructive female-feline desire at once encodes, displaces and re-tells a historical allegory of trade, mercantile hunger, and violence. The symptoms of this displacement are to be discovered in the fissured, multiple forms of its telling—the fabular and the mock-heroic—even as its uncomfortable effects are dissipated and contained by the homiletic idiom of the final stanza. Such a retelling serves both imperial and domestic ideological interests. It gestures toward the actual overseas theatre of mercantile conquest in reductive, trivial terms but denies genuine perception by refusing to represent that arena adequately. Simultaneously, it creates a normative representational code for women that historically characterises the British eighteenth-century consolidation of the domestic (both family and national) spheres. The process of mystification, then, is two-fold: men's anxieties about the progress of Britain as a trading empire are systematically re-written as narratives of women's lust and depravity, and the potential awkwardness of such a rewriting is dissolved into heavily stylized textual play.

A comment on this distancing effect, which operates throughout the ode, may be in order here. There is no denying (indeed most critics have celebrated) the postured charm of this poem, its 'gentlemanly' archness, its hyperbolic humour, its desire to be read as an elaborate literary joke, a witty jeu d'esprit. To overwhelm that playfulness in a reading designed to tease out the historical and ideological implications of the poem may seem like critical overkill. We must keep in mind though, that notions of the cultured, the charming or the gentlemanly (like all other aesthetic categories of discrimination) can be shown, in their historical deployment, to derive their substance not from any essential codes of literature and reading but from mechanisms of social and ideological consolidation. Thus the form and tone of the poem (which are precisely how the poem 'means' its meanings), far from being proof against any serious discussion, must offer the exact ground which a historically sensitive critical reading maps.

Gray was no jingoist, but he was certainly part of the burgeoning, occasionally anxious, more usually bullish public scenario of British empire that was materializing throughout the eighteenth century. The writing of this master script took many forms, causing, among many more serious and powerful effects, an occasional ode on the loss of a pet to turn into a somewhat baroque effort whose form, figures and rhetoric bear eloquent witness to the influence of the imperial ideal. The ripples of Selima's death by water, then, become in Gray's vision fabular versions of the waves that Britain's imperial progress generated—waves of desire, waves of warning. His little poem, much like the goldfish tub that Selima drowned in, was meant to allow a sparkling, untarnished, *aestheticized* view of its piscine and feline drama. It now appears to us rather as an old curiosity, a somewhat misshapen and oddly appealing literary artifact, its textures and surfaces to be read for evidence of ideological overdeterminations and rhetorical determinations.

We are only now beginning to become aware of how multifaceted and all-absorbing the discourses of British nationalism and empire were, especially in their efflorescence in the eighteenth century. The grand theme of a British national destiny is the discursive center not only for the efforts of the spokesmen of commercial and mercantile interests, for the political machinations of parliamentary chauvinists, and for the rhetorical zeal of the proselytizing missionaries of Christianity or 'civilization,' but also for the far more local (and perhaps more ideologically powerful) attempts by writers, teachers, and purveyors of daily culture to create a consensual national ideology. There is thus scarcely a poet in the period who did not, in public and in private verse, treat (or indirectly represent) the conjunction of the patriotic and the poetic.

A representative example of the forms this conjunction took is George Lyttleton's 'An Epistle to Mr. Pope. (From Rome, 1730).' Early on, the poem contains a thumbnail sketch of political and cultural history, a capsule 'progress of poesy':

> To thee from Latian realms this verse is writ,
> Inspir'd by memory of ancient wit;
> For now no more these climes their influence boast,
> Fall'n is their glory, and their virtue lost;
> From tyrants, and from priests, the muses fly,
> Daughters of reason and of liberty!
> . . . .
> To Thames's flowery borders they retire,
> And kindle in thy breast the Roman fire. (ll. 7–16)[31]

The poem goes on to mourn the decline of Italy as a political, scientific and cultural power (ll. 23–33), and then describes Lyttleton's efforts (in part by kissing, with 'lips devout, some mouldering stone') to rediscover this classical heritage (ll. 33–42). Then, in quite the most interesting development in an otherwise conventional and unimaginative poem, the ghost of Virgil appears before his worshipper's eyes, and proceeds to dictate to him a message for Pope:

> 'Great bard, whose numbers I myself inspire,
> 'To whom I gave my own harmonious lyre,
> 'If, high exalted on the throne of wit,

'Near me and Homer thou aspire to sit,
'No more let meaner satire dim the rays
'That flow majestic from thy nobler bays;
'In all the flowery paths of Pindus stray,
'But shun the thorny, that unpleasing way;
'Nor, when each soft engaging muse is thine,
'Address the least attractive of the nine.
'Of thee more worthy were thy task, to raise
'A lasting column to thy country's praise;
'To sing the land, which yet alone can boast
'That liberty corrupted Rome has lost;
'Where science in the arms of peace is laid,
'And plants her palm beneath the olive's shade.
'Such was the theme for which my lyre I strung,
'Such was the people whose exploits I sung;
'Brave, yet refin'd, by arms and arts renown'd,
'With different bays by Mars and Phoebus crown'd;
'Dauntless opposers of tyrannic sway,
'But pleased a mild Augustus to obey.[32]
'If these commands submissive thou receive,

. . . .

'Approving time will consecrate thy lays,
'And join the patriot's to the poet's praise. (ll. 51–78)

Lyttleton's poem makes it possible to see the warp and the woof of the fabric of nationalist consciousness that was then being woven. There is first the need to establish a cultural continuity with classic achievement, but to do so in terms that insist on the priority of the political; because England is the new home of 'liberty,' science and the muses can follow.[33] There is then the need to define a contemporary literary project: Pope is exhorted 'to raise/'A lasting column to thy country's praise;/'To sing the land' (ll. 61–63). This general poetic exhortation contains a more specific injunction, one that demands that the poet see the connections between formal choices and ideological ends. Pope must no longer write 'meaner satire'

(l. 55), but should walk in 'the flowery paths of Pindus' (l. 57), or otherwise write panegyrical and perhaps epic (l. 54) verse. And finally, there is the promise of poetic authority, power, and achievement. If Pope will obey these 'commands' (l. 73), public acknowledgement will 'join the patriot's to the poet's praise' (l. 78).

In *Liberty and Poetics*, Michael Meehan demonstrates the centrality of 'the idea of liberty [and] . . . the idea . . . of an active history, a national character founded in freedom and a matchless constitution,' to both the political theory and the cultural practice of eighteenth-century England.[34] These ideas emerged from and achieved their fullest and most fervent forms in Whig populism, and went on, in spite of more conservative suspicions of their 'levelling rationalism,' to achieve a sort of national consensus: 'The invocation of liberty, even in the most abstract guise, had a powerful incantatory quality to it and so broad a popular appeal that those promoting either their interest or their ideas under its banner could lay claim to a special disinterest, a truly 'national' mission. That fact alone made those manipulations, in Hume's and Johnson's eyes, all the more entrenched, and all the more insidious.'[35]

As Meehan points out, there were good reasons for the particular rhetorical forms, the 'incantatory quality' of the appeals to the 'new political order,' which invited, especially among the Shaftesburyans, 'enthusiastic rapture at its heavenly symmetries and its kinship with such weighty entities as Truth and Order.' The compelling power of such philosophical sloganeering 'bred a heady rhetoric in mid-century aesthetic contexts; British liberty, dwelling with Concord, Harmony and Order, might act as a pledge, the guarantee of an effective Pythagorean translation of eternal harmonies into local, British forms . . . that would forge of Britain that "new Rome in the West".' This positive aesthetic rapture did not of course have any equivalence in political freedoms: 'poets and panegyrists through the century showed a marked preference for the delineation of more abstract political entities, the "Genius", the "Spirit" of the "Idea" sustaining the political frame rather than the frame itself . . . Liberty in Britain was discernible far more readily there, in the realm of active desire, than in fragile legal forms.' As Meehan notes, in most eighteenth-century usage the term liberty 'refers to the British achievement of personal, or *civil* liberty—the security that comes with the rule of law—rather than that broader kind of freedom, *political* liberty, which offers democratic participation in government.'[36]

As Meehan's readings of several eighteenth-century theorists show, such 'patriotic ideas . . . reached far behond the bounds of specifically political verse, and early century panegyric towards a general reshaping of national artistic character.'[37] The idea of a national political and cultural identity in the making (and to be made) is an enormously enabling one, particularly, as we shall see, if the sense of national identity can be predicated upon a prior idea of an international destiny. Meehan's formulation is persuasive: 'This assertion of national singularity, and the attempts to read in the nation's political fortunes the outlines of a new aesthetic, did promote a national confidence among writers, and offered a powerful theoretical urgency to a growing ideal of independence, of taking aesthetic character and artistic ideals from within the culture, from the directives offered in the national history, from the demands of local government and from the demonstrated strengths of local achievement.'[38]

One of the most easily recognisable tropes of this nationalistic, even jingoistic, aesthetic is the conflation of patriotic subject-matter and poetic inspiration. Taking their cue from devotional poetry, poets like Milton, Marvell, Dryden, Pope, Thomson, Young, and Dyer (and this list includes only the best known poets of the time) claimed that their muse was contingent on the leadership of the ruler, or on domestic prosperity, or on the success of British foreign policy and its commercial and imperial ventures overseas.[39] Pope, for instance, wrote of Windsor Forest as the seat of both the Monarch and the Muse. Thomson, in 'To His Royal Highness the Prince of Wales' (1737), was even more categoric about the connections between poetic felicity and national power:

What though, by years depressed, my muse might bend?
    My heart will teach her still a nobler strain:
How with recovered Britain will she soar,
When France insults, and Spain shall rob no more.
(ll. 27–30)[40]

Perhaps the best example of this poetry of power is Edward Young's *Imperium Pelagi*. In the 'Preface,' Young claims that he is going to write a Pindaric, 'the most spirited kind of Ode,' on Trade, a better subject not being available to an Englishman: 'Trade is a very noble subject in itself, more proper than any for an Englishman, and particularly seasonable at this juncture.' Young is quite clear about why he writes this poem: 'If, on reading this Ode, any man has a fuller idea of the real interest or possible glory of his country than before, or a stronger impression from it, or a warmer concern for it, I give up to the critic any further reputation.'[41] Then, in the 'Prelude,' the syntax of key lines creates a wilful confusion between the winds that transport George II home, the divine inspiration that 'transports' the poet (l. 6), and the trade winds that are the cause of England's commercial power. In all this, though, the poet's position is clear. His song will allow the 'Pine' (the ship bearing George II) to achieve her real immortal destiny:

    Or teach this flag like that to soar
    Which gods of old and heroes bore;
Bid her a British constellation rise—
    The sea she scorns, and now shall bound
    On lofty billows of sweet sound;
I am her pilot, and her port the skies. (ll. 31–36)

THE ALLIANCE OF EDUCATION AND GOVERNMENT

All of Gray's important early poems, including the *Elegy*, demonstrably lack a sense of this new aesthetic of 'national confidence,' and consequently do not share many of the cultural and social strengths that other contemporary authors derived from this confidence. However, in lesser poems like 'Luna Habitabilis' and the Drowned Cat *Ode*, Gray did respond in whimsical ways to the rhetorical and ideological imperatives of this British will to identity as an imperial power and a nation-state, and in other, unfinished work, he in fact attempts to participate in the politico-cultural theorising that enunciated the historical 'singularity' of British nationhood.

In 'The Alliance of Education and Government,' Gray began an ambitious project to chart the political and cultural history of ancient and contemporary civilisations according to currently fashionable theories of the influence of environmental, especially climatic, factors on the development of social, political, and cultural systems.[42] Gray provides a capsule version of such theories in lines 84–87:

> Not but the human fabric from the birth
> Imbibes a flavour of its parent earth:
> As various tracts enforce a various toil,
> The manners speak the idiom of their soil.

Gray abandoned the poem by March 1749. Lonsdale lists several possible reasons (including Gray's own) for this, and accepts William Mason's explanation that when Gray read Montesquieu's *L'Esprit des Loix* (which is, in part, a full exposition of the environment-culture hypothesis), he realised 'that the Baron had forestalled some of his best thoughts.'[43] While this is entirely plausible, it is also significant that Gray's unfinished poem differs from many other English versions of similar theories precisely in what it leaves out. That is, it does not get around to articulating the explicit historical and ideological agenda of these poems, which is the demonstration of the uniqueness of British soil and of its balanced climate, and hence the 'naturalness' of the contemporary British achievement of liberty at home and power abroad.[44] By itself this omission (if we can call it that) means little, but when we remember that the writing of such national histories provided contemporary writers with their most powerful and enabling tropes of authority, it seems strange, if symptomatic, that Gray would have stopped short of exploiting that possibility.[45]

In the 1760's, when asked why he had not finished the poem, Gray, characteristically, offered an aesthetic explanation. Norton Nicholls reports him as saying that 'he had been used to write only Lyric poetry in which the poems being short, he had accustomed himself, & was able to polish every part; that this having become habit, he could not write otherwise; & that the labour of this method in a long poem would be intolerable, besides which the poem would lose its effect for want of Chiaro-Oscuro; for that to produce effect it was absolutely necessary to have weak parts.'[46] While there is no question that Gray was fastidious about his poetry (this is the traditional reason given to explain why he wrote as few poems as he did), this critical fastidiousness can surely not be an adequate answer. Gray had prepared well for this poem; he had been reading about its subject matter, and he had prepared notes on his project, 'hints for his own use in the prosecution of this work,' as Mason called them.

One of Gray's 'maxims' related to this work is the following:

'Those invasions of effeminate Southern nations by the warlike Northern people, seem (*inspite of all the terror, mischief, and ignorance which they brought with them*) to be necessary evils; in order *to revive the spirit of mankind, softened and broken by the arts of commerce, to restore them to their native liberty and equality*, and to give them again the power of supporting danger and hardship; so a comet, with all the horrors that attend it as it passes through our system, brings a supply of warmth and light to the sun, and of moisture to the air' (my italics).[47]

This maxim can function equally as a theory of historical explanation and as an apologetics for imperialism, and in 'The Alliance of Education and Government,' it does both. Gray writes of 'The blue-eyed myriads from the Baltic coast' who make the 'prostrate south' yield 'her boasted titles and her golden fields' (ll. 51–53). This scenario of conquest by hardy Northerners is parallel to another which features the 'iron-race [of] the mountain cliffs,' whose homelands—'rocky ramparts'—are 'the rough abode of *want and liberty*' (my italics), and who are therefore led to ravage and 'insult the plenty of the vales below' (ll. 88–99).

These abstacted, near allegorical, accounts of the history of warfare in the European theatre are interesting particularly in that they bring into play Gray's ideas about how the 'arts of commerce' lead to social decline, to the softening of 'the spirit of mankind.' The 'effeminate' South, in luxurious decay, *needs* the 'warlike' spirit of the 'North' ('inspite of all the terror, mischief, and ignorance' that accompanies it), in order to be restored to its 'native liberty and equality.' This ingenious and somewhat contradictory argument might suggest only historical oddity were it not for the fact that its axes of value and power also structure another conceptual divide, that between Europe (North) and Asia (South), thus rendering it part of the contemporary search for a general apologetics for imperialism. The equation is not quite that simple though; and in Gray's poem it is rendered more complicated by the threatening presence of contemporary non-European empires, that of the Islamic monarchies of Asia (India?) and Turkey:

> Proud of the yoke and pliant to the rod,
> Why yet does Asia dread a monarch's nod,
> While European freedom still withstands
> The encrouching tide, that drowns her lesser lands,
> And sees far off with an indignant groan
> Her native plains and empires once her own?
> Can opener skies and suns of fiercer flame
> O'erpower the fire that animates our frame,
> . . . .
> Need we the influence of the northern star
> To string our nerves and steel our hearts to war?
>
> (ll. 58–69)[48]

Gray's mapping of the North-South equation onto this contemporary geopolitical situation is just as defensive as John Brown's claim that the climate of Britain would ensure that Britons would never remain 'slaves' (see n. 44). The 'northern star' (l. 68) will oversee 'European freedom' (l. 60) and guard it from becoming Asian servitude, 'proud of the yoke and pliant to the rod' (l. 58). The call to arms (ll. 68–69) is thus defensive, but also, if one were to work out the full logic of this North-South, freedom-slavery equation, a potential rationalisation for the European presence in enslaved Asia: the 'warlike' Northerners would 'restore to them their native liberty and equality.' (In our discussion of lines 58–65 of Gray's 'Progress of Poesy,' we will see how such a logic makes possible the argument that the replacement of one imperial presence—that of Spain—by another—Britain—will actually be the replacement of 'tyranny' by 'law.')

Little of this, of course, gets worked out in the fragment of the poem Gray completed. What the poem in its present form shows us is Gray's particular interest in the connections between geo-politics, 'nature' (human and environmental) and culture. What it also promises is that Gray would have had to work through a variety of conceptual contradictions if he had tried to develop more fully the scheme of the poem. He chose never to do that, citing (to Norton Nicholls) the difficulties of aesthetic resolution rather than the more recalcitrant, less conscious problems of conceptual ambiguity. Gray was never quite certain of his position vis-a-vis the ideology of empire in Europe or elsewhere, and the 'Alliance between Education and Government' emphasises his inablity to come to terms easily with cultural, environmental or historiographical explanations of the rise and fall of empires. Some years later, however, having become, in James Steele's words, 'a confirmed patriot and a diffident imperialist'[49] Gray came back to the same themes, this time with much greater success.

THE PROGRESS OF POESY

Gray wrote 'The Progress of Poesy. A Pindaric Ode' between late 1751 and December 1754. In its attempt to resolve the problematic of literary authority, to find a position and a discourse from within which the poet can speak with power, this poem is similar to Gray's earlier 'Ode to Adversity.' Here too, the opening address is to the ritual figures and old goddesses of poetry, who are invoked in their most benign and enabling aspects. The first strophe, according to Gray's note to line 3, is about the 'various sources of poetry, which gives life and lustre to all it touches . . . its quiet majestic progress enriching every subject':

> Awake, Aeolian lyre, awake,
> And give to rapture all thy trembling strings.
> From Helicon's harmonious springs
> A thousand rills their mazy progress take:
> The laughing flowers, that round them blow,
> Drink life and fragrance as they flow.
> Now the rich stream of music winds along,
> Deep, majestic, smooth, and strong,
> Through verdant vales and Ceres' golden reign:
> Now rolling down the steep amain,
> Headlong, impetuous, see it pour:
> The rocks and nodding groves rebellow to the roar.
>
> (ll. 1–12)

The (un)remarkable fact about this stanza is its calm conventionality. The invocation of Pindar (l. 1) and Mount Helicon, and the depiction of poetry as 'the rich stream of music' that flows 'deep, majestic, smooth, and strong,' through 'verdant vales and Ceres' golden reign,' suggests an unruffled, non-agonistic relationship between the poet and the (topoi that signify) the traditional discourses of poetic origin and achievement. In fact, every detail is so comfortable and harmonious, so conventional, that even the figuration of the poetic sublime (which is at once the natural sublime) in lines 10–12 carries little power. The cataract of sound ('*Now* rolling down . . .') is scarcely built up, and has in any case been prepared for three lines before ('*Now* the rich stream of music winds along'), the opening repetition of 'now' connecting, making continuous, taming. Indeed, as Lonsdale points out about these three lines, most 'such descriptions contain 'headlong' and/or 'impetuous', as well as echoing rocks'[50]—Gray's language here rebellows to the roar of poetic convention just as surely as his rocks do.

The antistrophe furthers the celebration of the powers of poetry and poetic inspiration. Gray's note to l. 13 says that the address to the 'Sovereign of the willing soul' is about the 'Power of harmony to calm the turbulent sallies of the soul.' Both Mars and Jove are lulled into peace by the power of music:

On Thracia's hills the Lord of War
Has curbed the fury of his car,
And dropped his thirsty lance at thy command.
Perching on the sceptred hand
Of Jove, thy magic lulls the feathered king
With ruffled plumes and flagging wing:
Quenched in dark clouds of slumber lie
The terror of his beak and lightnings of his eye.
(ll. 17–24)

The sentiment, especially when phrased this way, is largely conventional. In fact, as Gray himself notes, lines 20–24 are 'a weak imitation of some incomparable lines' in the first Pythian of Pindar.[51] At the level of diction, as much as at the level of sentiment or figure, these lines are meant to echo powerful moments in the classical tradition.

The epode continues to elaborate themes similar to those of the strophe and the antistrophe, invoking Aphrodite (l. 29) and her companion Loves (l. 28) and Graces (l. 37) in an enactment of how 'voice' and 'dance' are both 'tempered to thy warbled lay' (ll. 1–2):

Frisking light in frolic measures;
Now pursuing, now retreating.
Now in circling troops they meet:
To brisk notes in cadence beating
Glance their many-twinkling feet. (ll. 31–35)

The 'frolic measures' of these lines offer an effective metrical contrast to the 'slow melting strains' of lines 36–41, in which the queen approaches and

> With arms sublime, that float upon the air,
> In gliding state she wins her easy way:
> O'er her warm cheek and rising bosom move
> The bloom of young desire and purple light of love.

Not just in theme and image, but also in cadence and form, Gray's verses pay homage to the Muse they address, and whose poetic attributes they incorporate and enact.

Perhaps the best indication of just how completely 'The Progress of Poesy' attempts to come to terms with its precursors (both poems by other poets and earlier poems by Gray) is the second strophe (stanza II. 1). In much the same way as lines 25–48 of the 'Ode to Adversity' rewrote lines 51–100 of the Eton *Ode* (see discussion in Chapter II), lines 42–47 now read, in the figures of poetry, sustaining and didactic possibilities:

> Man's feeble race what ills await,
> Labour, and penury, the racks of pain,
> Disease, and sorrow's weeping train,
> And death, sad refuge from the storms of fate!
> The fond complaint, my song, disprove,
> And justify the laws of Jove.

The threatening 'ministers of human fate' (l. 56) of the Eton *Ode* are here contained within a quatrain whose end-stopped last line creates a pause strong enough to set these lines off from the rest of the strophe, to present them within quotation marks, as it were. The displacement is now complete. The 'fond complaint' (notice the benign condescension of the 'fond') is no longer the poet's; he is raised above it in fuller poetic comprehension. His song is in fact going to 'disprove' this complaint; his voice, one with that of Milton's, will 'justify the laws of Jove' (l. 47).

At this moment, the voice of the poet appears as the canonical voice of the poetic tradition, ventriloquising all its figural and metaphysical force, claiming for it a full explanatory power: 'Say, has he [Jove] given in vain the heavenly Muse?' (l. 48). However, the rhetorical form of this question, which knows an answer but does not speak it, should give us pause, especially as the next lines work by extended figural indirection to make their point:

> Night and all her sickly dews,
> Her spectres wan and birds of boding cry,
> He gives to range the dreary sky:
> Till down the eastern cliffs afar
> Hyperion's march they spy and glittering shafts of war.
> (ll. 49–53)

Gray's later gloss is quite necessary to make sense of these lines: 'To compensate the real and imaginary ills of life, the Muse was given to Mankind by the same Providence that sends the Day by its chearful presence to dispel the gloom and terrors of the Night.' This elaborate diurnal, and naturalising, analogy for the healing powers of poetry is meant as a convincing answer to the question posed in line 48. Rather than do that, however, these lines succeed primarily in emphasising that Gray was never able to ventriloquise easily, or without discordance, the voices of poetic authority. For him, imitation and echo never quite turned into assertion or statement. Rather, the anxiety of other voices spoke elaborate figures and a somewhat baroque rhetoric, as here, when the powers of the 'heavenly Muse' are established in lines 49–53 only through an obscure piling up of images and topoi derived from canonical representations of 'the heavenly Muse.'[52]

At this point, from stanza II. 2, 'The Progress of Poesy' becomes an orthodox progress piece, which traces the geographical movement of the Muse through (cultural) history.[53] The desire to universalise the presence of poetry produces an ingenious itinerary for the Muse as she moves from the 'ice-built mountains' (l. 55) of the North to 'Chile's boundless forests' (l. 59). In each case, the moral is the same:

Her track, where'er the goddess roves,
Glory pursue and Generous Shame,
The unconquerable Mind and Freedom's holy flame.
(ll. 63–65)

Johnson objected to the cultural geography of this stanza ('The caverns of the North and the plains of Chile are not the residences of "glory" and "generous shame"'), but forgave all because this stanza so resolutely linked 'poetry and virtue,' 'the goddess' and 'Freedom's holy flame.'[54]

Both these geographical references are informed by contemporary ideological resonances. In his study of 'the Goths in England,' Samuel Kliger points out that the 'Whig aesthetic' included a theory of British genealogy and psychology that was based on their being a 'branch of the Gothic-Teutonic folk,' whose 'vigor, hardiness, and zeal for liberty' were explained by 'the frigid temperature of the Gothic habitat in the northern regions.'[55] To have the Muse visit the frozen North, in order to teach the glories of 'The unconquerable mind' (l. 65), is thus to establish a 'whiggish,' nationalistic genealogy for British liberty and poetics.[56] Similarly, as James Steele points out, 'Gray had . . . very good reason, quite apart from any love of the exotic, for cherishing primitive Creole art.' Admiral Anson, who had sailed across the globe between 1740 and 1744, expressly attacking Spanish shipping and settlements in Mexico, Peru, and Chile, had reported that 'the recurring theme of the Chilean natives' "recitals and representations" was revenge against their tyrannical Spanish masters and their French allies.' Their 'enthusiatic rage' convinced Anson that 'alliance with the Creole natives would [enable] Britain to challenge Spanish tyranny and establish British law on the continent of South America.'[57] Gray's recovery of a cultural alliance with 'the savage youth' (l. 60), then, parallels Anson's discovery of a potential political alliance with them.

After this detour through the primitive and the exotic (and by implication, through nationalist genealogy and imperial possibility), the second epode describes, in Gray's words, the 'Progress of Poetry from Greece to Italy, and from Italy to England,' that is, the progress of the classical Muse. As Johnson first suggested, this stanza is both burdened with weighty signifiers of the classical tradition and unsound in its mapping of cultural and political history: 'The third stanza sounds big with 'Delphi,' and 'Aegean,' and 'Ilisus,' and 'Maeander,' and 'hallowed fountain,' and 'solemn sound'; but in all Gray's odes there is a kind of cumbrous splendour which we wish away. His position is at last false: in the time of Dante and Petrarch, from which he derives our first school of poetry, Italy was overrun by 'tyrant power' and 'coward vice'; nor was our state much better when we first borrowed the Italian arts.'[58] Johnson's quick Tory eye sees clear through the whiggish pretensions of Gray's scheme, and refuses the schematic association of 'liberty' and poetic achievement in lines 77–83:

> Till the Sad Nine in Greece's evil hour
> Left their Parnassus for the Latian plains.
> Alike they scorn the pomp of tyrant power,
> And coward Vice that revels in her chains.
> When Latium had her lofty spirit lost,
> They sought, oh Albion! next thy sea-encircled coast.

What Johnson sees as two separate problems, the 'cumbrous splendour' of the verse and the falsity of its historical scheme, are more profitably understood as connected, the former produced by the poet's discomfort about the latter. This is not to claim that Gray is deliberately, but uneasily, falsifying history, but to remind us that each time Gray's poems thematise his relation to poetic traditions, and so include topoi, figures and allusions which predominantly signify the prior usages and conventions of poetic practice, the language of the poems seems overwhelmed by a (near-hysterical) piling up of detail. This results in the grotesque, obsessively enumerated figures of the Eton *Ode*, but also in the more benign catalogue of Adversity's attendants in the 'Ode to Adversity,' and the roll-call of resonant names—Delphi, Aegean, Ilissus, Maeander,

Greece, Parnassus, Latium, Albion—that marks the 'Progress of Poesy.' For Gray, to write poems meant always engaging with the actual, conventional *writing* of poetry, and this transaction, even when determinedly non-agonistic, still ripples the surface of his texts.

The last three stanzas of the poem define and celebrate, after the arrival of the Muse in Albion, a nationalist and English canon.[59] The third strophe, dedicated to Shakespeare, gives us the Bard as an infant—'Nature's darling'—by the banks of the 'lucid Avon' (ll. 84–85):

> To him the mighty Mother did unveil
> Her awful face: the dauntless child
> Stretched forth his little arms and smiled. (ll. 86–88)

This vignette of the *magna mater* and the 'dauntless child,' as in the portrayals of Milton and Dryden that follow, encodes the moment of daring that seems prerequisite for great poetic achievement. Shakespeare reaches instinctively to embrace the 'awful face' of the Muse, and is rewarded with immortality and the 'golden keys' of poetic ability:

> 'This can unlock the gates of joy;
> Of horror that and thrilling fears,
> Or ope the sacred source of sympathetic tears.'
> (ll. 91–94)

This representation of Shakespeare's abilities and achievement is derived from ideas about literary genius that the Longinian revival in the eighteenth century propagated. This combination of Longinian aesthetics of the sublime and the impassioned figuration associated with the Pindaric results in a 'pomp of machinery'[60] that celebrates rhetorical and figural excess. The muse is portrayed as 'the mighty Mother' with 'awful face' (ll. 86–87); poetic affects are described in terms of the unlocking of the 'gates of joy;/ Of horror . . . and thrilling fears' (ll. 92–93) or the opening of 'the sacred source of sympathetic tears' (l. 94): the sheer excitement of poetic possibility here is far removed from the contemplative, subdued Muse of the 'Ode on the Spring,' or the 'fruitless' mourning that characterises the poetic voice in the West *Sonnet*. However, this does not mean that there is an unproblematic identification between the poet-figure and the representation of canonical poetic power. For him, the Muse is no nurturing madonna, but is a potentially threatening figure whose awful aspect must be countenanced before success will be granted. Also, the vocabulary of sublime achievement in the poem is spoken not so much by the poet as by the 'mighty Mother'—the poet only quotes her in lines 89–94.

This potentially threatening aspect of the accession to poetic power continues in the antistrophe on Milton, who

rode sublime
Upon the seraph-wings of Ecstasy,
The secrets of the abyss to spy.
He passed the flaming bounds of place and time:
The living Throne, the sapphire blaze,
Where angels tremble while they gaze.
He saw; but blasted with excess of light,
Closed his eyes in endless night. (ll. 95–102)

Milton, in poetic ecstasy, sees what angels tremble to gaze on, but is struck blind by that vision. Ironically, as Lonsdale's annotations emphasise, much of the diction and most of the allusions are under debt to Milton, especially to *Paradise Lost*. In these lines, the language of Gray's poem enacts a compelling flirtation with (a rhetorical form of) poetic power—in the post-Miltonic tradition, it is no longer possible to speak of sublime or ecstatic poetic moments without Miltonic figures, but to be Miltonic is also, potentially, to be blinded, disfigured.

The same tension structures the depiction of Dryden, whose 'less presumptuous car' is drawn 'Wide o'er the fields of glory' by

Two coursers of ethereal race,
With necks in thunder clothed, and long-resounding
pace. (ll. 103–06)

His glorious flight takes the form not only of heroic couplets, but also of lyric, irregular odes:

> Hark, his hands the lyre explore!
> Bright-eyed Fancy hovering o'er
> Scatters from her pictured urn
> Thoughts that breathe and words that burn. (ll. 107–10)

This is a powerful iconography: Dryden riding in a speeding chariot pulled by spirited (and spirit-like) horses, his hands exploring the instrument symbolic of poetry, his inspirational angel hovering over, illuminating and ennobling him. Too powerful, perhaps—in an instant, the image is gone, the harsh mid-sentence break of the next line emphasising the fleeting, ethereal quality of the vision:

> But ah! 'tis heard no more—[61]

These 'words that burn' have an Icarian quality. High-flying certainly, but broken in mid-course, lost in the brief moment of a sigh. As with Shakespeare and even more with Milton, the sublime is paid for dearly.

The dialectic of identification and distancing that is enacted in these representations of the powers and the perils of poetry is next thematised, the muse addressed directly with a question:

> Oh! lyre divine, what daring spirit
> Wakes thee now? (ll. 112–13)

Once again, we are squarely within the problematic of all of Gray's poems: discursive position and poetic authority. To wake the 'lyre divine' is itself a daring act (l. 112), but to aspire to the poetic condition or cultural status of Shakespeare, Milton, or Dryden is far more daunting. Thus, ironically, even in the writing of a Pindaric ode, the poet-figure disavows sublime flight and suggests a less magnificent persona:

> Though he inherit
> Nor the pride nor ample pinion,

That the Theban eagle bear
Sailing with supreme dominion
Through the azure deep of air:
Yet oft before his infant eyes would run
Such forms that glitter in the Muse's ray
With orient hues, unborrowed of the sun. (ll. 113–20)

Towards the end of his Pindaric, the poet disclaims the soaring pride and 'supreme dominion' of the 'Theban eagle,' Pindar. Fly he does, but not too high, and the visionary forms his 'infant eyes' see 'glitter' with hues 'unborrowed of the sun.' In this last image, the Icarian sub-text resonates again. In the ode, to be too near the sun is to risk all, yet the sun remains the powerful image for poetic inspiration. The double-edged nature of inspiration, its enabling and its disabling quality, is constantly emphasised: when the Muse is Hyperion, its supposedly illuminating and 'chearful presence' is transfigured into the 'glittering shafts of war' (l. 53). Milton's gaze is 'blasted with excess of light,' and his blindness represented as the absence of sun-light: 'Closed his eyes in endless night' (ll. 101–02). Even Dryden's 'less presumptuous car' (l. 103) nevertheless borrows from traditional representations of the daily race of Hyperion's or Apollo's chariot.

Exemplary poetic achievement is fraught with danger, and emulation carries with it the fear of disfigurement. Thus, it is safer not to smile into the awful face of the *magna mater*, not to spy into the secrets of the abyss, not to race over the fields of glory, not to soar with supreme dominion—this series of negations cumulatively suggests how not to achieve the sublime authority of Shakespeare, Milton, Dryden, and Pindar. This disavowal of powerful inheritance is marked (in a manner similar to that of the fissuring of the deictics of the self in lines 93 and 96 of the *Elegy*) by the shifting of the integrated first-person form in line 46 ('The fond complaint, my song, disprove') to the distanced, third-person representation of the poet-figure in 113–23: 'Though he inherit,' 'his infant eyes,' 'Yet shall he mount and keep his distant way.' The Miltonic confidence of line 43 had permitted the 'my' that encourages the identification of the poet-figure and the author, the subject of the enounced and the subject of the enunciation. The subsequent recognition of the obverse, or the awful consequences, of this confidence (ll. 86–111) now leads to a splitting—the poet-figure thematised as abjuring such confidence, with the author enacting precisely such a soaring flight by writing a Pindaric.[62] And Gray's is no lesser Pindaric either; it is, after all, about the Progress of Poesy, about the *translatio* of cultural achievement that, historically, leads to British power and national poetic pride.

Yet the poet-figure is not left with a 'not quite' or 'less than' status. The grounds of his discursive authority are shifted away from the aesthetics of sublimity to what sound like the truisms of morality:

> Yet shall he mount and keep his distant way
> Beyond the limits of a vulgar fate,
> Beneath the Good how far—but far above the Great.
>
> (ll. 121–23)

He is not to be quite the 'Theban eagle,' but he definitely mounts above 'a vulgar fate.' The long distance between canonical apotheosis and the practices of Grub Street is suggested here. Exactly what this quick cultural and literary positioning has to do with the last line is not clear, though it is tempting to read the sudden (and unwarranted) invocation of the priorities of ethical discourse as necessary to lend authority to the attempt to distance the 'limits of a vulgar fate.' Finally, however, there is no way to avoid the repetition of the uneasiness that had accompanied the position of the poet-figure in the *Elegy* too: constituency-less, somewhere between the 'Good' and the 'Great,' solitary in his 'distant way,' separated from the vulgar crowd. No matter that Gray tries strongly to speak the canonical or the prophetic voice; his ideologically contradictory condition lingers. Threatened by the bourgeois forms of social and cultural consensus in eighteenth-century England, Gray's representations of the poet enact a flirtation with various forms of public power, but then dwindle into the aloof, the marginal, the solitary.

Johnson's criticism of 'The Progress of Poesy' is based on an engaging, insistently literal reading of the poem. Form, his remarks imply, can only be justified by function and meaning. His objections to the 'pomp of machinery' in the Shakespeare stanza (III. 1) could characterise his entire critique of the poem: 'Where truth is sufficient to fill the mind, fiction is worse than useless; the counterfeit debases the genuine.'[63] Gray writes a particular form of 'counterfeit' precisely because he is less confident of being able to enact the 'truth' than Johnson, and his choice of the Pindaric is appropriate for a variety of reasons. The form allows thematic discontinuities and syntactic and metrical irregularities, and is thus suited to the kind of highly qualified, internally dialogic, panegyric that is Gray's subject. Traditionally, the Pindaric is a form sharing the public concerns of the epic and the private explorations of the lyric, the exact combination Gray requires. Also, in contemporary usage, the Pindaric had an appreciably high-cultural tone, one that Gray clearly has in mind when he inserts, as the epigraph to 'The Progress of Poesy' and 'The Bard,' a phrase from Pindar: 'vocal to the Intelligent alone.'[64]

Carol Maddison, in her history of the Ode, describes the Pindaric in terms that make it easy to see why this form must have had the fascination it did for Gray at this stage of his poetic career:

> The Pindaric ode was characterized by passages of gnomic wisdom, and by what may seem strange at first, considering its public performance and semi-sacred character, by references to the poet's private feelings, to his inspiration, his artistic intent, his poetic rivals, and the jealously he rouses. These personal references are not so strange, however, if we recollect the particular function of the epinician, which was to celebrate the glorious achievements of the Greek race recalled through this latest example of prowess, beauty, and divine grace. The poet, like the hero, was part of the glory of Greece . . . He, too, was god-inspired and as much a part of the great deed as the victorious athlete. Therefore it is not inappropriate that he should comment on his inspiration and how it is working, that he should celebrate his triumph too.[65]

For Gray, the very history of this form offers its poet a public, even a national voice and presence. A celebration of the glories of Albion involved a simultaneous glorification of the poet, and thus offered an intrinsic or a structural basis for the authority of the poetic voice. However, as our analysis of the ambivalences in Gray's attitudes toward the domestic and imperial glory of Britain has shown, Gray could no more write an unqualified national panegyric than he could locate himself (as a poet) within an enabling socio-cultural consensus or community. Hence, he could never fully commit himself to the soaring flight of the 'Theban eagle,' but had to fly his separate, aloof way. Constantly, in themes and forms, Gray's poems enact larger ideological discontinuities, surging towards affirmations of poetic, even prophetic power, eddying away into moments of self-reflexive doubt that stem from the lack of a constituency to authorise such a powerful presence.

THE BARD

Louis Kampf, in his provocative challenge to 'The Humanist Tradition,' offers this reading of Gray's 'The Bard': the poem 'suggests an image of the poet desperate to be part of the life of a whole people; it is an image which can become real only in an egalitarian and classless society. Gray could not look forward to—indeed, could not fathom—such a society. However, he at least knew how to look back.'[66] In its retrospect of English history, 'The Bard' also looks back to a figure from one of Gray's earliest translations, the 'wondrous sage' with 'awful . . . mien' of Tasso's *Gerusalemme Liberata* (see Chapter II, pp. 54–55). That figure, one of the first representations of prophetic vision and power ('no common guide') in Gray's poetic canon, wears the halo of extra-poetic authority that comes from being inscribed within a socio-cultural and discursive system that designated an important role to the oracular and the vatic.[67] That is, in order for (the powers of) the Bard to be credible, he has to be shrouded in the sublime obscurities of a historically earlier and less well known period, and represented as not so much *within* this period, as transcendent of it, rising above it.

The particular form this transcendence takes in 'The Bard' is prophecy. Mason reports Gray's 'original argument' to 'The Bard':

'The army of Edward I as they march through a deep valley, are suddenly stopped by the appearance of a venerable figure seated on the summit of an inaccessible rock, who, *with a voice more than human,* reproaches the King with all the misery and desolation which he had brought on his country; foretells the misfortunes of the Norman race, and *with prophetic spirit declares,* that all his cruelty shall never extinguish *the noble ardour of poetic genius* in this island . . . His song ended, he precipitates himself from the mountain, and is swallowed up by the river that rolls at its foot' (my italics).[68]

The Bard is portrayed as foretelling several centuries of English history, and even more significantly, telling this history primarily as a narrative of revenge for the wrongs done to him and his fellow poets. Gray's wry comment to Stonhewer about this is self-consciously apt: 'I annex a piece of the Prophecy; which must be true at least, as it was wrote so many hundred years after the events.'[69] The familiar tension between the 'truth' of the discourse of poetic power and Gray's discomfiture about its rhetorical and representational claims is evident here, as it is perhaps in the song-ending, spectacular, suicidal leap of the Bard.

Accordingly, a complete identification with the Bard is constantly avoided in the poem. The drama of the poem is communicated in a counterpoint of several voices. There is that of the poet-figure, who does little more than describe the Bard's initial appearance (ll. 9–22) and death (ll. 143–44), and who recognises the power of the Bard's song:

> And, with a master's hand and prophet's fire,
> Struck the deep sorrows of his lyre. (ll. 21–22)

He is granted the insight (the historical hindsight?) to recognise the sublime authority of the Bard's utterance, but is also witness to the Bard's plunge 'to endless night.' In all this, he can know himself as less than, but also more secure than, the figure of ultimate inspiration; a knowledge that he shares with the poet-figure of 'The Progress of Poesy,' who could recognise soaring poetic flight (Shakespeare, Milton, Dryden, and Pindar) but also knew that such Icarian power was not for him.

This limited presence for the poet-figure is emphasised further both by the slightness of his reporter's role in the enounced of the poem and by the huge contrast between his dull, though somewhat awe-struck voice and the awe-inspiring intensity of the speech of the Bard and of the bardic chorus. The poem opens in the full, raw power of the Bard's voice:

> 'Ruin seize thee, ruthless king!
> 'Confusion on thy banners wait,
> 'Though fanned by Conquest's crimson wing
> 'They mock the air with idle state.
> 'Helm nor hauberk's twisted mail,
> 'Nor even thy virtues, tyrant, shall avail
> 'To save thy secret soul from nightly fears,
> 'From Cambria's curse, from Cambria's tears!' (ll. 1–8)

This immediacy of tone is, consistently, the power of the poem. As Fredric Bogel points out, the 'dimmest region of speech in the poem is in fact the present. The poet says relatively little, and what he does say is not immediate and dramatic, like the bard's address, but narrative and descriptive. As a present utterance, then, the poem directly acquires its vocal strength from the past, from the voice of the bard.'[70]

The source of the Bard's power, and this is particularly important to our discussion of Gray's ideas about cultural and discursive consensus, is not just (demonic) inspiration, but an entire community of bards and fellow-sufferers. The roll-call of dead bards (ll. 28–33) is a naming into being of community and tradition: Hoel, Llewellyn, Cadwallo, Urien, Modred—the names recall not so much individuals as voices that could (and do, in the poem) speak together. Also emphasised is the pathos of their connection to their land. Cambria's mountains, 'each giant-oak and desert cave' (l. 23), mourn with the Bard for those 'whose magic song/ 'Made huge

Plinlimmon bow his cloud-topped head' (ll. 33–34). 'Cambria's fatal day' (l. 27) is marked by the loss of its freedom and the slaughter of its bards, who now lie 'smeared with gore and ghastly pale' (l. 36).

Similarly, the Bard finds consolation, and quite literally, new life, in the enabling conjunction of the patriotic, the poetic, and the prophetic:

> 'Dear lost companions of my tuneful art,
> 'Dear as the light that visits these sad eyes,
> 'Dear as the ruddy drops that warm my heart,
> 'Ye died amidst your dying country's cries—
> 'No more I weep. They do not sleep.
> 'On younder cliffs, a grisly band,
> 'I see them sit, they linger yet,
> 'Avengers of their native land;
> 'With me in dreadful harmony they join,
> 'And weave with bloody hands the tissue of thy line.'
> (ll. 39–48)

Because they die for and with their country, their story (and the prophetic narrative they now weave) can avenge their native land. The history of their past embodies them with voice in the present, and power over the future. They can stand for the rejuvenated future of their communities precisely because they were sacrificed as symbols of that community.

The second strophe, antistrophe, and epode are all spoken by the bardic choir, and prophesy the 'misfortunes of the Norman race' of conquerors and kings in England. This massed voice utilises all the heavy machinery of the oracular tone, all that Johnson (as have many readers since) found unacceptable and described as the 'glittering accumulations of ungraceful ornaments; they strike, rather than please; the images are magnified by affectation; the language is laboured into harshness. The mind of the writer seems to work with unnatural violence . . . His art and his struggle are too visible, and there is too little appearance of ease and nature.'[71] The laboured harshness and violence of the language is better understood in the terms that Bogel sets out, as symptoms of Gray's need for 'an image of such a past,' than as a sorry error of poetic technique. The language of prophecy here, full with performative excess, is witness to the contemporary urgency of poetic desire for (the fiction of) a time when poets could declaim, and in the very act of declamation, move mountains and men, *make history happen*. The recovery of such a speech, then, is scarcely unproblematic—a speaking of a language that no one has ever heard but all know to exist—and results in the kinds of gothic excess that Johnson, somewhat tautologically, found not 'truth.'

In 'The Bard,' this tone certainly helped obscure the historical references, such that Gray was forced to append explanatory notes to the 1768 edition. He complained to James Beattie that the allusions in the poem were 'to a few common facts to be found in any six-penny History of England by way of question & answer for the use of children.'[72] (It is likely though, that his peevishness stems less from being thought obscure than from being reminded that the performative sublimities of oracular discourse were in fact no match for the specific realities of the expectations of contemporary readers.) The three stanzas of the bardic chorus work their way through predictions of the lonely death of Edward II and his son the Black Prince; the death through starvation of Richard II; the 'ruinous civil wars of York and Lancaster'; the many secret murders supposed to have been perpetrated in the Tower of London; the gory deeds of Richard III, finally ending in a couplet that emphasises the agency of the bards in getting under way this pageant of horrors:

> 'Now, brothers, bending o'er the accursed loom,
> 'Stamp we our vengeance deep and ratify his doom.
>
> (ll. 95–96)

Their work done, the spectral chorus disappears from the Bard's sight (ll. 99–104).

The poem then shifts, in the third strophe, from these negative prophecies to an ideologically far more potent mode—the prophetic celebration of English history and power. This shift is enacted in a manner representative of the complex connections between Gray's experience of contemporary poetic deprivation and the compensations offered by the articulation of a poetics of British patriotism. Having woven the fate of the Norman line, the bards vanish, reminding the surviving Bard of his solitariness in the face of the enemy:

> 'Stay, oh stay! nor thus forlorn
> 'Leave me unblessed, unpitied, here to mourn.
>
> (ll. 101–02)

This moment of his loneliness is, however, also the moment of his greatest (historical) insight. He sees 'solemn scenes' descending from 'Snowdon's height' (ll. 105–06), and marvels at what he sees:

> 'Visions of glory, spare my aching sight,
> 'Ye unborn ages, crowd not on my soul!
> 'No more our long-lost Arthur we bewail.
> 'All hail, ye genuine kings, Brittania's issue, hail!
>
> (ll. 107–10)

This vision of the glories of Brittania's future that would begin with the ascension of the Tudors crystallises around the 'form divine' of Elizabeth:

> 'Her eye proclaims her of the Briton-line;
> 'Her lion-port, her awe-commanding face,
> 'Attempered sweet to virgin-grace.
> 'What strings symphonious tremble in the air,
> 'What strains of vocal transport round her play!
>
> (ll. 115–20)[73]

There is a reciprocity between the figure of the monarch and the musical halo that surrounds and celebrates her—the power of one is the power of the other. In the seventeenth and eighteenth centuries, Elizabeth was always the symbol of the strong ruler in whose reign England first developed a powerful commercial and military presence overseas. In this vision of her surrounded by the powers of music ('strings symphonious,' 'strains of vocal transport') the Bard thus projects the fantasy of the instrumental connection between poetry and (national) power that Gray's later poems encode.[74]

The fantasy is powerful enough to breathe life into the dead Taliessin (ll. 121–22), whom Gray described as 'Chief of the Bards, flourished in the VIth Century.' Taliessin is invoked in order that his powers should

> 'The verse adorn again
> 'Fierce war and faithful love,
> 'And truth severe, by fairy fiction dressed. (ll. 125–27)

This Spenserian four-point combination of militarism and romance, the moral and the imaginative, is a prelude to the Bard's sketch of English literary achievement, beginning with Shakespeare:

> 'Pale Grief and pleasing Pain,
> 'With Horror, tyrant of the throbbing breast.
> 'A voice as of the cherub choir
> 'Gales from blooming Eden bear. (ll. 129–32)[75]

In his 'original argument' to the poem, Gray had the Bard promising Edward II that 'men shall never be wanting to celebrate true virtue and valour in immortal strains, to expose vice and infamous pleasure, and boldly censure tyranny and oppression.'[76] However, Lonsdale reports Mason as believing that Gray 'was unable in practice to persuade himself that the English poets from Spenser to Addison had been preoccupied with the celebration of "true virtue and valour"; and Mason remembered that "the Ode lay unfinished by him for a year or two on this very account".'[77] Gray's ambivalence is played out in the poem in the distancing of this song of English literary achievement—the vision of the literary future is lost 'in long futurity' (l. 134) and expires for the Bard. (Gray's 1768 note said this fading vision concerned the 'succession of Poets after Milton's time').

The prophetic vision of an authentic 'Briton' national and poetic achievement is now directed against Edward, 'Fond impious man,' fond in that he believes that poetic power can be vanquished (ll. 135–40). The Bard now knows differently:

> 'Enough for me: with joy I see
> 'The different doom our fates assign.
> 'Be thine despair and sceptred care;
> 'To triumph, and to die, are mine. (ll. 139–42)

The fateful conjunction of triumph and death is ennobling, but it also captures the contradictory dynamic of the prophetic and the historical, of the enabling power of the poetic imagination and the debilitating reality of the poet bereft of constituency.[78] As Bogel puts it, while the Bard 'is in one sense the poem's principal exemplar of substantial experience, [he] is nevertheless isolated from the full flourishings of heroic poetry and permitted to triumph only in memory or prospect. His suicide . . . is therefore less a gesture of romantic defiance than an emblem or fulfillment of his true situation.'[79] Once more, the ending of Gray's poem brings us back to the problematic of poetic and discursive authority that he, acutely sensitive to the socio-historical urgencies of his day, was always concerned with.

'THE TRUE TRAGEDY OF AN EIGHTEENTH-CENTURY GENTLEMAN.'[80]

David Garrick, trying to compensate for the lack of public enthusiasm (or rather the loud public confusion)[81] about the *Odes*, wrote a poem '*To* Mr. Gray, *on the Publication of his* Odes *in* 1757.' The most interesting verses are the first and the last two (v and vi):

> Repine not, GRAY, that our weak dazzled eyes
> Thy daring heights and brightness shun;
> How few can track the eagle to the skies,
> Or like him gaze upon the sun! (ll. 1–4)

. . . .

Yet droop not, GRAY, nor quit thy heav'n born art,
Again thy wond'rous powers reveal;
Wake slumb'ring virtue in the Briton's heart,
And rouse us to reflect and feel!
With antient deed our long chill'd bosoms fire,
Those deeds which mark'd Eliza's reign!
Make Britons Greeks again—then strike the lyre,
And Pindar shall not sing in vain. (ll. 21–28)[82]

Garrick saw clearly the nationalistic imperative in Gray's *Odes*, particularly the 'Englishing' of Celtic cultural topography in the apotheosis of Elizabeth in 'The Bard.' The song of Pindar that Gray wrote was meant as the precise form for the announcement of national history and poetic destiny, for the poet's flirtation with public power. However, Garrick could not in any way avoid the problem, which Gray too knew well, that the reading public who had so avidly purchased copies of the *Odes* had pronounced them to be obscure and difficult. Interestingly, Gray had known that such a reaction might indeed develop. Before the poems were printed, even Walpole had complained about obscurity, and had suggested notes. Gray's response was somewhat standoffish: 'I do not love notes, though you see I had resolved to put two or three. They are signs of weakness and obscurity. If a thing cannot be understood without them, it had better be not understood at all. If you will be vulgar, and pronounce it *Lunnun*, [see 'The Bard,' l. 87] instead of London, I can't help it.'[83]

Lonsdale includes a full survey of this issue in his notes to the *Odes*.[84] He suggests that Gray, perhaps 'embarrassed by the great popularity of the *Elegy* . . . seems to have been determined to puzzle all but the most learned of his readers, as is clear from the brief motto . . . "*vocal to the Intelligent alone*".' Lonsdale also reports Gray's comment in his copy of the 1757 *Odes*: 'The words of Pindar prefixed to them . . . were prophetic of their fate: Very few understood them; the multitude of ranks called them unintelligible.' Also worth quoting here is a summary comment Gray made to Mason (in a letter dated September 7, 1757) shortly after the publication of the *Odes*:

> I would not have put in another note to save the souls of all the *Owls* in London. it is extremely well, as it is. nobody understands me, & I am perfectly satisfied. even the Critical review . . . that is rapt, & surprised, & shudders at me; yet mistakes the Aeolian Lyre for the *Harp of Aeolus* . . . if you hear anything (tho' it is not likely, for I know, my day is over) you will tell me. Ld Lyttleton & Mr Shenstone admire me, but wish I had been a *little clearer*. M^{r} (Palmyra) Wood owns himself disappointed in his expectations. your Enemy, Dr Brown, says I am the best thing in the language. M^{r} F:^{x}, supposing the Bard sung his song but once over, does not wonder, if Edward the Ist did not understand him . . . 'tis very well: the next thing I print shall be in Welch. that's all.[85]

'[F]or I know, my day is over,' Gray writes, and suggests a poem in Welsh would be as culturally intelligible as the *Odes* and 'The Bard' had been—there is condescension here, and resentment, and a proleptic sense that the world of poetry had expanded beyond his classical compass, his dated navigational methods.

Gray's response is typical of the contradictions that bedevilled his career as a poet. Even as he wrote to locate himself within the national aspiration for power, even as these later poems make clearly defined attempts to sing of public themes in public ways, he could not shake himself of the fear that such poetry would submerge him in a sea of vulgar readers, till he would be, at least culturally, one of them. He could not take any but a snobbish tone about such proceedings. In 1768, eleven years after the first edition, Gray included both an expanded commentary, and this sour 'Advertisement,' in the new edition: 'When the Author first published this . . . he was advised, even by his Friends, to subjoin some few explanatory Notes; but he had too much respect for the understanding of his Readers to take that liberty.'[86]

Gray wrote at a time when the celebration of nationalistic pride and imperial strength began to assume a significant place in the ideological project of a 'Great Britain.' Gray's *Odes* suggest his awareness of the scope, and the enabling power, of this poetic and cultural project. However, his choice of form, and the determined density of recondite historical and poetic allusions which comprise 'The Progress of Poesy' and 'The Bard,' suggest his ambivalent, complicated relationship with the idea of a public culture. As this analysis has shown, these poems function within, and derive a great deal of their energy and performative force from, the contemporary drive towards a consolidated thematics of British cultural, social and political power. In their complex repetition of themes, arguments and formal features, however, these odes also enact a fear of the assimilatory, cooptative features of the bourgeois culture in the making. The attractions of a public poetic authority based on a nationalistic and patriotic poetics beckoned one way; the fear of cultural cooptation pointed to another. The *Odes* are riven by such fissures. In these poems, Gray proved at best a reluctant public prophet; in fact, in his choice of representational methods, in his marginalia, in all his peevish editorial comments, Gray seems to be looking distastefully at the large mass of his readers and saying: there, but for the obscure grace of the Pindaric, go I.

NOTES

1. Gray to Horace Walpole, March 1, 1747, *Correspondence*, i. 272. Lonsdale records the details of the writing of this ode in *Gray*, pp. 78–79.
2. See, for instance, W.J. Courthope, *History of English Poetry*, 6 vols. (London: Macmillan, 1910), v. 20–43; C.A. Moore, 'Whig Panegyric Verse, 1700–1760: A Phase of Sentimentalism,' *PMLA* 61 (1926), pp. 362–401; Bonamy Dobrée, 'The Theme of Patriotism in the Poetry of the Early Eighteenth Century,' *Proceedings of the British Academy* 35 (1949), pp. 49–65; A.D. McKillop, *The Background of Thomson's Liberty*, Rice Institute Pamphlet 38 (Houston: Rice Institute, 1951).
3. See Dobrée, 'Theme of Patriotism,' pp. 60–63; Hugh Cunningham, 'The Language of Patriotism, 1750–1914,' *History Workshop* 12 (1981), p. 11.
4. For an full survey of such poems, see George deF. Lord, et al., eds. *Poems on Affairs of State: Augustan Satirical Verse, 1660–1714*, 7 vols. (New Haven: Yale University Press, 1963–75).

5. Ellen Pollack, *The Poetics of Sexual Myth: Gender and Ideology in the Verse of Swift and Pope* (Chicago: Chicago University Press, 1985), p. 2.
6. Pollack, *Poetics of Sexual Myth,* p. 8.
7. Addison, *Works,* ii. 263, 265.
8. John Sekora, *Luxury: The Concept in Western Thought, Eden to Smollet* (Baltimore: Johns Hopkins University Press, 1977), p. 67.
9. Quoted by Lonsdale in *Gray,* p. 91.
10. John Dyer, *The Ruins of Rome: A Poem* (London: Gilliver, 1740), p. 28.
11. Goldstein, *Ruins and Empire,* p. 44. Goldstein's book is a fine study of 'The Evolution of a Theme ["Ruins and Empire"] in Augustan and Romantic Literature.'
12. Laura Brown, *Pope,* p. 43.
13. Landa, 'Pope's Belinda,' p. 223.
14. Landa, 'Pope's Belinda,' p. 223. Landa also specifies a contemporary political-economic reason for the contradictory simultaneous celebration, and satire, of the figure of the woman consumer: 'Belinda as a consumer, the embodiment of luxury ... was ... recognisably the final point in a vast nexus of enterprises, a vast commercial expansion which stirred the imagination of Englishmen to dwell on thought of greatness and magnificence . . . This would be an affirmative response, which very likely would be leavened by a negative one. Wheneas in foreign silks Belinda goes, she could not please the austere mercantilist. Defoe would see her . . . as one who has "dethroned your True-born English Broadcloth and Kerseys"' (p. 234).
15. Laura Brown, 'Commodity Fetishism and Neoclassical Aesthetic Theory: An Essay in Feminist Poetics.' Unpublished essay. 1986.
16. As we might expect, these ideological forms structured poems written by working women no less than they did those written by gentlemen. In her essay on the politics of Mary Collier's work, Donna Landry indentifies a similar rhetorical move in *The Three Wise Sentences, from the First Book of Esdras, Chap. III and IV,* a text 'published with, and conservative ballast to' the poet's more radical *The Woman's Labour: An Epistle to Mr. Stephen Duck* (1939). Landry analyses lines 132 to 235 as enacting 'a displacement of the [the poem's own earlier] discourse of "Woman" as agent of both production and reproduction, indeed also as chief subject of history. Displaced first, we notice, by "Man" in his accumulative and imperialist mode, industrious at home or "wandering" armed abroad in search of "Booty" (164) to bestow on

the woman at home. "Woman" is thus transposed from material producer to consumer.' 'The Resignation of Mary Collier. Some Problems in Feminist Literary History,' in *The New Eighteenth Century*, eds. Felicity Nussbaum and Laura Brown (New York: Methuen, 1987), p. 119.

17. John Gay, *Poetical Works*, ed. G.C. Faber (London: Oxford University Press, 1926), p. 135.

18. The somewhat improbable preposition 'on' in the opening line of the poem seems momentarily to project the drama of fishes and cat, of desire, death and exemplarity onto the painted sides of the China jar. The hesitant, confusing, use of this trope of aesthetic distance, artistic self-conciousness, and cultural displacement might be our first suggestion that the assured, cavalier tone of the ode need not be read on its own terms. On the presence of the China jar see A.R. Humphreys' fine survey of the effect the trade with the East—China, India, Arabia, Persia—had on literary ethics and aesthetics, architecture and gardening, fashions and hobbies in eighteenth-century England. 'Lords of Tartary,' *Cambridge Journal* 3 (1949), pp. 19–31.

19. Gay's 'To A Lady on her Passion for *Old China*' (1725) develops the analogy at length: 'When I some antique Jar behold,/Or white, or blue, or speck'd with gold,/Vessels so pure, and so refin'd/Appear the types of woman-kind: . . . . /How white, how polish'd is their skin,/And valu'd most when only seen!/ She who before was highest priz'd/Is for a crack or flaw despis'd' (ll. 29–40). *Poetical Works*, p. 180.

20. Brown, *Pope*, p. 9.

21. Humphreys sees goldfish as 'a sign of the times. They were brought from China in the seventeenth century—whether early or late is disputed. In the eighteenth, still curious and delightful evidence of alien beauty, they were fit presents for a King's mistress—Mme de Pompadour received some as a gift.' 'Lords of Tartary,' p. 19. This last reference finds an echo in the poem under discussion, when the innuendo in Selima's description as a 'favourite' (l.36) transforms her into another example of female sexual and moral illegitimacy.

22. Louis A. Landa, 'Pope's Belinda,' p. 222.

23. Alexander Catcott, *The Antiquity and Honourableness of the Practice of Merchandize* (1744), qtd. in Landa,' Pope's Belinda,' p. 222. John Edwards also identifies Tyre with London: Tyre 'was deservedly reckon'd the Greatest Mart and Empory of that part of the Universe: Thither was brought the Riches of *Asia, Europe,* and *Africa.* In this also

Britain resembles her, and was justly stiled by *Charles the Great* the Store-House and Granary of the Western World. The Great City of this our Isle may be call'd the Mart of Nations, as Tyre is, Isai. xxiii. 3.' 'That Decay of Trade and Commerce, and Consequently of Wealth, is the Natural Product and Just Penalty of Vice in a Nation,' in *Sermons on Special Occasions and Subjects* (London, 1698), quoted in Landa, pp. 221–22.

24. Johnson, 'Thomas Gray,' p. 466.
25. The 'natural' connection between cat and fish is designed to prove the previous question ('What female heart can gold despise?') purely rhetorical. At this point in the poem, however, it is not clear which equation—female-gold or cat-fish—is 'natural' and which 'rhetorical.'
26. This connection between a woman's death and women's desire is emphasized when the warrior Arruns, who eventually kills Camilla, prays to Apollo for success: 'I seek no plunder and no trophy,/no spoils for defeating the maiden—my fame will come to me/from other deeds' (xi. 790–92). Virgil, *The Aeneid*, trans. James H. Mantinband (New York: Ungar, 1964).
27. The last two paragraphs of Lonsdale's translation of Gray's college poem (written in 1737) are quoted as the epigraph to this chapter. See Lonsdale, *Gray*, p. 303.
28. For a spirited anti-Johnsonian defence of the 'double subject' of the poem, see Geoffrey Tillotson, who reads the subjects as Selima and Homer's Helen. 'Gray's "Ode on the Death of a Favourite Cat, Drowned in a Tub of Gold Fishes",' *Augustan Studies* (London: Athlone Press, 1961), pp. 216–33.
29. The general problematic is of the anxieties attendant upon the voyeuritistic male gaze as it guiltily enjoys the spectacle of female exposure, often as the prelude to enjoying further violence done to that female body. As Edward Snow remarks while discussing the ethical narratives contained in some traditional representations of the biblical Susanna and the Elders (such as Tintoretto's painting), there is a 'convention that justifies male voyeuristic desire by aligning it with female narcissistic self-involvement.' ('Theorizing the Male Gaze: Some Problems,' *Representations* 25 (1989), p. 38.) The depiction of woman's narcissism, then, is meant to attract moral censure, and thus to direct attention from (even perhaps to explain and excuse) the scenarios of violation that follow. As Snow suggests, the pleasure of

the viewer or reader is 'fixed' and rendered complicit via this manoeuvre.

30. John Barrell and Harriet Guest, 'On the Uses of Contradiction: Economics and Morality in the Eighteenth-Century Long Poem,' in *The New Eighteenth Century*, eds. Nussbaum and Brown, p. 136.
31. George Lyttleton, *Poetical Works*, in *The Works of the British Poets*, ed. Robert Anderson, 13 vols. (London: John & Arthur Arch, 1795), x. 256.
32. For a brief account of this poem as one of 'numerous attempts to rescue Augustan art from its unfortunate political associations,' see Michael Meehan, *Liberty and Poetics in Eighteenth Century England* (London: Croom Helm, 1986), pp. 67–68.
33. John Crider calls this belief, 'that the arts move in liberty's train,' a 'great commonplace of Augustan poets.' 'Structure and Effect in Collins' Progress Poems,' *Studies in Philology* 60 (1963), p. 64.
34. Meehan suggests that one index of this centrality is that contemporary writers constantly turn 'for inspiration from more philosophically rigorous views towards the simplest exhortations, and the most deeply mythologised readings of the national history.' *Liberty and Poetics*, p. 19.
35. Meehan, *Liberty and Poetics*, p. 13. On 'the assimilation of ideas from early Whig polemic into aesthetic debate, and the role of definition and redefinition of the nature and effects of liberty, in the evolution of British cultural theory,' see also pp. 20–23.
36. Meehan, *Liberty and Poetics*, pp. 16, 10, 15.
37. Meehan, *Liberty and Poetics*, p. 8.
38. Meehan, Preface to *Liberty and Poetics*.
39. See Laurence Goldstein: 'It is no accident that in *The Ruins of Rome* Dyer describes Julius Caesar in terms he had used previously for his own poetic flight: "he soars in thought/Above all height" . . . As in Spenser's case, the comparison of Roman to English empire, explicit in all elegies of this type, enables the poet to discover his vocation in society.' Goldstein also points out that after *The Ruins of Rome*, Dyer 'chooses in *The Fleece* to "attune the old Arcadian reed" so that it pipes a system of political theory adaptable to the democratic opportunities of the age. It is a salvation of pastor more than flock.' *Ruins and Empire*, pp. 39–40, 42.
40. James Thomson, *Poetical Works*, ed. J. Logie Robertson (London: Oxford University Press, 1908), p. 465.
41. Young, *Works*, ii. 335–36.

42. For reviews of the nature of these theories, and of their practitioners, see Lonsdale, *Gray*, pp. 88–91; Rene Wellek, *The Rise of English Literary History* (Chapel Hill: The University of North Carolina Press, 1941), pp. 31–33, 54–60; John G. Hayman, 'Notions on National Characters in the Eighteenth Century,' in *Huntington Library Quarterly* 35 (1971–72), pp. 1–17.
43. Lonsdale, *Gray*, p. 86.
44. Meehan quotes as an example John Brown, *An Estimate of the Manners and Principles of the Times* (1757): 'Degenerate Englishmen, though free, may be subdued by Foreigners, though Slaves: but the Climate will conquer in its turn: the Posterity of those Slaves will throw off the Yoke, and defy the servile Maxims of their Forefathers' (*Liberty and Poetics*, p. 17). Another good example of the polemical thrust of such ideas is James Thomson's *Liberty* (1735–36), in which the Goddess of Liberty speaks of her naturalisation as British Liberty, and includes, in 'Britain' (Part IV), an 'abstract of the English history, marking the several advances of Liberty, *down to her complete establishment at the Revolution* (my italics).' *Poetical Works*, p. 357.
45. Gray begins 'A Long Story (1750), a ballad-like poem, with an account of 'Lady Cobham's Manor House' at Stoke Poges that goes back to one of its earliest Elizabethan occupants, the 'grave Lord-Keeper' (l. 11) whose dancing skills 'Moved the stout heart of England's Queen / Though Pope and Spaniard could not trouble it' (ll. 15–16). The next stanza, however, disavows even this brief facetious excursus into local and nationalistic English history, and does so in language that might fruitfully be read as expressing Gray's discomfort with contemporary poetic retellings of similar themes, particularly those that utilised a popular poetic form or a colloquial vocabulary:

    What, in the very first beginning!
    Shame of the versifying tribe!
    Your history whither are you spinning?
    Can you do nothing but describe? (ll. 16–20)

46. 'Norton Nicholls' Reminiscences of Gray,' 'Appendix Z,' in *Correspondence*, iii. 1291.
47. Quoted by Lonsdale in *Gray*, p. 91.
48. Lines 62 and 63, in which Europe indignantly groans for the loss of 'Her native plains and empires once her own' are glossed by Lonsdale, as follows: 'Turkey's offensive power diminished after the peace of

Karlowitz in 1699 but she continued to win and lose territory in Europe for several decades. She was victorious over the Austrians and Russians in 1738, crossed the Danube and at the peace of Belgrade in 1739 regained Belgrade and other places which she had lost earlier in the century.' *Gray*, p. 97.

49. Steele, 'The Season for Triumph', p. 215. For a full account of this process, which traces Gray's 'great interest [in] Britain's changing fortunes in the war overseas and related political developments at home', see pp. 214–35.
50. Lonsdale lists examples from Spenser, Dryden, Pope and Thomson. *Gray*, p. 163.
51. Johnson's is the appropriate comment: 'The second stanza, exhibiting Mars' car and Jove's eagle, is unworthy of further notice. Criticism disdains to chase a schoolboy to his commonplaces.' 'Thomas Gray,' p. 467.
52. Ironically, the language of line 53, about Hyperion marching accompanied by 'glittering shafts of war,' is at odds with Gray's prose gloss about 'the Day' and 'its chearful presence.' The presentation of Hyperion, then, derives more from the re-presentation of canonical figures than it does from the local theme of the illuminating presence of the Muse. Johnson's comment is apt: this stanza 'endeavors to tell something, and would have told it had it not been crossed by Hyperion.' 'Thomas Gray,' pp. 467–68.
53. On this issue generally, see Geoffrey H. Hartman, 'Romantic Poetry and the Genius Loci,' in *Beyond Formalism* (New Haven: Yale University Press, 1970), pp. 311–336. Hartman writes about the English attempt, in the seventeenth and eighteenth centuries, 'to create a native poetry which would express the special destiny of the nation. The poetical genius should reflect the genius loci, the spirit of England's religion, history, and countryside. From Milton through Thomson, Gray, Collins, and the Romantics, the idea of a Progress of Poetry from Greece or the Holy Land to Britain is essential' (pp. 317–18).
54. Johnson, 'Thomas Gray,' p. 468.
55. Samuel Kliger, *The Goths in England: A Study in Seventeenth and Eighteenth Century Thought* (Cambridge: Harvard University Press, 1952), p. 2.
56. John Crider, in 'Collins' Progress Poems,' usefully qualifies Aubrey Williams' suggestion that 'the true source of the [Progress Piece]

convention' is the 'medieval and renaissance idea of *translatio studii*, the idea of a transplantation from age to age and from country to country of cultural treasure,' by suggesting that 'underlying this idea is that of *translatio imperii*, the westward movement of empire' (p. 57). (Cf. Williams, *Pope's Dunciad: A Study of Its Meaning* (London: Methuen, 1955), p. 44).

57. Steele, 'The Season for Triumph,' p. 219.
58. Johnson, 'Thomas Gray,' p. 468.
59. Hartman writes that between 'the time of Milton and Gray . . . a formula arose which . . . suggested that the demonic, or more than rational, energy of imagination might be tempered by its settlement in Britain—its naturalization, as it were, on British soil . . . The poem becomes, in a sense, a seduction of the poetical genius by the genius loci: the latter invites—subtly compels—the former to live within via media charms.' 'Genius Loci,' p. 319. As Gray's representations of Shakespeare, Milton, Dryden, and Pindar in 'The Progress of Poesy' show, Hartman's is a usefully diagnostic reading of the precarious domestication of the demon of poetic inspiration.
60. The phrase is Johnson's, who, predictably, objected to Gray's inflated language. 'Life of Gray,' p. 468.
61. James Steele suggests that Gray mourns here 'the hard historical fact that . . . many years had elapsed since great men of Britain had provided the Muses with acts of glory worth singing about in a high Pindaric ode.' This is also the reason why Gray could not complete the poem (started in September 1751), could not wake 'the heroic lyre of Dryden before the autumn of 1754. By that time, a few Britons—with Gray's approval—were once more pitching the tents of war, and winning on '"fields of glory".' 'The Season for Triumph,' p. 220.
62. This dialectic of identification and resistance is played out between the epigraph to the poem and the disavowal of the 'Theban eagle' too. The epigraph, 'vocal to the Intelligent alone,' is taken from the same passage from Pindar (*Olympic Odes*, ii. 81–88) that the identification of Pindar as the eagle is taken from (see Lonsdale, *Gray*, p. 176, n. 115). Gray's ode, like those of Pindar, is 'vocal to the Intelligent alone,' but the poet-figure refuses a similar likeness with Pindar.
63. Johnson, 'Thomas Gray,' p. 468. George N. Schuster, in his summary of the differences between 'eighteenth-century Pindarists and their foes,' suggests that 'the issue was first of all between "lucidity" and "turgidity," between rhetoric conceived of as the learned enrichment

of utterance and rhetoric viewed as the science of simplifying relationships between the maker of discourse and his audience.' In this struggle, the 'irregular ode assumed a recondite, philosophical character.' *The English Ode from Milton to Keats* (New York: Columbia University Press, 1940), p. 170.

64. Gerald MacLean offers a provocative Foucauldian reading that suggests that the 'progress' in the poem is that of English literary history. That is, the poem constructs an allusive genealogy of English poetry, one whose difficult references can only be teased out by those informed in the proper canons of taste. Most readers would read the poem and discover not its 'determinate meanings' so much as their own 'failure of understanding,' thus ratifying a specialist cultural discourse—that of literature—as well as their own subordination to its higher protocols of meaning. MacLean sees Gray's progress poem as part of the process by which 'untold numbers of teachers, writers and talkers—developed the discipline of literary history to be not only a humanistic legitimation of their own will to power, but also as a self-determining political mechanism that carefully marked out the man of taste from the rabble of illiterates, aristocrats and women.' 'So What *Does* Thomas Gray's "Progress of Poesy" Have To Do with Progress?' *Postscript* 2 (1985), pp. 70–71.

65. Carol Maddison, *Apollo and the Nine: A History of the Ode* (Baltimore: The Johns Hopkins Press, 1960), p. 8.

66. Louis Kampf, 'The Humanist Tradition in Eighteenth-Century England—And Today,' in *Fearful Joy*, eds. Downey and Jones, p. 253.

67. Fredric V. Bogel's comment on Burke's ideas of historical inheritance could apply equally to Gray here: 'The past is necessary to us not because it is past but because it is the chief repository of that embodied circumstantiality that can alone make our experience both real and significant. It is a repository of *authority*, and there is desperate need in human life for an authority weightier than that of reason and logic.' *Literature and Insubstantiality in Later Eighteenth-Century England* (Princeton: Princeton University Press, 1984), p. 116.

68. Quoted by Lonsdale in *Gray*, p. 178.

69. August 21, 1755. *Correspondence*, i. 432–33.

70. Bogel, *Literature and Insubstantiality*, p. 94. Bogel's reading of 'The Bard' emphasises its 'splendid but ontologically displaced visions of source and fulfillment, past and future' (p. 96), and its subordination of 'the question of the historical actuality of [the] past . . . to an

exploration of our need for an image of such a past, the effects on present experience of that need, and the nature of the image itself' (p. 97).

71. Johnson, 'Thomas Gray,' p. 470.
72. February 1, 1768. *Correspondence*, iii. 1002.
73. The entire representation of Elizabeth is as awe-inspiring for the Bard as his presence was for the poet-figure. Even within this visionary identification of the poetic with the political or the national, we can see preserved the priority of the latter.
74. James Steele suggests that 'at the heart of the Bard's vision lies the wager that it will be the destiny of post-Norman Britain to prevail in the world', and that Gray 'in "The Bard" expressed the zealous hopes of a patriotic Pittite at a time when British forces were being mustered for their impending worldwide challenge to the *ancien régime* of France.' 'The Season for Triumph,' pp. 223–24. As before, my reading sees hesitations and dialogic uncertainties where Steele sees zeal and fervour.
75. See also 'The Progress of Poesy,' ll. 91–94.
76. Quoted by Lonsdale in *Gray*, p. 178.
77. Lonsdale, *Gray*, pp. 178–79.
78. In a letter to Mason, June 11, 1757, Gray wrote that some friends 'dislike the conclusion of the Bard, & mutter something about Antithesis and Conceit in *To triumph, to die*, w[ch] I do not comprehend . . . pray, think a little about this conclusion, for all depends on it. The rest is of little consequence.' *Correspondence*, ii. 504.
79. Bogel, *Literature and Insubstantiality*, pp. 95–96.
80. This phrase is the sub-title to W. Powell Jones's biography, *Thomas Gray, Scholar*.
81. For an excellent account see W. Powell Jones, 'The Contemporary Reception of Gray's *Odes*,' *Modern Philology* 28 (1930–31), pp. 61–82. Toynbee and Whibley record a 1760 parody of Gray's style, called, somewhat predictably, 'Ode to Obscurity,' whose opening stanza is a good instance of the public reception of Gray's *Odes*:

    Daughter of Chaos and Old Night,
        Cimmerian Muse, all hail!
    That wrapped in never-twinkling gloom canst write,
    And shadowest meaning with thy dusky veil!
        What Poet sings, and strikes the strings?

It was the mighty Theban spoke.
He from the ever-living lyre
With magick hand elicits fire.
Heard ye the din of Modern Rhimers bray?
It was cool M[aso]n: or warm G[ra]y
Involv'd in tenfold smoke.

Correspondence, ii. 674.

82. David Garrick, *The Poetical Works*, 2 vols. (London: George Kearsley, 1785), rpt. (London: Benjamin Blom, 1968), ii. 511–12.
83. July 11, 1757. *Correspondence*, ii. 508.
84. Lonsdale, *Gray*, pp. 157–58, 179–80.
85. Gray, *Correspondence*, ii. 522–24.
86. Quoted by Lonsdale in *Gray*, p. 158.

V

Had I But The Torrent's Might . . .

> . . . to supply the place of [*The Long Story*] in bulk, lest *my works* should be mistaken for the works of a flea, or a pismire, I promised to send him an equal weight of poetry or prose: so, . . . I put up about two ounces of stuff; viz. The Fatal Sisters, The Descent of Odin . . . a bit of something from the Welch, and certain little notes . . . This is literally all; and with all this I shall be but a shrimp of an author.
>
> —Gray to Walpole,
> about the 1768 edition of his Collected Poems[1]

Gray wrote very little poetry after his Pindaric odes. There are brief epitaphs, a few translations from Norse and Welsh poetry, two pastoral airs, two satires and a congratulatory 'Ode for Music' performed at the installation of the Duke of Grafton as Chancellor of Cambridge University on July 1, 1769. Gray was never a prolific poet, but it is important to note that these occasional poems, for the most part, do not share in the import, scope or power of his earlier poems. The later poems are not as internally conflicted and dialogic, nor do they explore questions of poetic and cultural authority in the same way that the earlier poems do. The questions do not disappear though, and my analysis will show that they still frame the production, dissemination and reception of the later poems. There is however a falling off of poetic ambition and production, and perhaps that was inevitable, or at least prepared for, within the scenario of cultural marginality and poetic positioning that Gray's poems enact.

This is not to suggest that we should understand Gray's career as a poet in Arnoldian terms, and bemoan the frustration of a poet born into an age of prose.[2] The contexts of literary production and reception certainly changed during Gray's lifetime, and he co-existed uneasily (largely via a series of engagements and withdrawals) with these changes—but he had a powerful other creative possiblity, one that he exercised increasingly in the last decade and a half of his life. Thomas Gray, gentleman-poet, transformed himself into Thomas Gray, gentleman-scholar, perhaps 'the most learned man in Europe,'[3] enormously knowledgeable in a number of fields, particularly History and Entomology. His Commonplace Books, letters, and conversations reported by his friends bear out the extent of his learning; characteristically, even as Regius Professor of Modern History at Cambridge (he was appointed in 1768), Gray published no work at all. His research and writing remained private, compensation for a life in retreat from the public sphere rather than the prelude to a more public, if only academic, contribution to the affairs of the university or the nation.

I have argued in the preceding chapters that all of Gray's pastoral and lyric poems incorporate displaced or reflexive responses to the literary history of their genres and to their socio-cultural moment, and are structured around poetic versions of a public/private cultural dichotomy. This dichotomy also informs the production and dissemination of Gray's satires and his translations from the Old Norse and Welsh, and to that extent, these poems, while different in language and theme, continue to inhabit the vexed cultural space demarcated by the earlier poems. The form of satire, and the idiom the satires are written in, suggest a desire for public performance, and yet they were never published, only circulated within an extremely restricted circle of intimates. Even as the translations work towards the presentation of strong, vatic voices, they do so in internally qualified ways, and only by ventriloquising the strengths of the originals. These contradictions, I will attempt to show, are in keeping with the general logic of Gray's poetic production.

To write satire is to choose a genre of public opposition, and even if the poem is meant only for a few selected readers, there is no gainsaying the impulse towards engagement that has, historically, made this the most contestatory of poetic forms. Even more importantly, Gray's surviving satires, 'The Candidate' and 'On Lord Holland's Seat,' share many formal and linguistic features with the popular practices of contemporary satirists. Ironically, the presence of these recognisably 'popular' elements make them precisely the kind of poems that he would not have wanted to make public. There are of course many reasons, both personal and politic, why a poem, even a satire on public issues, is best kept private. In the case of Gray's satires, however, there is a *poetic* logic at work too, one that is grounded in the socio-literary context: to write in a public voice and manner is to become available and assimilable to a large audience, and to publish is to become part of the circuit of commodified literary relations—to become, in fact, an author professed.

Any discussion of Gray's satires must recognise that his literary executors, Mason and Walpole, were responsible for the suppression (and destruction) of many of them, a task made easy by the fact that most of the satires existed only as closely circulated manuscripts. Indeed neither of the two that survive, 'The Candidate' and 'On Lord Holland's Seat near Margate, Kent;' were published by Mason in his 1775 edition of Gray's poems. Ketton-Cremer lists titles like 'A Character of the Scotch,' 'The Mob Grammar,' 'A History of Hell' (whose conclusion 'concerning *King-craft*' Mason thought prescient enough to suggest that Gray was 'prophet as well as poet'), and 'The Duke of Newcastle's Journal Going to Hanover,' as having been destroyed by Mason.[4] Judging from the potent ease and fluency of the two surviving poems, it seems possible that the combined weight of the lost satires might have modified the biographical-critical sense of Gray as an isolated lyric poet, and that these satires, in their partisan engagement with contemporary issues, would have suggested a poet who could write fluently in a genre and an idiom characteristic of the popular literary culture of the early and mid-eighteenth century. Gray clearly did not intend these satires for publication, and certainly their publication would have thrust him into the kind of public, if not popular, attention that he drew away from. Perhaps to that extent, Mason's edition, which included his *Memoires* of Gray, only sought to perpetuate the *cordon sanitaire* that the poet had himself put in place. The general tone of Mason's project is best summed up in a letter Walpole wrote to him: 'You know that my idea was that your work should consecrate his name. To ensure that end, nothing should be blended with it that might make your work a book of party and controversy . . . it will be policy; if the book appears without its sting, Gray's character will be established, and unimpeached. Hereafter let them decry him if they can.'[5]

THE CANDIDATE

Gray's 'The Candidate' was an intervention in the controversy surrounding the contest for the High Stewardship of Cambridge in 1764. The Government candidate was John Montague, Earl of Sandwich, who was opposed by the Whigs in the university as well as by many Fellows who believed that the High Steward should be known more for his public virtues than for his profligacy. Sandwich, as First Lord of the Admiralty, brought to his campaign a minister's power of patronage and the promise of future preferment for those who supported him, arguments that key members of the Divinity Faculty, in particular, found irresistible. After a bitter and prolonged contest, Sandwich eventually (in April 1765) lost the election to Lord Royston, the son of the deceased High Steward.[6]

Sandwich's public profile as a dissolute lecher provided the satiric idiom for many of the attacks against him. Journalists and poets alike compared him to a rake seducing an elderly woman (the university), who seemed in danger of giving in, and Gray's method and vocabulary is not different. In fact, Gray 's satire is the closest he ever came to writing in an entirely popular vein, both in terms of form and language:

> When sly Jemmy Twitcher had smugged up his face
> With a lick of court whitewash and pious grimace,
> A-wooing he went, where three sisters of old
> In harmless society guttle and scold. (ll. 1–4)

From the use of the nick-name 'Jemmy Twitcher' for Sandwich, to words like 'smugged' and 'guttle' (which Johnson's *Dictionary* lists as a 'low' word), this poem employs a vocabulary indistinguishable from contemporary popular satiric practices.

In fact, 'The Candidate' gains its dramatic energy and satiric bite from its representation of the Cambridge Faculties of Medicine, Jurispudence and Divinity as three common scolds, two of whom catalogue Jeremy Twitcher's deficiencies on the way to rejecting him as a suitor, while Divinity excuses his failings in deciding to become 'Mrs Twitcher' herself. An everyday misogyny shapes these characters, caricaturing them in ways made familiar by contemporary novels or cartoonists like Hogarth. Here is Physic (Medicine), speaking to Law:

> 'Lord! Sister,' says Physic to Law, 'I declare
> Such a sheep-biting look, such a pick-pocket air,
> Not I, for the Indies! you know I'm no prude;
> But his nose is a shame and his eyes are so lewd!
> Then he shambles and straddles so oddly, I fear—
> No; at our time of life, 'twould be silly, my dear.'
> (ll. 5–10)

Here ridicule achieves its ends by ventriloquising the exclamatory and syntactical forms of popular speech, reducing Sandwich to the shifty, possibly syphylitic (l. 8), beau of these sisters.

Like most eighteenth-century satire, 'The Candidate' strives for cultural verisimilitude via a socially differentiated linguistic register, 'low' speech and manner providing the basis for satire. However, we should remember that such differentiation does not simply establish the parodic internal contrast between the Cambridge Faculties and the characters of 'Phyzzy' (l. 13), Law and Divinity, but also allows the high-cultural text to maintain its superior and ironising distance from the spectacle it stages. Apart from its idiom, the overtly dialogic, dramatised nature of this satire sets it apart from Gray's preceeding poetry, energising it in the manner of the best of Dryden's or Pope's satires. Divinity's response to her sisters' discussions is in character, as she argues forgiveness for Jemmy Twitcher based on a specious invocation of Biblical parallels:

> Divinity heard, between waking and dozing,
> Her sisters denying and Jemmy proposing;
> From dinner she rose with her bumper in her hand,
> She stroked up her belly and stroked down her band.
> 'What a pother is here about wenching and roaring!
> Why David loved catches and Solomon whoring.
> Did not Israel filch from the Egyptians of old
> Their jewels of silver and jewels of gold?
> The prophet of Bethel, we read, told a lie;
> He drinks: so did Noah; he swears: so do I.
> To refuse him for such peccadilloes were odd;
> Besides, he repents, and he talks about God.[7] (ll. 19–30)

This combination of the vulgar and the perverse is further emphasised in the last four lines of the poem, as Divinity acts aggressively on the twin principles of self-interest and Christian compassion:

> 'Never hang down your head, you poor penitent elf!
> Come, buss me, I'll be Mrs Twitcher myself.
> Damn ye both for a couple of Puritan bitches!
> He's Christian enough that repents and that stitches.'
> (ll. 31–34)

This poem might have demonstrated nothing more to us than that Gray had a healthy ear for the vulgar, as also the ability—largely underutilised, of course—to write in a popular form and idiom. However, the surprising, obscene directness of the last couplet ('stitch' was slang for 'lying with a woman'[8]) was so uncharacteristic of Gray's work that it led instead (not surprisingly) to an editorial problem, one which resonates ironically with the delicate dynamic that governed the public and the private, the published and the privately circulated, in Gray's poetic career.

Gray circulated the poem in manuscript to only a few friends (even Mason did not see it till after Gray's death), and it was not printed in an unexpurgated form till it was included in the Yale edition of Walpole's correspondence in 1955. Walpole believed that it was not proper to print the last couplet in the edition of Gray's works that Mason was planning, and wrote to Mason to suggest a revision: 'Methinks I wish you could alter the end of the last line, which is too gross to be read by any females, but such cock bawds as the three dames in the verses—and that single word is the only one that could possibly be minded. P.S. Might it not do thus?

> Damn you both! I know each for a Puritan punk.
> He is Christian enough that repents when he's drunk.'[9]

Mason agreed to the need for change, even though he held that Gray's rhymes could not be bettered: 'The couplet which you wish me to alter is one of those that can only be altered, not improved; the utmost one can hope is a passable alteration. However I think with you (and always did) that the lines ought to be altered.'[10]

Eventually, Mason did not include the poem in his 1775 edition, and as Lonsdale points out, the couplet was 'simply omitted from all texts intended for the general public and the last offending word omitted by Walpole from the flysheet and one of his MS copies.'[11] The 'bitches'/'switches' rhyme, which is Gray's most drastic celebration of the vulgar, and the moment in the poem when it emphatically confirms its identity with the obscene and scatological broadsides and lampoons characteristic of eighteenth-century popular culture, is precisely what needed to be edited before the poem could be, as it were, made public. This is not to argue that Gray had meant this satire for public circulation, because he certainly had not. In fact, this poem reads as it does probably because Gray had not meant it to be seen except by a few friends.

The certainty of private circulation, that is, enables Gray's use of the idiom of popular satire, of the kind of language that differentiates 'The Candidate' from Gray's other poems. (The *Elegy*, was of course remarkably popular, but the poem itself does not contain any socially differentiated speech. Even the language of the illiterate 'hoary-headed swain' bears no inflections indicative of his peasant origins, and is in fact dictated by the conventional usages of the polite pastoral tradition). Walpole, on the other hand, and this is appropriate for a man who was himself a publisher, was wary of the chances of ensuring privacy (which is possibly why he wished to have an altered version published). 'We will preserve copies,' he wrote to Mason, 'and the devil is in it, if some time or other it don't find its way to the press.'[12] These then are the ironies that make 'The Candidate' an apt exhibit in Gray's *ouevre*: a private intervention in a public debate, written in a popular form and idiom for the delectation of a closed high-cultural circle, deemed unfit for posthumous editions of Gray's poetry so that the public image of a private scholar not be threatened.

ON LORD HOLLAND'S SEAT

It is no surprise then that Walpole and Mason also suppressed Gray's 'On Lord Holland's Seat near Margate, Kent,' (written in 1768) from Mason's 1775 edition. Walpole's reasons combined a concern for the state of Holland's health with concern for Gray's reputation as a poet: 'I think you determined not to print the lines on Lord H[olland]. I hope it is now a resolution. He is in so deplorable a state, that they would aggravate the misery of his last hours, and you yourself would be censured . . . As Gray too seems to have condemned all his own satirical works, that single one would not [?give] a high idea of his powers, though they were great in that walk; you and I know they were not inferior to his other styles.'[13] 'On Lord Holland's Seat' confirms, if anything, this tantalising report of Gray as an assured satirist who abjured his powers and curtailed his production.

The beginning of the poem tropes ironically on the twin themes of virtuous retirement and the cultivation of the ethical life popularised by the *beatus vir* theme in pastoral and georgic verse. In Horace and Juvenal, Pope and Johnson, the good statesman-citizen, disgusted by the corrupt city, moves to a country estate, there to cultivate his garden and his soul. In 'On Lord Holland's Seat,' Holland too retires, but his retreat is precipitated when he is 'abandoned by each venal friend' (l. 1), their betrayal forcing him to a

pious resolution
To smuggle some few years and strive to mend
A broken character and constitution. (ll. 2–4)[14]

Holland is no different from those he leaves behind; in fact, as the word 'smuggle' (l. 3) suggests, his own motives for moving to the country are less than virtuous, and perhaps even underhanded and criminal.

The 'congenial spot' (l. 5) he finds (his country estate) is off treacherous sandbanks on the Kentish coast:

Here sea-gulls scream and cormorants rejoice,
And mariners, though shipwrecked, dread to land.
Here reign the blustering North and blighting East,
No tree is heard to whisper, bird to sing: (ll. 7–10)

This blighted landscape is to be home to Holland's seat, suffused not with *beatitus* but its malefic opposite. The buildings that are erected only confirm the natural horrors of the estate:

Yet nature cannot furnish out the feast,
Art he invokes new horrors still to bring.
New mouldering fanes and battlements arise,
Arches and turrets nodding to their fall,

Unpeopled palaces delude his eyes,
And mimic desolation covers all. (ll. 11–16)

Key to this description of the perverse architecture that Holland spawns is the phrase 'mimic desolation' (l. 11), which seems at first to refer only to the process described in lines 11 and 12, that is, to the way in which 'Art' adds new horrors to those furnished by 'nature.' But the 'New mouldering fanes and battlements,' and the 'Arches and battlements' that go 'nodding to their fall' (ll. 13–14) mimic not simply the examples of nature but also literary representations of the ruins of ancient Rome. As Lonsdale suggests, Gray's lines repeatedly echo Pope's 'To Mr Addison,' and its description of Roman ruins:

With nodding arches, broken temples spread!
The very Tombs now vanish'd like their dead!
Imperial wonders rais'd on Nations spoil'd,
Where mix'd with Slaves the groaning Martyr toil'd;
Huge Theatres, that now unpeopled Woods,
. . . .
Fanes, which admiring Gods with pride survey,
Statues of Men, scarce less alive than they;
Some felt the silent stroke of mould'ring age. (ll. 3–11)[15]

In the discussion of 'Ode on the Death of a Favourite Cat' in Chapter IV, I had shown how the ruins of imperial Rome were often allegorised by eighteenth-century English poets to serve as historical warnings about the downfall inevitable to those imperial civilisations that allowed new-found wealth to corrupt their social and moral values. Holland's architectural aping of the *ruins* of ancient Rome (in particular Cicero's estate) thus seems particulary perverse, as well as largely apt—the enactment of a vision of historical degeneration apposite to one whose corrupt moral values prefigure and make possible such destruction. In the poem, then, Holland's ruins are figures not so much for the degenerative processes of nature (and time) as for the historical desolation attendant upon the collapse of corrupt empires.

That Gray's lines speak in Pope's satirical idiom is appropriate; the predecessor poet had provided, in the closing of *The Dunciad*, a compelling, indeed apocalyptic, example of the overtaking of an empire by the forces of cultural darkness. Both Pope and Gray, as partisan satirists, represent historical personalities as the agents of this darkness, portraying their cultural and moral bankruptcy as enabling the crisis. Thus, Holland is shown as grieving that his betrayal by his comrades-in-arms has prevented the execution of his grand plan:

> 'Ah', said the sighing peer, 'had Bute been true,
> Nor Shelburne's, Rigby's, Calcraft's friendship vain,
> Far other scenes than these had blessed our view
> And realised the ruins that we feign.
> Purged by the sword and beautified by fire,
> Then had we seen proud London's hated walls:
> Owls might have hooted in St Peter's choir,
> And foxes stunk and littered in St. Paul's.'
>
> (ll. 17–24)

The sham ruins on Holland's estate are thus a prospectus for a failed plan to bring ruin to London, and mimic both the collapse of past empires and the potential desolation of England. As John Chalker says, the last two quatrains are 'satiric hyperbole, a grotesque caricature of Holland's intentions; but the extraordinary emotional power of the lines springs from Gray's Augustan sense that London is no more permanent than Rome, and that its churches could easily become the resting places of wild creatures . . . It is not the inevitable transitoriness of life that Pope or Gray laments, but the avoidable transitoriness of civilization.'[16]

It is ironic to think about Gray and Pope together in the context of satire, to think that they shared, even briefly, an apocalyptic idiom of civilisational decay. After all, Pope is the dominant, the most *public*, literary figure of his age, a dominance achieved during a long, embattled career of poetic controversy. Gray, on the other hand, is our very type of retiring poet, shying away from a public profile, restricting the circulation of his satires. Yet the language of cultural contestation speaks in Gray's early verse too (as I have sought to show in preceeding chapters), and in a sense the surviving satires only extend this socio-cultural engagement. In displaced or in more direct ways, via mediated or more immediately accessible dialogues, Gray's poems offer a response to urgent cultural and historical questions, some of which we will return to in an analysis of Gray's translations from the Norse and Welsh.

In *Thomas Gray, Scholar*, his study of Gray's scholarly and intellectual interests, William Jones describes, *inter alia*, Gray's growing interest after 1753 in the origins and history of English poetry. In order to further his project, Gray began, in his usual meticulous manner, an extensive study of Romance, Germanic and Celtic poetics. However, in a pattern by now familiar, he was to give up this projected history of English poetry, and shift his enquiries away from poetics to antiquities, but not before he wrote articles in his Commonplace Book 'on early English poetry, on Welsh lore, and on things Norse.'[17] Gray's search for origins, for a genealogy for English poetics, led him to Old Norse and Welsh poems, a few of which he translated as examples of precursor poetic styles. It is these fragmentary translations, the products of Gray the poet and, as he was increasingly and exclusively becoming, Gray the scholar, that I will discuss briefly in this concluding account of Gray's career as a poet.

As literary historians have pointed out, Gray's 'The Fatal Sisters. An Ode,' 'The Descent of Odin. An Ode,' 'The Triumphs of Owen. A Fragment,' and three untitled fragments from the Welsh poem, the *Gododdin* (which Lonsdale titles 'The Death of Hoel,' 'Caradoc' and 'Conan'), are all part of the contemporary vogue for antiquity.[18] Most antiquarian enquiry was conducted into 'rude' cultures, elements of which could be selectively claimed as the pre-history of English culture. Greek and Roman architecture, art and literature were of course mined for many of the same reasons, but they were seen as providing models of a far more cultured achievement. Pre-literate cultures (including Homeric Greece), on the other hand, provided a different socio-cultural model, one which authorised a more public poetry, that of inspirational force, of powerful voice, of vatic performance. Bishop Percy, for instance, prefaces his *Five Pieces of Runic Poetry* with the claim that 'the study of ancient northern literature' is justified even 'if those kinds of studies are not always employed on works of taste or classic elegance, [as] they serve at least to unlock the treasures of native genius; they present us with sallies of bold imagination, and constantly afford matter for philosophical reflection by showing the workings of the human mind in its most original state of nature.'[19]

This need to generate genealogical models is, for instance, the express reason for Goldsmith's piece on 'The History of Carolan, the last Irish Bard': 'to be acquainted with the ancient manners of our own ancestors, we should endeavour to look for their remains in those countries, which, being in some measure retired from an intercourse with other nations, are still untinctured with foreign refinement, language, or breeding.' He thus turns to Ireland, Britain's first imperial hunting ground, and describes it (in language that we recognise as foundational to the historical imaginary of empire) as frozen in time, outside of history: 'in several parts of that country [they] still adhere to their ancient language, dress, furniture, and superstitions; several customs that still speak their original; and, in some respect, Caesar's description of the Ancient Britons is applicable to these.'[20] Hence, though Carolan was an eighteenth-century figure (he died in 1738), his career provides Goldsmith an example of the important place of the bard in English cultural pre-history.

Attempts to understand the bardic function often employed the language of historical paradox—commentators stressed the strange centrality of poets (bards, scalds) to 'unrefined' social systems, indeed to people whose skill in warfare was occasionally responsible for the destruction of more literate cultures. That is how Percy's 'Preface' presents the 'ancient inhabitants of the northern parts': they 'are generally known under no other character than that of a hardy and unpolished race . . . Their valour, their ferocity, their contempt of death, and passion for liberty, form the outlines of the picture we commonly draw of them.' He emphasises one remarkable feature, their 'amazing fondness for poetry. It will be thought a paradox, that the same people, whose ferocious ravages destroyed the last poor remnants of expiring genius among the Romans, should cherish it with all possible care among their own countrymen: yet so it was.'[21]

Percy, like other contemporary antiquarians and poets, emphasised the quasi-religious fervour attendant upon ancient bardic practices. 'The invention of [poetry] was attributed to the gods, and ranked amongst the most valuable gifts conferred on mortals. Those that excelled in it, were distinguished by the first honours of the state: were constant attendants on their kings, and were often employed on the most important commissions.'[22] Percy, like Gray, found in the Bard a figure for the empowered poet, one whose poetry demands and is granted the greatest cultural respect, and who is in turn elevated in social prestige and state honours. At their prophetic best, these bards seemed to make things happen; not only were they secure of their place in their social hierarchy, but they also seemed assured of their role in the history they presaged.

Percy does not, however, see the bards purely as oracles, who spoke in divine voice. They were, first and foremost, *poets*, and he points out that the Icelandic bards were 'called by the significant name of SCALD, a word which implies a "smoother or polisher of language".' He comments at length on the language of their poetry, suggesting that the poems

'tho quite original and underived, are far from being so easy and simple as might be expected: on the contrary, no compositions abound with more laboured metaphors, or more studied refinements. A proof that poetry had been cultivated among them for many ages. That daring spirit and vigour of imagination, which distinguished the northern warriors, naturally inclined them to bold and swelling figures . . . It was the constant study of the northern SCALDS to lift their poetic style as much as possible above that of their prose. So that they had at length formed to themselves in verse a kind of new language, in which every idea was expressed by a peculiar term, never admitted into their ordinary converse.

In a footnote, Percy says that this 'new language' was called 'by them, in the manner of the ancient Greeks, (Asom-maal,) THE LANGUAGE OF THE GODS.'[23]

When eighteenth-century antiquarians studied or translated bardic verse, they were especially charmed by what they perceived to be its magical qualities, its 'bold and swelling' metaphors and charged, incantatory rhythms. They found in this poetry a language that seemed no longer responsible to the idiom of everyday cultural functioning, yet played a significant role in the culture. To poets like Gray, who were already deeply dissatisfied with the new cultural vocabularies being put into place by socio-economic transformation in eighteenth-century England, this discourse, transcendent of social forms yet authoritative within them, offered seductive and enabling possibilities. On the one hand, there was the excitement of ventriloquising the voice of wondrous power, and on the other, the more mundane attraction of being able to confuse less-knowledgeable contemporary critics! It would be possible, Gray wrote to Mason, 'to graft any wild picturesque fable absolutely of one's own invention upon the Druid-stock, I mean upon those half-dozen of old fancies, that are known to have made their system. this will give you more freedom and latitude, & will leave no hold for the Criticks to fasten on.'[24]

Gray's oft-quoted reaction to James Macpherson's *Fragments of Ancient Poetry, collected in the Highlands of Scotland and translated from the Galic or Erse Language* (published in 1760) and to a manuscript copy of Evan Evans's *Some Specimens of the Poems of the Antient Welsh Bards* (published in 1764), is representative of one kind of response (there were of course more sceptical reactions) to the growing number of translations from, and treatises on, one or other ancient literature: 'I am gone mad about them,' he wrote to Wharton, and declared himself '*extasié* with their infinite beauty.' Even if Macpherson was to prove a forger, Gray was enthusiastic about the poems: 'in short this man is the very Demon of Poetry, or he has lighted on a treasure hid for ages.' The 'Welch Poets are also coming to light,' he went on to write, 'I have seen a Discourse in Mss. about them . . . with specimens of their writings. this is in Latin, &, tho' it don't approach the other, there are fine scraps among it.' [25]

In Chapter IV, in the discussion of 'The Progress of Poesy' and the 'Bard,' I had suggested that Gray's poems participate in a more extensive project, the eighteenth-century English construction of nationalist cultural and historical genealogies. The former poem lays claim to a classical poetic inheritance as part of a larger historical model of the westward movement of culture ('When Latium had her lofty spirit lost,/ [The Muses] sought, oh Albion! next thy sea-encircled coast.'), and then suggests Shakespeare, Milton and Dryden as exemplars of the English artistic genius. 'The Bard' enshrines a similar nationalistic imperative, and its excursus into Celtic culture constructs a pre-history for England that celebrates the untutored, wild, *prophetic* songs of its first poets, the Welsh Bards. Gray's use of the Pindaric encourages, rhetorically and formally, the celebration of national history and cultural achievement, as it does the poet's flirtation with public place and power. Gray's poems engage both thematically and structurally with the problem of poetic authority, and, in each case, it is the displacement of poetic voice which particularly indicates self-reflexive concerns with cultural positioning and socially viable literary practice.

Gray's translations from the Norse and the Welsh respond to these concerns too, though not in the same way. In many ways, they are more sure-footed than Gray's early poems, their structure and syntax less fissured by anxieties about poetic voice and performance—though that of course is due largely to the nature and quality of the original verse. However, to the extent that they share in contemporary efforts to derive an ancient and vigorous genealogy for English culture (Gray conceived of them as specimen-translations from ancient literatures which had influenced the history of English poetry), they benefit from the ideological certainties of that nationalist credo. Also, their alien mythology, and the strangeness of their versification, allow a license of voice, tone and phrase missing in contemporary poetic modes. The anxiety about poetic authority that surfaces in Gray's other poems is masked by the declamatory, prophetic stance of the Norse and Welsh originals. If we have any sense of the precariousness of the poetic exercise undertaken by Gray, then, it must come from our sense of the displaced linguistic and cultural anxieties attendant upon translation. Gray's translation of fragments also suggests interesting interpretive questions, some of which will be taken up in the analysis that follows.

Both sets of originals, Norse and Welsh, share themes and poetic archaisms that derive from feudal cultures. All the poems sing of war, heroism and death, and in each case, fulfil a prophetic, celebratory or elegiac function. For eighteenth-century antiquarians, this context of production seemed uniquely socially sanctioned, indeed part of popular ritual. The assured quality of cultural reception must have been particularly attractive to high-cultural poets like Gray, who would have been drawn to the fact that the poetic voices in the poem seemed to bear few obvious traces of uncertainty about their role, or about the tone appropriate to their performance. Gray's translation of these poems, then, is a complex and overdetermined literary exercise: the disenfranchised eighteenth-century poet ventriloquising the voice of ancient cultural empowerment, finding in a feudal poetics a nostalgic celebration of bardic potency (but also romantic examples of the death of the poet), discovering in the swansongs of the past dying echoes of his present.

TRANSLATIONS FROM THE NORSE AND WELSH

'The Fatal Sisters. An Ode' (1761) is centered around weaving as a metaphor for poetic creativity and power. The poem is the weaving song of the Valkyries ('wierd sisters' in the mode of the witches in *Macbeth*), and the work of their voices and hands is the work of fate:

We the reigns to slaughter give,
Ours to kill and ours to spare:
Spite of danger he shall live.
(Weave the crimson web of war.) (ll. 33–36)

The sisters are not dispassionate oracles; they weave war, their tools and their handiwork the materials of death and destruction:

Glittering lances are the loom,
Where the dusky warp we strain,
Weaving many a soldier's doom,
Orkney's woe, and Randver's bane.

See the grisly texture grow,
('Tis of human entrails made,)
And the weights that play below,
Each a gasping warrior's head.

Shafts for shuttles, dipped in gore,
Shoot the trembling cords along.
Sword, that once a monarch bore,
Keep the tissue close and strong! (ll. 5–16)

They weave the outcome of the battle—'Hail the task, and hail the hands! / Songs of joy and triumph sing! (ll. 53–54)—but also sing of future mourning and of history-in-the-making:

They, whom once the desert-beach
Pent within its bleak domain,
Soon their ample sway shall stretch
O'er the plenty of the plain.

Low the dauntless Earl is laid,
Gored with many a gaping wound:
Fate demands a nobler head;
Soon a King shall bite the ground.

Long his loss shall Eirin weep,
Ne'er again his likeness see;

Long her strains in sorrow steep,
Strains of immortality! (ll. 37–48)

In his 'Preface,' Gray called the song of the sisters 'dreadful': the spectacle of witch-like women singing, with bloodthirsty vigour, in a prophetic strain sets in play disturbing cultural and gender anxieties. The context of superstition which informs the Norse original creates a threatening aura around the Fatal Sisters, which is not dissipated in translation. If anything, it is emphasised within the English representational tradition, where (for instance) the witches of *Macbeth* provide a resonant pre-text. Thus, the Fatal Sisters are rendered not quite ideal as figures of the empowered poet, even though (or perhaps precisely because) their vision encompasses present and future. In so far as they translate, for the eighteenth-century poet, into unstable figures of powerful women, they need to be contained somehow. Appropriately for a poem by Gray, this containment stems from a moment of direct poetic address incorporated into the poem, a rhetorical feature not present in the original:[26]

Mortal, thou that hears't the tale,
Learn the tenor of our song.
Scotland, through each winding vale
Far and wide the notes prolong. (ll. 57–60)

The song of the Fatal Sisters is heard, learned and perpetuated by a man (whom Gray described in his 'Preface' as a curious 'native of Caithess' who spots and follows the 'twelve gigantic figures resembling women'), and passes into the historical and cultural vocabulary of all of Scotland via him. The prophetic voices of the sisters are thus *mediated* into popular performance and memory by a male interlocutor. Further, his invoked humanity—his 'mortality'—offsets the sinister aspect of the singers, just as his assimilation and dissemination of their song 'through each winding vale' recasts it within the mold of cultural and social tradition. This male auditor (and, presumably, singer), that is, recuperates the sisters and their song; his instrumental presence transforms them and their craft into an acceptable figure for compelling poetic performance.

The connection between female prophecy and destruction is repeated in 'The Descent of Odin. An Ode' (1761), in which the prophetess of the underworld, roused from her deathly sleep by Odin, foretells the death of Balder as the prelude to the epic downfall of the gods. She is brought to life, conjured up via poetry, by the disguised god, the 'King of Men' (l. 1):

> where long of yore to sleep was laid
> The dust of the prophetic maid.
> Facing to the northern clime,
> Thrice he traced the runic rhyme;
> Thrice pronounced, in accents dread,
> The thrilling verse that wakes the dead;
> Till from out the hollow ground
> Slowly breathed a sullen sound. (ll. 19–26)

Her prophetic voice is here already rendered a function of Odin's magic verse, and the dialogue between them that follows confirms his power, even though he is the supplicant and she the seer. His runic spells force her to answer his questions, and the dialogic balance between them slowly but surely tilts in his favour. Finally, when she discovers his true identity, and hails him as the 'King of Men,' the 'Mightiest of a mighty line' (ll. 82–83), Odin's response is only to denigrate her. He denies her utterance a divine provenance and instead demonises her:

> No boding maid of skill divine
> Art thou, nor prophetess of good;
> But mother of the giant brood! (ll. 84–86)

In 'The Descent of Odin,' then, the poem's staged dialogue establishes differential, gendered values for poetic voice: male/divine versus female/demoniacal. The instabilities attendant upon the enactment of prophetic power in a woman's voice are sharply quelled. Yet not entirely, for the final vision is that of the prophetess, one that confirms her as vengeful and perverse. Her 'iron-sleep' (l. 89) will never be broken again, she says, not

> Till Lok has burst his tenfold chain;
> Never, till substantial Night
> Has reassumed her ancient right;
> Till wrapped in flames, in ruin hurled,
> Sinks the fabric of the world. (ll. 90–94)

The end of the *Dunciad* provides a spectacular instance of the contemporary currency of such apocalyptic discourse in eighteenth-century English poetry[27]—here too disfigured, devastating female power is implicated in the ruin of civilisation.

The point I am making in this analysis of Gray's translations from the Norse is not that he mis-translated, or rewrote the originals in his own image (though all translation involves some of that[28]), but that his translations echo, in themes and rhetorical forms, issues made familiar in his earlier poetry. Insofar as his poems always incorporate concerns about poetic empowerment, modes of address, and contexts of reception, these fragments from a feudal culture provide fine comparative examples. The translations emerge, that is, from Gray's declared project—the reconstruction of a genealogy for English poetry—but also exercise his less overt, though persistent, anxieties about poetic voice.

This continuity of poetic concerns has been commented upon by Arthur Johnston: 'The concept of the poet shown in the poems written between 1752 and 1761 grows naturally if surprisingly from the opposite concepts [Gray] had entertained from 1738 to 1750, from the poet as hidden and remembered only by a kindred spirit, to the poet as the sole surviving voice of liberty and virtue, from the poet as *memento mori* to the poet as celebrator of the noble dead, from the poet as "at ease reclined in rustic state", to the anguished poet "With haggard eyes" on a rock "o'er old Conway's foaming flood", from the poet as a "silken son of dalliance" to the poet as mental warrior.'[29] The irony of this transformation is, of course, that it was accomplished in a period when Gray virtually stopped writing poetry, and it is exemplified in translations rather than in original verse. The more public the voice, the more indirect the mode of achieving it—this seems to be one problematic resolution of the complexities of cultural marginalisation.

As the analysis of 'The Fatal Sisters' and 'The Triumphs of Owen' has suggested, the fantasy of cultural centrality, of extra-poetic authority, is subject to certain discriminations, most notably those attendant upon the construction of a masculine culture. The 'mental warrior' that Johnston sees in Gray's later poetry is a figure achieved via a formative detour: in these translations the circuit of poetic desire is profoundly male, and is arrived at (in part) by containing potentially threatening female voices. Gray's translations from the Welsh confirm the privileged masculinity of poetic power; this is one of the multiple determinations that guide Gray's excursus into the poetry of war and death, into the culture of feudalism. There is the mode of panegyric ('The Triumphs of Owen,' 'Caradoc' and 'Conan'), of celebration. But, as so often in Gray's earlier poems, poetic desire is also articulated in the language of loss, in the mourning song of one man for another ('The Death of Hoel'). In terms of genre, these poems offer the ideal format: that of the commemorative song of the bard for the victorious warrior, or for the warrior who has gone to a heroic death.

'The Triumphs of Owen. A Fragment,' like 'Conan,' celebrates the achievements of a warrior-hero, but also incorporates prominently a reference to the song, and by implication, the important position, of the poet: 'Owen's praise demands my song,/ Owen swift, and Owen strong' (ll. 1–2). 'Conan' begins:

> Conan's name, my lay, rehearse,
> Build to him the lofty verse,
> Sacred tribute of the bard,
> Verse, the hero's sole reward. (ll. 1–4)

The cultural fantasy at the heart of such sentiment is obvious: societies that recognise the commemorative function recognise equally the importance of the bard (this, as we had seen, is a theme central to the *Elegy*). And yet Gray's translations can only enact such claims within the context of historical loss; that time is past, and along with Owen, Caradoc and Conan, the bard can only be a figure for the nostalgia that informs aristocratic, high-cultural memory.

'The Death of Hoel' most explicitly engages with the themes of empowerment and loss that characterise much of Gray's poetry. The poem opens with the poet's wish for super-human strength in order to wreak revenge upon those who killed his friend:

> Had I but the torrent's might,
> With headlong rage and wild affright
> Upon Diera's squadrons hurled,
> To rush and sweep them from the world!
> Too, too secure in youthful pride,
> By them my friend, my Hoel, died. (ll. 1–6)

Since revenge is not possible, the memorial and mourning functions are all that are left to the poet, particularly as Hoel dies in a battle that wiped out 'Twice two hundred warriors' (l. 12):

> But none from Cattraeth's vale return,
> Save Aeron brave and Conan strong,
> (Bursting through the bloody throng)
> And I, the meanest of them all,
> That live to weep and sing their fall. (ll. 20–24)

This then is the paradox of the memorial poem: the exercise of the poet's cultural duty is predicated upon absence, upon the destruction of the hero or the heroic community. Here, once again in Gray's poetry, poetic life and song are reminders of the loss of an immediate community, and the mass death of the warriors an image of the passing of a way of life.

It might be appropriate to conclude this study of Gray's poetry on this elegiac note, especially after we have noticed how repeated elegiac moments in Gray signify his conflicted response to the fading of an enabling socio-cultural community larger than that provided by a few close friends and correspondents. We have seen how tropes of death and other markers of passing in his poems are figures for historical loss, but also that such transition is not simply mourned, but engaged with, contested. My analysis of the different poems has attempted to follow the specifically poetic impact of such cultural contestation, and such social transformation, in the work of Gray, reading rhetoric and form in conjunction with history and ideology. As I hope I have made clear, in Gray's poems (as indeed in much mid-eighteenth-century English poetry), poetic performance is riven by anxieties about the cultural and socio-historical place of poetry and the poet. The study of such poetics, then, is inevitably the study of the difficult invocation (and failing dissolution) of various tropes of authority, some sanctioned by contemporary cultural usage, others anchored in literary-historical practices.

As I have argued, it is not enough to be sensitive to the conflicted, convoluted tropology of voice and address in these poems without recognising that poetic forms carry with them their own historical and performative burdens, that poetic practice is ideologically overdetermined. Psychoanalytic and deconstructive modes of critical analysis have encouraged a welcome responsiveness to the play of rhetorical signification (as the play of desire), but we must not lose sight of the fact that the crucial forms and particulars of such signification are constituted by, and constitute, the history of their cultural moment. To write poetry, as to write in any other literary genre, is to intervene in a cultural process—equally, the thematics, rhetorical strategies and evocation of affect in poetry are no less responsive to the history of literary practice and the ideological compulsions of the occasion. Thus, critical discussion of issues of voice and of subjectivity in poetry should not end up collapsing one into the other, but should see both as registers of the complex relationship of text, author and context.

One quick instance of the latter problem can be seen in Wallace Jackson's study of the figurations of thwarted desire in Gray's poems, where he concludes that Gray 'is the most disappointing poet of the English eighteenth-century—disappointing, that is, in terms of what was expected of him . . . I attribute this failure to no cultural malaise, for it seems to me utterly and completely personal.' Jackson denies the validity of any socio-cultural explanations, and offers instead a near-mythologised, quasi-psychological account of Gray's 'failure' as a poet: 'Rather, it appears, Gray could not fully serve the muse of his own dedication, the figure he deliberately wills into existence and to whom he dedicates his powers.'[30] At one level, Jackson's critical vocabulary and concerns are far removed from those of the humanist critics whose readings of Gray I briefly discuss in Chapter II. He is sensitive to the traumatic shifts in voice and figure in the poems, and aware that the ultimate ground of such trauma is a more or less self-reflexive poetic concern with the tropes of literary authority. However, in his refusal to consider any but an 'utterly and completely personal' account of Gray's impasse, he returns us once more to a critical model of the man who suffers (desire) and the poetic imagination that closes in upon itself.

In contrast, I have argued that Gray's 'disappointments' are best read in historical and cultural terms, and that the figures for poetic inspiration, voice, and achievement in his poems add up to more than 'the muse of his own dedication,' and in fact help to dramatise an analytical, contestatory response to changing literary practices and socio-cultural formations. I have argued that there are structuring continuities between Gray's class position, cultural assumptions and prescriptions, and poetic practices; further, that his personal and poetic responses to cultural marginalisation are symptomatic of larger crises in the world of letters brought about by the expansion of the literary market. In the analysis of his poems, I have shown that even their enactment of isolation and loneliness is a product of ideological engagement, and that there are many moments in Gray's poems, including in the lyrics, when 'failure' follows upon an attempt to articulate large cultural and nationalist agendas.

If this project has succeeded, it will have demonstrated that the reading of poetry is rewarding not only for the pleasure of unravelling meanings and discovering canny (and uncanny) instances of tropological and rhetorical complexity. Indeed, it will have shown that the critical analysis of such complex meanings must also be an account of conflicted cultural and literary-historical transitions. It will have suggested, that is, the necessity of a critical method sensitive to the interplay of ideology and poetic form. To that extent, I have paid the small, occasional poem attention in the same way that I have the weightier Pindaric or elegy, in part to suggest that different cultural artifacts can offer rich gleanings to readers who are attentive to their differential formal qualities and modes of representation. The fissured complexities of poetic enunciation express, and are subject to, not only the problems of representation but also cultural and historical contradictions. Historicising the text, while respecting its cultural protocols, its *literariness,* allows a fuller account of its construction and affect. In the present instance, it enables us to see Gray's poetry as lacking only in volume, not in substance. Even more importantly, it encourages us to read in ways that remind us that the making of culture, like the making of history, is a contested and vital process, and one in which poetry (and criticism) always attempt to make things happen.

NOTES

1. February 25, 1768. *Correspondence,* iii. 1017–18.
2. Arnold's explanation of Gray's lack of productivity takes the form of a comment on the poet's socio-cultural context, except that his critical terminology obfuscates, rather than clarifies, the issue: 'Gray, a born poet, fell upon an age of prose. He fell upon an age whose task was such as to call forth in general men's powers of understanding, wit and cleverness, rather than their deepest powers of mind and soul.' Matthew Arnold, 'Thomas Gray,' in *English Literature and Irish Politics,* ed. R.H. Super, vol. ix of *The Complete Prose Works,* 11 vols. (Ann Arbor: University of Michigan Press, 1977), p. 200.
3. This assessment is that of William John Temple, who wrote a biographical sketch of Gray in the *London Magazine* in March 1772: 'He knew every branch of history, both natural and civil; had read all the original historians of England, France, and Italy; and was a great antiquarian. Criticism, metaphysics, morals, politics made a principle

part of his plan of study; voyages and travels of all sorts were his favourite amusement; and he had a fine taste in painting, prints, architecture, and gardening.' Quoted by Jones, *Thomas Gray*, p. vii.

4. R.W. Ketton-Cremer, *Thomas Gray* (Cambridge: Cambridge University Press, 1955), p. 204. Ketton-Cremer derives these titles from a list written by Mason at the end of a letter to him from Walpole on August 23, 1774. Walpole, *Correspondence*, i. 165–66.
5. Walpole to Mason, April 17, 1774, in Walpole, *Correspondence*, i. 151–52. Walpole was writing to dissuade Mason from including in his notes to Gray's letters several contentious observations about the works of Ossian, on the grounds that in 'Gray's own letters there is enough to offend; your notes added will involve him in the quarrel, every silly story will be revived and his ashes will be disturbed to vex you' (p. 151), but his comments, as he suggests himself, are meant as a statement of editorial and biographical policy.
6. Lonsdale provides an account of this election in *Gray*, pp. 243–49. See also Leonard Whibley's 'The Contest for the High Stewardship and Gray's Verses on Lord Sandwich,' 'Appendix P' in *Correspondence*, iii: 1236–242.
7. Divinity's argument parallels the opening lines of Dryden's *Absalom and Achitophel*, in that both use selective examples of morally suspect behaviour from the Bible to make their case:

   In pious times, e'er Priest-craft did begin,
   Before *Polygamy* was made a sin;
   . . . .
   Then *Israel*'s Monarch, after Heaven's own heart,
   His vigorous warmth did, variously, impart
   To Wives and Slaves: And, wide as his Command,
   Scatter'd his Maker's Image through the Land. (ll. 1–10)

   The Poems and Fables of John Dryden, ed. James Kinsley (London: Oxford University Press, 1962), p. 190.
8. Grose, *Classical Dictionary of the Vulgar Tongue*. Quoted by Lonsdale in *Gray*, pp. 251–52.
9. Walpole to Mason, September 16, 1774. Quoted by Lonsdale in *Gray*, p. 252. Lonsdale records the details of the variant printings of 'The Candidate,' including Walpole's and Mason's emendations of the last couplet on pp. 245–48, 251–52.
10. Mason to Walpole, October 2, 1774. Walpole, *Correspondence*, i. 171. Quoted by Lonsdale, *Gray*, p. 252.

11. Lonsdale, *Gray*, p. 252.
12. Walpole to Mason, 16 September 1774. Walpole, *Correspondence*, i. 168. Quoted by Lonsdale, *Gray*, p. 245.
13. Walpole to Mason, December 1, 1773. Walpole, *Correspondence*, i. 118. Quoted by Lonsdale, *Gray*, p. 261. The poem was first printed from an unauthorised copy in *The New Foundling Hospital for Wit* (1769), and its authorship denied by Gray and his friends. Lonsdale lists the details of this and other printings in *Gray*, pp. 260–61.
14. Henry Fox, later Lord Holland, had an extraordinary political career, whose salient details are recorded by Lonsdale in *Gray*, pp. 259–60. Of significance here is the fact that he parlayed his post of Paymaster-General into an impressive fortune, broke with his political allies between 1763 and 1765, and constructed his estate near Margate, which featured representations of ruined classical buildings and facades.
15. Alexander Pope, 'To Mr. *ADDISON*, Occasioned by his Dialogues on MEDALS,' in *Minor Poems*, ed. Norman Ault (New Haven: Yale University Press, 1954), pp. 202–203. Pope's poem is not simply a warning against the transitoriness of empire. Somewhat contradictorily, it also urges Britain on to mercantile and imperial power:

    Oh when shall Britain, conscious of her claim,
    Stand emulous of Greek and Roman fame?
    In living medals see her wars enroll'd,
    And vanquished realms supply recording gold? (ll. 53–56)

16. John Chalker, *The English Georgic* (Baltimore: The Johns Hopkins Press, 1969), pp. 11–12.
17. Jones, *Thomas Gray*, p. 85. Jones offers a detailed account (some of which I summarise here) of Gray's reading and writing on these topics in a chapter entitled 'Notes for the First History of English Poetry,' (pp. 84–107). Lonsdale also discusses (as background to the composition of 'The Fatal Sisters') Gray's interest in writing a history of English poetry, and the fact that Gray might have planned to include these translations in his 'History.' *Gray*, pp. 210–213.
18. See, for instance, C.J. Nordby, *The Influence of Old Norse Literature Upon English Literature* (New York: Columbia University Press, 1901); Frank Edgar Farley, *Scandinavian Influences in the English Romantic Movement* (Boston: Ginn & Company, 1903); Edward D. Snyder, *The Celtic Revival in English Literature 1760–1800* (Cambridge: Harvard Univer-

sity Press, 1923); William Cragie, *The Northern Element in English Literature* (Toronto: University of Toronto Press, n. d.). For a more analytical account of the construction of 'antiquity' in eighteenth-century literary and historiographical discourse see Ian Haywood, *The Making of History* (Rutherford: Fairleigh Dickinson University Press, 1986).

19. 'Preface' to *Five Pieces of Runic Poetry. Translated from the Icelandic Language* (London: R & J Dodsley, 1763), n. p. These translations were published anonymously, but are now known to be authored by Bishop Percy.
20. Oliver Goldsmith, 'The History of Carolan, the last Irish Bard,' in *Collected Works*, ed. Arthur Friedman, 5 vols. (Oxford: Clarendon Press, 1966), iii. 118.
21. Percy, 'Preface' to *Runic Poetry*, n. p.
22. Percy, 'Preface' to *Runic Pieces*, n. p.
23. Percy, 'Preface' to *Runic Pieces*, n. p.
24. Gray to Mason, March 24, 1758. *Correspondence*, ii. 568.
25. Gray to Wharton, c. June 20, 1760. *Correspondence*, ii. 680. For an account of Gray's response to Macpherson see Leonard Whibley's 'Gray and James Macpherson,' 'Appendix L' to Gray, *Correspondence*, iii: 1223-229. Evans's volume was entitled *Some Specimens of the Poetry of the Antient Welsh Bards, translated into English; with explanatory notes on the historical passages, and a short account of men and places mentioned by the Bards: in order to give the curious some idea of the tastes and sentiments of our Ancestors, and their manner of writing*, a title which quite effectively spells out the general rubric under which the vogue for antiquity was developed in the eighteenth-century.
26. Cf. Lonsdale's note: 'G. evidently refers to Dorruðr, the eavesdropper named in the *Njals Saga* and mentioned in his "Preface". The corresponding passage in the original poem may have been addressed to listeners is general.' *Gray*, p. 220, n. 57. Gray was aware that the name Dorruðr was the result of a corruption in the Latin translation of the Norse phrase 'vef darraðar' (which means 'web of the dart'): 'So Tormodus interprets it, as tho' *Daradr* were the name of the Person, who saw this vision, but in reality, it signifies a *range of spears*, from *Daur*, hasta, & *Radir*, ordo', etc.' Quoted by Lonsdale in *Gray*, p. 218, n. 25.
27. For comparison, we have the last four lines of the *Dunciad*:

    Lo! thy dread Empire, CHAOS! is restor'd;

Light dies before thy uncreating word:
Thy hand, great Anarch! lets the curtain fall;
And Universal Darkness buries All. (iv. 653–56)

Alexander Pope, *The Dunciad*, p. 409.

28. William Cragie suggests that eighteenth-century translations of ancient poetry 'amplified' the originals to suit contemporary taste: 'Scholars might be attracted by the Old Norse and Icelandic poetry in its original form, or even in Latin translations, and might venture like Hickes and Percy, to produce plain prose versions of it, but anyone who attempted to render it in verse felt it necessary to make it conform to the taste of the day by introducing epithets and phrases entirely lacking in the original.' *The Northern Element*, pp. 113–14. Similarly, Arthur Johnston's analysis of 'The Triumphs of Owen' shows that 'Gray substitutes specific images for general terms . . . both ornamenting and heightening the style, and supplying the figurativeness of language that was expected of "primitive" poetry.' However, Johnston does feel that 'there have been few translations of medieval Welsh poems that have so successfully captured the spirit of the original.' 'Gray's "The Triumphs of Owen",' *RES* 11 (1960), pp. 280, 284.
29. Johnston, 'Thomas Gray, Our Daring Bard,' in *Fearful Joy*, p. 63.
30. Wallace Jackson, 'Thomas Gray and the Dedicatory Muse,' *ELH* 54 (1987), p. 277. Jackson's essay notices many of the same rhetorical fissures—the symptoms of performative anxiety—that are explored in my analysis of Gray's poems, but our methods and interests are very different. Jackson's primary concern is with the working out of psychological and imaginative scenarios. Gray's early poems, for instance, 'dramatize the various rejections of desire as the major adventure of the resident ego within the poems,' and function to create 'a poetry that is beginning to announce itself in the special sense of a clarified and dramatized relation between poet and muse, a drawing out of a particular imaginative province, a space within which, like Coleridge's honey-dew drunken visionary, the poet enacts his own magic' (p. 281). Even though Jackson has a sharp sense of the tenuous and repressive resolutions of the poet's 'magic' in Gray, his refusal to think about the cultural and literary-historical dimensions of this poetic problem, or even to follow through the psychoanalytic or semiotic implications of his own analyses, limits the force and scope of his conclusions.

Bibliography

Abrams, M. H. 'Art-as-Such: The Sociology of Modern Aesthetics.' *Bulletin of The American Academy of Arts and Sciences*. 38 (1985): 8-33.

Addison, Joseph. *The Spectator*. In Vol. 2 of *Works*. 6 vols. Ed. Richard Hurd. London: George Bell & Sons, 1880–83.

Alpers, Paul. *The Singer of the Eclogues*. Berkeley: University of California Press, 1979.

Arnold, Matthew. 'Thomas Gray.' In *English Literature and Irish Politics*. Vol. 9 of *The Complete Prose Works*. 11 vols. Ed. R. H. Super. Ann Arbor: University of Michigan Press, 1960–77.

Aubin, Robert A. *Topographical Poetry in XVIII–Century England*. New York: The Modern Language Association of America, 1936.

Barrell, John. *English Literature in History, 1730–80: An Equal, Wide Survey*. London: Hutchinson, 1983.

——. *The Dark Side of the Landscape: The Rural Poor in English Painting 1730-1840*. Cambridge: Cambridge University Press, 1980.

Barrell, John and Harriet Guest. 'On the Uses of Contradiction: Economics and Morality in the Eighteenth-Century Long Poem.' In *The New Eighteenth Century*. Ed. Nussbaum and Brown.

Bateson, F. W. *English Poetry and the English Language*. Oxford: The Clarendon Press, 1973.

Beljame, Alexandre. *Men of Letters and the English Public in the Eighteenth Century*. Trans. E. O. Lorimer. London: Kegan Paul, Trench, Trubner & Co., 1948.

Bloom, Harold. *The Anxiety of Influence*. New York: Oxford University Press, 1973.

Bogel, Fredric V. *Literature and Insubstantiality in Later Eighteenth–Century England*. Princeton: Princeton University Press, 1984.

——. *The Dream of my Brother: An Essay on Johnson's Authority*. English Literary Studies Monograph 47. British Columbia: University of Victoria, 1990.

Brewer, John. 'Commercialization and Politics,' in *The Birth of a Consumer Society: The Commercialization of Eighteenth-Century England*. Ed. Neil McKendrick, John Brewer, and J. H. Plumb. Bloomington: Indiana University Press, 1985.

Brown, Laura. *Alexander Pope*. London: Basil Blackwell, 1985.

——. 'Commodity Fetishism and Neoclassical Aesthetic Theory: An Essay in Feminist Poetics.' Unpublished essay, 1986.

Brown, John. *An Estimate of the Manners and Principles of the Times*. London: L. Davis and C. Reymers, 1757.

Burke, Edmund. *A Philosophical Enquiry into the Origin of our Ideas of the Sublime and Beautiful*. Ed. J. T. Boulton. London: Routledge and Kegan Paul, 1958.

Catcott, Alexander. *The Antiquity and Honourableness of the Practice of Merchandize*. Bristol: 1744.

Chalker, John. *The English Georgic*. Baltimore: The Johns Hopkins Press, 1969.

Clark, S. H. ' "Pendet Homo Incertus": Gray's Response to Locke. Part One: Dull in a New Way.' *Eighteenth-Century Studies* 24 (1991): 273-91.

Cohen, Ralph. 'On the Interrelations of Eighteenth-Century Literary Forms.' In *New Approaches to Eighteenth-Century Literature*. Ed. Phillip Harth. New York: Columbia University Press, 1974.

Coleridge, Samuel T. *Biographia Literaria*. 2 vols. Ed. J. Shawcross. Oxford: The Clarendon Press, 1907.

Collins, A. S. *Authorship in the Days of Johnson*. London: Robert Holden & Co., 1927.

Courthope, W. J. *History of English Poetry*. 6 vols. London: Macmillan, 1895-1910.

Coward, Rosalind and John Ellis. *Language and Materialism*. London: Routledge and Kegan Paul, 1977.

Cragie, William. *The Northern Element in English Literature*. Toronto: University of Toronto Press, n.d.

Crider, John. 'Structure and Effect in Collins' Progress Poems.' *Studies in Philology* 60 (1963): 57-72.

Culler, Jonathan. *Structuralist Poetics*. Ithaca: Cornell University Press, 1975.

——. 'Apostrophe.' In *The Pursuit of Signs*. Ithaca: Cornell University Press, 1980.

Cunningham, Hugh. 'The Language of Patriotism, 1750-1914.' *History Workshop* 12 (1981): 8-33.

Davie, Donald. *Purity of Diction in English Verse*. London: Routledge and Kegan Paul, 1967.

De Man, Paul. 'Review of Harold Bloom's *Anxiety of Influence*.' In *Blindness and Insight*, 2nd rev. edn. Minneapolis: University of Minnesota Press, 1983.

——. 'The Rhetoric of Temporality.' In *Blindness and Insight*.

——. 'Intentional Structure of the Romantic Image.' In *The Rhetoric of Romanticism*. New York: Columbia University Press, 1984.

——. 'Autobiography as De-Facement.' In *Rhetoric of Romanticism*.

——. 'Anthropomorphism and Trope in the Lyric.' In *Rhetoric of Romanticism*.

——. 'Lyrical Voice in Contemporary Theory.' in *Lyric Poetry: Beyond New Criticism*. Ed. Patricia Parker and Chavira Hosek. Ithaca: Cornell University Press, 1985.

——. 'Hypogram and Inscription: Michael Riffaterre's Poetics of Reading.' *Diacritics* 11 (1981): 17-35.

Dobrée, Bonamy. 'The Theme of Patriotism in the Poetry of the Early Eighteenth Century.' *Proceedings of the British Academy* 35 (1949): 49-65. London: Oxford University Press, 1949.

Downey, James and Ben Jones, ed. *Fearful Joy: Papers from the Thomas Gray Bicentenary Conference at Carleton University*. Montreal: McGill-Queen's University Press, 1974.

Dryden, John. *The Poems and Fables of John Dryden*. Ed. James Kinsley. London: Oxford University Press, 1962.

Dyer, John. *Grongar Hill*. Ed. Richard C. Boys. Baltimore: The Johns Hopkins Press, 1941.

——. *The Ruins of Rome: A Poem*. London: Gilliver, 1740.

Eagleton, Terry. 'Frère Jacques: The Politics of Deconstruction.' *Semiotica* 63 (1987): 351-58.

Easthope, Anthony. *Poetry as Discourse*. London: Methuen, 1983.

Edwards, John. 'That Decay of Trade and Commerce, and Consequently of Wealth, is the Natural Product and Just Penalty of Vice in a Nation.' In *Sermons on Special Occasions and Subjects*. London: J. Robinson, 1698.

Edwards, Thomas. *Imagination and Power: A Study of Poetry on Public Themes*. London: Chatto & Windus, 1971.

Elioseff, Lee. *The Cultural Milieu of Addison's Literary Criticism*. Austin: University of Texas Press, 1963.

Empson, William. *Some Versions of Pastoral*. London: Chatto & Windus, 1935.

——. *Seven Types of Ambiguity*. London: Chatto & Windus, 1949.

Evans, Evan. *Some Specimens of the Poetry of the Antient Welsh Bards, translated into English; with explanatory notes on the historical passages, and a short account of men and places mentioned by the Bards; in order to give the curious some idea of the tastes and sentiments of our Ancestors, and their manner of writing*. London: R. & J. Dodsley, 1764.

Farley, Frank Edgar. *Scandinavian Influences in the English Romantic Movement*. Boston: Ginn & Company, 1903.

Feather, John. *A History of British Publishing*. London: Croom Helm, 1988.

Foladare, Joseph. 'Gray's "Frail Memorial" to West.' *PMLA* 75 (1960): 61-65.

Foss, Michael. *The Age of Patronage*. Ithaca: Cornell University Press, 1971.

Foucault, Michel. 'What is an Author?' In *Language, Counter-Memory, Practice*. Ed. Donald F. Bouchard. Trans. Donald F. Bouchard and Sherry Simon. Ithaca: Cornell University Press, 1977.

Freud, Sigmund. 'Medusa's Head.' In *Sexuality and the Psychology of Love*. Vol. 3 of the *Collected Papers of Sigmund Freud*. 10 vols. Ed. Philip Rieff. New York: Collier Books, 1963.

——. 'Fetishism.' In *Sexuality*. Ed. Rieff.

Fussell, Paul. *The Rhetorical World of Augustan Humanism: Ethics and Imagery from Swift to Burke*. Oxford: The Clarendon Press, 1965.

Garrick, David. *The Poetical Works*. 2 vols. London: George Kearsley, 1785. Rpt. London: Benjamin Blom, 1968.

Gay, John. *Poetical Works*. Ed. G. C. Faber. London: Oxford University Press, 1926.

Goldgar, Bertrand A. *Walpole and the Wits*. Lincoln: University of Nebraska Press, 1976.

Goldsmith, Oliver. 'The History of Carolan, the last Irish Bard.' In Vol. 3 of *Collected Works*. 5 vols. Ed. Arthur Friedman. Oxford: The Clarendon Press, 1966.

Goldstein, Laurence. *Ruins and Empire*. Pittsburgh: University of Pittsburgh Press, 1977.

Graham, Walter. *English Literary Periodicals*. New York: Thomas Nelson & Sons, 1930.

Gray, Thomas. *The Poems of Thomas Gray, William Collins, Oliver Goldsmith*. Ed. Roger Lonsdale. London: Longman, 1969.

——. *Correspondence of Thomas Gray*. 3 vols. Ed. Paget Toynbee and Leonard Whibley. Oxford: The Clarendon Press, 1935.

Grose, Francis. *Classical Dictionary of the Vulgar Tongue*. London: S. Hooper, 1785. Fac. Rpt. Menston: The Scolar Press, 1968.

Hagstrum, Jean. *The Sister Arts*. Chicago: The University of Chicago Press, 1958.

——. 'Gray's Sensibility.' In *Fearful Joy*. Ed. Downey and Jones.

Hartman, Geoffrey H. 'Romantic Poetry and the Genius Loci.' In *Beyond Formalism*. New Haven: Yale University Press, 1970.

——. 'Wordsworth, Inscriptions and Romantic Nature Poetry.' In *Beyond Formalism*.

Hayman, John G. 'Notions on National Characters in the Eighteenth Century.' In *Huntington Library Quarterly* 35 (1971-72): 1–17.

Haywood, Ian. *The Making of History*. Rutherford: Fairleigh Dickinson University Press, 1986.

Helgerson, Richard. *Self-Crowned Laureates*. Berkeley: University of California Press, 1983.

Hirschman, Albert O. *The Passions and the Interests: Political Arguments for Capitalism before Its Triumph*. Princeton: Princeton University Press, 1977.

Hohendahl, Peter U. 'Literary Criticism and the Public Sphere.' In *The Institution of Criticism*. Ithaca: Cornell University Press, 1982.

Holub, Robert C. 'The Rise of Aesthetics in the Eighteenth Century.' *Comparative Literature Studies* 15 (1978): 271-83.

Hume, David. 'Of the Standard of Taste.' In *Four Dissertations*. London: A. Millar, 1757. Rpt. New York: Garland Publishing Inc., 1970.

Humphreys, A. R. 'Lords of Tartary.' *Cambridge Journal* 3 (1949): 19-31.

Jack, Ian. 'Gray in his Letters.' In *Fearful Joy*. Ed. Downey and Jones.

Jackson, Wallace. 'Thomas Gray and the Dedicatory Muse.' *ELH* 54 (1987): 277-98.

Johnson, Samuel. 'Alexander Pope.' In *Lives of the English Poets*. Ed. John Wain. London: J. M. Dent & Sons, 1975.

——. 'Thomas Gray.' In *Lives*. Ed. Wain.

——. *Poems*. Ed. David N. Smith and Edward L. McAdam. Oxford: The Clarendon Press, 1974.

Johnston, Arthur. 'Thomas Gray: Our Daring Bard.' In *Fearful Joy*. Eds. Downey and Jones.

——. 'Gray's "The Triumphs of Owen." ' *RES* 11 (1960): 275-85.

——. ' "The Purple Year" in Pope and Gray.' *RES* 14 (1963): 389-93.

Jones, William Powell. *Thomas Gray, Scholar: The True Tragedy of an Eighteenth-Century Gentleman*. Cambridge: Harvard University Press, 1937.

——. 'The Contemporary Reception of Gray's *Odes*.' *Modern Philology* 28 (1930-31): 61-82.

Kampf, Louis. 'The Humanist Tradition in Eighteenth-Century England—And Today.' In *Fearful Joy*. Ed. Downey and Jones.

Kernan, Alvin. *Printing Technology, Letters and Samuel Johnson*. Princeton: Princeton University Press, 1987.

Ketton-Cremer, R. W. *Thomas Gray*. Cambridge: Cambridge University Press, 1955.

Kliger, Samuel. *The Goths in England: A Study in Seventeenth and Eighteenth Century Thought*. Cambridge: Harvard University Press, 1952.

——. 'Whig Aesthetics: A Phrase in Eighteenth Century Taste.' *ELH* 16 (1949): 135-50.

Krapp, Robert M. 'Class Analysis of a Literary Controversy.' *Science and Society* 10 (1946): 80-92.

Landa, Louis A. 'Pope's Belinda, The General Emporie of the World, and the Wondrous Worm.' *South Atlantic Quarterly* 70 (1971): 215-35.

Landry, Donna. 'The Resignation of Mary Collier: Some Problems in Feminist Literary History.' In *The New Eighteenth Century*. Ed. Nussbaum and Brown.

Locke, John. *Two Treatises of Government*. Ed. Peter Laslett. Rev. edn. New York: New American Library, 1965.

Lonsdale, Roger. 'The Poetry of Thomas Gray: Versions of the Self.' *Proceedings of the British Academy* 59 (1973): 105-23. London: Oxford University Press, 1975.

Lord, George deF. *et al.* ed. *Poems on Affairs of State: Augustan Satirical Verse, 1660-1714*. 7 vols. New Haven: Yale University Press, 1963-75.

Lowenthal, Leo and Marjorie Fiske. 'The Debate over Art and Popular Culture: English Eighteenth Century as a Case Study.' In Leo Lowenthal. *Literature, Popular Culture and Society*. Englewood Cliffs: Prentice-Hall, 1961.

Lyttleton, George. *Poetical Works*. In Vol. 10 of *The Works of the British Poets*. 13 vols. Ed. Robert Anderson. London: John & Arthur Arch, 1795.

Maclean, Norman. 'From Action to Image: Theories of the Lyric in the Eighteenth Century.' In *Critics and Criticism*. Ed. R. S. Crane. Chicago: Chicago University Press, 1952.

MacLean, Gerald. 'So What *Does* Thomas Gray's "Progress of Poesy" Have To Do with Progress?' *Postscript* 2 (1985): 67-74.

Maddison, Carol. *Apollo and the Nine: A History of the Ode*. Baltimore: The Johns Hopkins Press, 1960.

Mallet, David. *Excursion*. Ed. Robert B. Pearsall. Cornell University Thesis, 1953.

Marx, Karl. *Capital: A Critique of Political Economy, Vol. I*. Trans. Ben Fowkes. New York: Random House, 1977.

Mason, William. *The Poems of Mr. Gray. To Which are Prefixed Memoires of his Life and Writings by W. Mason, M. A.* York: A. Ward, 1775.

McFarland, Thomas. 'Poetry and the Poem: The Structure of Poetic Content.' In *Literary Theory and Structure*. Ed. Frank Brady, John Palmer and Martin Price. New Haven: Yale University Press, 1973.

McKillop, A. D. *The Background of Thomson's 'Liberty'*. Rice Institute Pamphlet 38. Houston: Rice Institute, 1951.

Meehan, Michael. *Liberty and Poetics in Eighteenth Century England*. London: Croom Helm, 1986.

Mell, Donald C. *A Poetics of Augustan Elegy*. Amsterdam: Rodopi N. V., 1974.

Mitford, J. 'Life of Young.' In Young, *Works*.

Montesquieu, Charles de Secondat, Baron de. *The Spirit of Laws*. Trans. Thomas Nugent. Rev. J. V. Prichard. Chicago: Encyclopedia Brittanica, 1955.

Moore, C. A. 'Whig Panegyric Verse, 1700-1760: A Phase of Sentimentalism.' *PMLA* 41 (1926): 362-401.

Mukarovsky, Jan. 'Standard Language and Poetic Language.' In *Essays on the Language of Literature*. Ed. Seymour Chatman and Samuel R. Levin. Boston: Houghton Mifflin Co., 1967.

Nordby, C. J. *The Influence of Old Norse Literature Upon English Literature*. New York: Columbia University Press, 1901.

Nussbaum, Felicity and Laura Brown, ed. *The New Eighteenth Century*. New York: Methuen, 1987.

O Hehir, Brendan. *Expans'd Hieroglyphics*. Berkeley: University of California Press, 1969.

Parrinder, Patrick. *Authors and Authority*. London: Routledge and Kegan Paul, 1977.

Percy, Thomas. 'Preface' to *Five Pieces of Runic Poetry. Translated from the Icelandic Language*. London: R & J Dodsley, 1763.

Pittock, Joan. *The Ascendancy of Taste*. London: Routledge and Kegan Paul, 1973.

Pollack, Ellen. *The Poetics of Sexual Myth: Gender and Ideology in the Verse of Swift and Pope*. Chicago: Chicago University Press, 1985.

Pope, Alexander. *The Dunciad*. Ed. James Sutherland. 3rd edn. Rev. New Haven: Yale University Press, 1963. Vol. 5 of the Twickenham Edition of *The Poems of Alexander Pope*. Ed. John Butt.

——. *Pastoral Poetry and An Essay on Criticism*. Ed. E. Audra and Aubrey Williams. New Haven: Yale University Press, 1961. Vol. 1 of the Twickenham Edition of *The Poems of Alexander Pope*. Ed. John Butt.

——. *Poems*. Ed. John Butt. New Haven: Yale University Press, 1963.

——. *Minor Poems*. Ed. Norman Ault. New Haven: Yale University Press, 1954. Vol. 6 of the Twickenham Edition of *The Poems of Alexander Pope*. Ed. John Butt.

——. *The Rape of the Lock*. Ed. Geoffrey Tillotson. 2nd edn. Rev. New Haven: Yale University Press, 1954. Vol. 2 of the Twickenham Edition of *The Poems of Alexander Pope*. Ed. John Butt.

——. *The Correspondence of Alexander Pope*. 5 vols. Ed. George Sherburn. Oxford: The Clarendon Press, 1956.

Quayle, Thomas. *Poetic Diction*. London: Methuen, 1924.

Reed, Amy L. *The Background of Gray's Elegy*. New York: Columbia University Press, 1924.

Reichard, Hugo M. 'Pope's Social Satire: Belles-Lettres and Business.' *PMLA* 67 (1952): 420-34.

Riffaterre, Michael. *Semiotics of Poetry*. Bloomington: Indiana University Press, 1978.

Rogers, Pat. *The Augustan Vision*. New York: Barnes and Noble, 1974.

——. *Grub Street*. London: Methuen & Co., 1972.

Rothblatt, Sheldon. *Tradition and Change in English Liberal Education*. London: Faber and Faber, 1976.

Rothstein, Eric. *Restoration and Eighteenth-Century Poetry 1660-1780*. London: Routledge and Kegan Paul, 1981.

Saccamano, Neil. 'Authority and Publication: The Works of "Swift".' *The Eighteenth Century* 25 (1984): 241-62.

Sacks, Peter M. *The English Elegy*. Baltimore: The Johns Hopkins Press, 1985.

Saunders, David and Ian Hunter. 'Lessons from the "Literatory": How to Historicise Scholarship.' *Critical Inquiry* 17 (1991): 479-509.

Schuster, George N. *The English Ode from Milton to Keats*. New York: Columbia University Press, 1940.

Scodel, Joshua. *The English Poetic Epitaph*. Ithaca: Cornell University Press, 1991.

Sekora, John. *Luxury: The Concept in Western Thought, Eden to Smollet*. Baltimore: Johns Hopkins University Press, 1977.

Sickels, Eleanor M. *The Gloomy Egoist*. New York: Columbia University Press, 1932.

Sitter, John. *Literary Loneliness in Mid-Eighteenth Century England*. Ithaca: Cornell University Press, 1982.

Snow, Edward. 'Theorizing the Male Gaze: Some Problems.' *Representations* 25 (1989): 30-41.

Snyder, Edward D. *The Celtic Revival in English Literature 1760-1800*. Cambridge: Harvard University Press, 1923.

Speck, W. A. 'Politicians, peers and publication by subscription 1700-50.' In *Books and their Readers in Eighteenth-Century England*. Ed. Isabel Rivers. New York: St. Martin's Press, 1982.

Stallybrass, Peter and Allon White. *The Politics and Poetics of Transgression*. Ithaca: Cornell University Press, 1986.

Steele, James. 'Thomas Gray and the Season for Triumph.' In *Fearful Joy*. Ed. Downey and Jones.

Steele, Richard. *The Correspondence of Richard Steele*. Ed. Rae Blanchard. London: Oxford University Press, 1941.

Sutherland, James. *A Preface to Eighteenth Century Poetry*. Oxford: The Clarendon Press, 1948.

Tasso, Torquato. *Gerusalemme Liberata*. Ed. Mario Sansone. Bari: Adriatica Editrice, 1963.

Thomson, James. *Poetical Works*. Ed. J. Logie Robertson. London: Oxford University Press, 1908.

——. *The Seasons*. Ed. James Sambrook. Oxford: The Clarendon Press, 1981.

Tillotson, Geoffrey. *Augustan Poetic Diction*. London: The Athlone Press, 1964.

——. 'Gray's "Ode on the Spring".' In *Augustan Studies*. London: The Athlone Press, 1961.

——. 'Gray's "Ode on the Death of a Favourite Cat, Drowned in a Tub of Gold Fishes".' In *Augustan Studies*.

Tovey, Duncan C, ed. *Gray and His Friends*. Cambridge: Cambridge University Press, 1890.

Toynbee, Paget, ed. *The Correspondence of Gray, Walpole, West and Ashton*. 2 vols. Oxford: The Clarendon Press, 1915.

Virgil. *The Aeneid*. Trans. James H. Mantinband. New York: Ungar, 1964.

Walpole, Horace. *Correspondence with William Mason*. 2 vols. Ed. W. S. Lewis, Grover Cronin Jr. and Charles H. Bennett. New Haven: Yale University Press, 1955. Vols. 28 and 29 of the Yale Edition of *Horace Walpole's Correspondence*. 42 vols. Ed. W. S. Lewis. 1937-80.

Watt, Ian. *The Rise of the Novel*. Berkeley: University of California Press, 1957.

——. 'Two Historical Aspects of the Augustan Tradition.' In *Studies in the Eighteenth Century*. Ed. R. F. Brissenden. Canberra: Australian National University Press, 1968.

——. 'Publishers and Sinners: The Augustan View.' *Studies in Bibliography* 12 (1959): 3-20.

Weinfield, Henry. *Poet Without a Name: Gray's 'Elegy' and the Problem of History*. Carbondale: Southern Illinois University Press, 1991.

Wellek, Rene. *The Rise of English Literary History*. Chapel Hill: The University of North Carolina Press, 1941.

Whalley, George. 'Thomas Gray: A Quiet Hellenist.' In *Fearful Joy*. Ed. Downey and Jones.

Whibley, Leonard. 'The Contest for the High Stewardship and Gray's Verses on Lord Sandwich.' In Gray, *Correspondence*.

——. 'Gray and James Macpherson.' In Gray, *Correspondence*.

Williams, Aubrey. *Pope's Dunciad: A Study of Its Meaning*. London: Methuen, 1955.

Williams, Raymond. *The Country and the City*. New York: Oxford University Press, 1973.

——. *The Long Revolution*. New York: Columbia University Press, 1961.

Woodmansee, Martha. 'The Genius and the Copyright: Economic and Legal Conditions of the Emergence of the "Author".' *Eighteenth-Century Studies* 17 (1984): 425-48.

Wordsworth, William. 'Appendix to the Preface (1802).' In *Literary Criticism of William Wordsworth*. Ed. Paul M. Zall. Lincoln: University of Nebraska Press, 1966.

——. 'Essay on Epitaphs.' In *Literary Criticism*. Ed. Zall.

——. 'Preface to *Lyrical Ballads* (1800).' In *Literary Criticism*. Ed. Zall.

Young, Edward. *Conjectures on Original Composition*. London: A. Millar and R. & J. Dodsley, 1759. Fac. Rpt. Leeds: The Scolar Press, 1966.

——. *Poetical Works*. 2 vols. London: Bell and Daldy, 1866.

Zionkowski, Linda. 'Bridging the Gulf Between: The Poet and the Audience in the Work of Gray.' *ELH* 58 (1991): 331-50.

Index